NEOLIBERALISM AND URBAN REGENERATION

London's Communities Finding
a Voice and Fighting Back

Roger Green and Keith Popple

First published in Great Britain in 2025 by

Bristol University Press
University of Bristol
1–9 Old Park Hill
Bristol
BS2 8BB
UK
t: +44 (0)117 374 6645
e: bup-info@bristol.ac.uk

Details of international sales and distribution partners are available at bristoluniversitypress.co.uk

© Bristol University Press 2025

British Library Cataloguing in Publication Data
A catalogue record for this book is available from the British Library

ISBN 978-1-5292-4394-9 hardcover
ISBN 978-1-5292-4395-6 paperback
ISBN 978-1-5292-4396-3 ePub
ISBN 978-1-5292-4397-0 ePdf

The right of Roger Green and Keith Popple to be identified as authors of this work has been asserted by them in accordance with the Copyright, Designs and Patents Act 1988.

All rights reserved: no part of this publication may be reproduced, stored in a retrieval system, or transmitted in any form or by any means, electronic, mechanical, photocopying, recording, or otherwise without the prior permission of Bristol University Press.

Every reasonable effort has been made to obtain permission to reproduce copyrighted material. If, however, anyone knows of an oversight, please contact the publisher.

The statements and opinions contained within this publication are solely those of the authors and not of the University of Bristol or Bristol University Press. The University of Bristol and Bristol University Press disclaim responsibility for any injury to persons or property resulting from any material published in this publication.

Bristol University Press works to counter discrimination on grounds of gender, race, disability, age and sexuality.

Cover design: Liam Roberts Design
Front cover image: iStock/Nirian

Contents

List of Figures		iv
Acknowledgements		v
Foreword by Marjorie Mayo		vii
Introduction		1
Roger Green and Keith Popple		
1	Neoliberalism and Increasing Inequality	8
	Keith Popple	
2	Challenging the Neoliberal Hegemony	29
	Keith Popple	
3	'Cranes in the Sky': The Remaking of London	53
	Roger Green, with Malcolm Cadman, Andy Turner,	
	Marion Briggs and Tony Nickson	
4	Deptford: Community and Change	77
	Roger Green, with Marion Briggs, Malcolm Cadman, Warda Farah,	
	Joyce Jacca, Richard Katona, Tony Nickson and Andy Turner	
5	Defiance and Resistance: The Voice4Deptford Campaign	90
	Roger Green, with Andy Turner, Malcolm Cadman, Marion Briggs,	
	Vanessa Celosse, Warda Farah, Joyce Jacca, Richard Katona,	
	Tony Nickson, Kenneth M. Thomas and other members and	
	supporters of the campaign	
6	Confronting the Developers	120
	Roger Green, with Malcolm Cadman	
7	Whose City? Communities versus Capital	137
	Roger Green and Keith Popple	
Notes		144
References		145
Index		178

List of Figures

5.1	Aerial view of Deptford Dockyard (Convoys Wharf)	114
5.2	Convoys Wharf site front gate	114
5.3	Convoys Wharf site looking to Canary Wharf	115
5.4	Convoys Wharf site from nearby council housing estate	115
5.5	Roger Green speaking at the Voice4Deptford 'pop-up shop' meeting	116
5.6	Voice4Deptford campaign meeting	116
5.7	Voice4Deptford logo	117
5.8	'Give Deptford a voice'	117

Acknowledgements

Books such as these are a collective enterprise, and therefore we would like to thank and acknowledge the many who have helped us deliver this book.

Sure, over the past few years one or two of us have written about neoliberalism, hegemony and counter-hegemony, however without relating these key concepts to the struggles faced by an emerging and now established community campaign group of this kind it would not have the meaning it does now. There is no doubt that without the input from the Voice4Deptford members, supporters, Deptford residents and many others who came and went over the past eleven years of the campaign's life it would have remained a community memory. Occasionally referred to in the Dog and Bell pub in Deptford while sipping a beer or over a coffee in the DeliX café along the Deptford High Street.

We start with a special mention and a big thanks to Malcolm Cadman, chair of Voice4Deptford, for getting the campaign on the road, his support in encouraging the completion of the book, and for his incredible commitment and knowledge of the Deptford community and its people. His 'stickability' in keeping the campaign on the rails especially during some of the not so good times when the campaign floundered under the heel of the powerful interests involved in the Convoys Wharf development is a lesson to us all.

A big thanks goes to all members of the campaign's original 'core group'. Andy Turner, who was in at the start of the campaign, Joyce Jacca, Sue Davies, Marion Briggs, Sue Davies, Vanessa Celosse, Warda Farrah, Tony Nixon, Kenneth M. Thomas and others. We couldn't have done it without you all. So many thanks.

A mention too to Richard Katona who sadly passed during the COVID-19 pandemic. He was a lovely, sincere, scholarly, quietly spoken and thoughtful man with Deptford running through his veins. Richard was an active member of the campaign and supported the 'pop-up' shop, banging off emails to Goldsmiths Warden arguing why we should get the shop, which we did, at no cost. His generosity knew no bounds. He was 'behind the scenes' a massive financial supporter of the V4D Crowd Justice campaign to fund the judicial review. A true Deptford community activist.

Thanks go to John Clarke, alias Jazzman John, poet, writer and performer, for introducing one of the authors, Roger Green, to the real Deptford music scene and opening his eyes to his take on Deptford, correctly forecasting the area as the developers' next gentrified South London hotspot.

We cannot forget those in Deptford and the surrounding neighbourhoods who came along to the community meetings, had their say, sometimes very loudly, and continue to make Voice4Deptford a necessary important campaign.

A big thanks must go to the other London campaigns who gave their time, agreeing to meet up and share what was happening with their campaigns against housing redevelopments.

Thanks to go to Goldsmiths, University of London colleagues who over the years supported the initial Deptford research projects, the campaign and the writing of the book. Special mention to Saugat Gurung, IT Services Assistant and final year student at Goldsmiths, for resolving a laptop malfunction.

We also thank our respective families and friends who have continually encouraged this project. One of our friends asked if we planned a sequel!

Thanks go to Emily Watt and Anna Richardson of Policy Press who always believed in the idea for the book and encouraged its completion.

Finally, we would like to thank all the many others who over the years who have wittingly and unwittingly contributed to our thinking on this radical approach to working with communities and led to us to write what you will read here. However, of course, responsibility for the content of the book rests with us alone.

Foreword

Marjorie Mayo

Emeritus Professor of Community Development, Goldsmiths,
University of London

The links between the local and the global have greater relevance than ever right now and not just in relation to the climate crisis. Far from it in fact. Urban regeneration processes need to be understood in precisely such terms too. And this is most especially so in a global city such as London. Social geographers such as Doreen Massey (Massey, 2007) and Saskia Sassen (2014) have pointed to precisely these interconnections already, identifying the brutality and complexity inherent in the global economy. This very complexity has been making it hard to trace lines of responsibility for the displacement, evictions and eradications that contemporary capitalism produces, with its logics of expulsion, logics that hit working-class communities with particular intensity in global cities such as London.

Which makes this book all the timelier. Communities need to be equipped to analyse these interconnections between the local and the global if they are to respond strategically, understanding the different levels and spaces of power, rooted in the power of global capital, along with the power of the property development industry, too often supported, rather than effectively challenged, by the state at both local and national levels.

The authors' case study of community action in Deptford, Southeast London, offers the basis for unpacking precisely these interconnections. This is the story of the power of global capital, on the one hand, and working-class communities' strategies to resist displacement, on the other – social cleansing in the context of 'feral capitalism', as David Harvey has so aptly described these processes (Harvey, 2013). These are struggles for the right to the city, struggles over contested values about the uses of urban spaces along with struggles over the right to affordable housing and sustainable environments.

While the book focuses on a particular place in a specific global city, the authors go on to raise wider questions too, by implication. These are questions of key relevance for communities and for those who support them in whatever roles, as professionals and/ or activists, engaging in community-based campaigns, in solidarity. Professionals and activists need to be raising these questions for themselves, in their own particular contexts. Who is standing to gain from this particular urban regeneration programme? And who is standing to lose, as a result? Whose side are you on? And how are you going to support communities effectively, campaigning for more equitable alternatives?

This takes the discussion back to the importance of understanding the interconnections between the local and the global. How to impact at different levels and spaces of power, on the basis of such understandings? And most importantly how to build strategies of resistance from the bottom up, working inclusively for sustainable cities of the future – while recognizing the limits as well as the possibilities of what can be achieved at different levels and spaces of power.

This book is to be particularly welcomed for addressing these questions. How to resist processes of social cleansing in a global city? How to develop strategic alliances in the pursuit of progressive alternatives – putting people rather than profits first? And how to widen and deepen forms of democratic representation for a more sustainable future?

This is more urgent than ever in the contemporary context, both locally and globally. Democratic rights are potentially threatened by the growth of authoritarian populism. And authoritarian populism tends to flourish when people feel unrepresented and unheard, disillusioned and disempowered, fearful for their futures in situations of increasing precarity and risk. *Neoliberalism and Urban Regeneration: London's Communities Finding a Voice and Fighting Back* focuses on community struggles for the right to the city, in response to neoliberal forms of urban regeneration. But the book's implications are wider still, in face of these far-right challenges.

Introduction

Roger Green and Keith Popple

Background

For far too long urban communities and neighbourhoods have been reimagined by corporate power, whether it is global developers, the super-rich, oligarchs, powerful institutions or other power brokers that influence key decisions taken at the highest level. The overriding vision and drive of this commanding and forceful group is to determine the urban future, which with its top-down development of our cities, has created and sustained poverty, dispossession and urban blight among the poorest of our populations. The strategy practised by this corporate power and the super-rich has brought into sharp relief the city as a commodity, where class, power and politics are interwoven to dominate the urban landscape. The outcome is a continuing housing shortage deepened by the increasing pursuit of huge profits rather than human need, which has created significant socio-spatial segregation and inequality between the super-rich, the rich and 'the rest' of us.

These outsiders, with their power, influence and money, are demolishing long-established communities and repopulated brownfield sites to make way for massive office blocks and sprawling retail parks while creating new urban neighbourhoods with high-density housing that is unaffordable for most to purchase. This powerful and massive juggernaut of change has side-tracked the token consultation processes involving existing communities. The result is that these rudimentary consultation processes are largely ignored, with community voices excluded by developers and the local politicians who collude with them. The outcome is that the promised benefits to existing communities fail to materialize, leading to residents feeling rejected and angry.

While we recognize this 'take over' of communities is not only UK-wide but is occurring in many other major cities around the world, we focus in this book on communities in London, and one in particular, Deptford in Southeast London. This is one of many urban communities across London where the regeneration and redevelopment process is well under way, with the construction of new expensive soulless housing developments with little or no social housing for local people. It is a community alongside London's River Thames that includes the historically important Convoys Wharf waterfront site, where a proposed housing development is being strongly contested by a Voice4Deptford campaign involving residents, community groups, academics and their supporters. A campaign that is seeking to change this process of a highly contested urban site undergoing significant change, where in a post-Brexit UK it faces a range of social, economic and physical environmental challenges. The lessons learned from this ongoing campaign have inspired the writing of this book, which has been co-produced by a coalition of academics, community activists and residents involved in the 'fight back' against a global developer.

By using the Voice4Deptford campaign as our case study of an organized community 'fight back' we propose an approach to working with communities based on these experiences and the ideas generated that adds to the established critiques of community action and community development. One that builds on the methods, theories and approaches that currently exist. We therefore propose a 'radical rethink' in working with communities, an approach where 'taking sides' against developers and their powerful corporate investors and supporters is fundamental. Our approach demands a reconstruction of thinking and action about working in communities and where economic and social injustices are central to our understanding of the need to 'fight back'.

Our theoretical position is informed by the Italian neo-Marxist theorist and political activist Antonio Gramsci's ideas of 'cultural hegemony' which applied to working with communities ask the key questions, what's going on and who benefits? We argue that when working with communities one cannot remain 'neutral', rather there is a need to take sides, which we consider is a fundamental requirement. It is a question we pose in the context of the wide-ranging detrimental impact of neoliberalism with its domination, exploitation and pursuit of ever-increasing profit and power. The ideology of neoliberalism, among many other similar regressive economic, social and political theories, is an anathema to the communities we work with, and where human need and a sense of community, collaboration, affiliation and sense of fairness are much more important.

In working with communities, we face the many global challenges which impact both urban and rural communities in countries across the world. These challenges include:

- The continuing and increasingly dangerous climate emergency that demonstrates we cannot allow global corporations and many nation states to continue to plunder Planet Earth's natural resources and create irreversible environmental damage, particularly in poorer communities.

- A recognition that existing forms of political representation do not bring about real structural social change, power or empowerment for communities.
- The evidence of the vast increases in wealth and the number of the 'super-rich', together with massive global corporations who hold sway with governments in their pursuit of expanding their wealth, power and influence to the detriment of communities.
- The impact of urbanization, with huge populations moving to urban settings away from rural areas. It is estimated that by 2050 over 70 per cent of Earth's population will be urban dwellers, a global phenomenon which results in significant socio-spatial segregation and inequality between the super-rich and 'the rest' of us.
- Global corporations who view ordinary people, families and communities as 'collateral damage' in their pursuit of financial rewards for their shareholders and chief executive officers.
- The impact of the global COVID-19 pandemic and its terrible destruction of communities around the world and the existing severe inequalities and social injustice that it has exposed locally, nationally, regionally and globally.

It is these disparities that we investigate and seek to uncover in this book, and to reveal the impact of inequality and different forms of socioeconomic exclusion on communities' ability to engage, participate and challenge planning and redevelopment processes. We explore and identify geographic proximities, spatial divisions and 'connectivities' to enable people working with communities to identify the different challenges they are facing. We uncover the fragmenting effects of globalization and 'austerity urbanism' as it manifests itself in the living spaces of communities under the guise of regeneration, redevelopment or local 'infrastructure gains'.

Finally, we address and challenge the continuing failure of neoliberalism to benefit the many. We argue that an ideological position and practice shift is required, which is embedded in a rejection of neoliberalism, and, in its place, we argue for a more progressive, just, equal and liberating theory and practice that genuinely includes rather than excludes the many.

How the book emerged

The idea for this book emerged following the continuing lessons being learned from the Voice4Deptford campaign as it has ebbed and flowed from its initial starting point in 2013 with its successes and failures from its onset through to where we are now. Countless discussions, meetings and conversations held in a variety of local community locations from a community centre, a Salvation Army hall, different local cafes, rooms in

Goldsmiths, University of London, and the bar in the locally famous Dog and Bell pub, facing the contested Convoys Wharf site, known previously in the 19th century as the 'Royal Marine pub' for serving the 'more respectable Marines' based in Deptford Dockyard. All these offered the creative space for our learning and actions.

This originated in a conversation that took place in late 2013 over a cup of tea at Pepys Community Forum, located in an old 19th-century rambling warehouse near to the River Thames in Deptford, between Malcom Cadman, director of Pepys Community Forum, a local resident and community activist, and Roger Green, an academic community researcher and activist from nearby Goldsmiths, University of London. The discussion centred on the local communities' concerns regarding proposed developments along the River Thames, Deptford waterfront, particularly the Convoys Wharf site. A brownfield site with a unique historical heritage, and where only limited community consultation had previously been undertaken with the local community.

This meeting, and the many others that followed, together with the subsequent development of the campaign, brought increasing numbers of Deptford residents and supporters into its fold, and who have also contributed to this book along with the authors, Roger Green and Keith Popple, Emeritus Professor at London South Bank University and writer in community development, social policy and social work.

The structure of the book

We offer the reader a structure that differs from other books in this area. Each of the chapters puts forward not only detailed examples and a critical analysis of the corrosive impact of neoliberalism, or capitalism at your 'front door', as one Deptford resident called it, but also, and importantly, we offer hope, ways forward, with both a critique and a promise.

In the first two chapters Keith Popple sets this scene, showing how neoliberalism has produced and spread severe inequality worldwide, and highlights London as an example of its corrosive impact. Along with increasing global climate challenges because of neoliberal economic forces, we examine how cronyism during the COVID-19 pandemic, the negative consequences of the country leaving the European Union, the influence of Russia and the role of the British establishment, have all contributed to the situation that the UK now inhabits.

Chapter 1 outlines the development of neoliberalism and how its powerful ruthless ideology has infiltrated our lives, becoming packaged as a 'common sense' or 'natural' way of viewing the world that we occupy. We see how this dominant hegemony has moved the focus from community and collective wellbeing to individual responsibility, and to corporate acquisitiveness and greed. It is this, we argue, that has severely damaged the complex fabric of our world and created and sustained poverty. In this chapter we introduce the insights of one of the most original and wide-ranging Marxist thinkers, Antonio Gramsci.

Chapter 2 examines the efforts to counter the neoliberal hegemony. To undertake this, we start by considering the impact of neoliberalism on democracy, which we argue is failing in many parts of the world, including the UK. This consideration includes the role of the powerful hegemony of vested interests where power, influence and money are concentrated in the hands of the few. A secret network supports this establishment, who benefit from neoliberalism and who are intent on excluding the majority. The failure of democracy to meet the needs of the many is a trend reflected globally, and which has increased with concerns over a less safe world, and with growing economic insecurity. The outcome is that people are looking for alternative platforms to express their grievances and have become involved in what can be termed as counter-hegemonic practices and visions. Probably the most conspicuous of these movements are those challenging the degradation of the planet largely driven by the fossil fuel industries. These counter-hegemonic movements are local, national and international, and have sought to broaden democracy, like those we discuss in this book and who are working in London to fight back against the developers, the super-rich and corporate acquisitiveness.

In Chapter 3, Roger Green explains in detail how the advocates of neoliberalism, the global property developers and foreign investors are bringing about an increasingly reimagined and segregated London in the pursuit of profits. How this is a corporate takeover of the city under the guise of redevelopment, regeneration or gentrification, with the destruction of working-class communities, and the creation of new expensive high-rise neighbourhoods and urban 'villages'. How this is occurring at the expense of ordinary Londoners and their need for secure social housing and community infrastructure that offers them equality and social justice.

In Chapter 4 Roger Green introduces the reader to Deptford, in Southeast London, less than five miles from arguably the financial capital of the world, the City of London. A demographically diverse community with a significant maritime past, including its hidden history of the slave trade at Convoys Wharf, a large empty post-industrial brownfield dockyard site facing the River Thames. It is this site that lies at the heart of a contested battle between a global developer and the local Deptford community. It explores how the community has historically fought back when their community is threatened. With examples, it will show how they have taken and supported both industrial action and community resistance against the imposition of capitalist forms and its injustices for their working-class community.

In Chapter 5 members of the Voice4Deptford campaign tell the story of the continuing Convoys Wharf campaign. How they organized a fight back against a global developer who has plans to redevelop this historically world-famous dockyard site.

It explains how the proposed development offers a high-rise, bland, out-the-box 'anywhere' design for primarily overseas investors and those with sufficient personal capital. While ignoring the severe need for locally socially rented housing and infrastructure growth and disregarding the site's important maritime heritage.

It will detail how a group of residents, activists and their supporters came together, organized public meetings and established a campaign planning group; how community action succeeded in diverting agency, power and knowledge away from 'experts' into the orbit of the community; how it challenged local power holders' entitlement to retain a hegemonic hold over communities by denying their voices, real participation and decision making; how it actively encouraged and supported residents to step forward and become community 'organic intellectuals'; and how it uniquely brought all the key stakeholders, the developer, the local Member of Parliament, the mayor and local politicians, and planning officers around the 'table'.

In Chapter 6 Roger Green and members of the Voice4Deptford campaign look at other examples of community resistance in organizing and 'fighting back' against top-down urban redevelopment occurring across London. They show that it has a continuing historical lineage. From the regeneration of the London Docks in the early 1980s until the present day, active campaigns by communities under threat of losing their homes, jobs, their sense of community and their 'way of life' are now a daily part of London's urban fabric.

Communities in London, the UK and indeed globally are challenging the right of 'outsiders' to determine their futures. Therefore, in this concluding chapter, Chapter 7, we will be returning to the arguments we have made throughout the book, including the concept of hegemony and the ideas and insights of the Italian theorist Antonio Gramsci. We offer a 'way forward'. An argument for real democracy, and community action, that involves resistance and change for urban communities that are facing forced change and destruction. It offers lessons learnt from both the unique Voice4Deptford campaign and other community campaigns by highlighting the practice of generating the voices of communities and acting when confronted by powerful external and internal forces, such as developers with a global reach and local power holders. We argue for an act of mobilizing embryonic social capital albeit in circumstances not of our choosing that produces an insurrection of subjugated knowledge. An organic community co-production engagement approach in urban community spaces such as Deptford that challenges both existing capitalist power arrangements and existing ideas of community action and community development.

And finally ...

While this book has focused on London, and particularly Deptford, we have linked the phenomenon impacting on the capital city, and the Deptford community, with the serious conundrums the whole globe is experiencing. What is happening in London and Deptford is being reproduced in cities, town and urban areas everywhere that neoliberalism has sunk its tentacles into the economic, political and social fabric.

We hope readers internationally will find much here that chimes with what is happening in your country and in your communities. Importantly we hope that you can take from our research and writings the sense that change is possible against even the most powerful dangerous cultural hegemony we have experienced in our lifetime. Neoliberalism is a cruel confidence trick. Communities, though, have right on their side and in the end truth will out.

1

Neoliberalism and Increasing Inequality

Keith Popple

Introduction

There is little doubt that we are living in a precarious, turbulent and uncertain period in our global history. A world where vast inequalities are increasingly opening between and within countries. This phenomenon is in parallel with, and often a significant contributor to, a series of dangerous outbreaks of conflict around the world as countries face down geopolitical threats. We are now living in a constantly changing strategic environment with more conflicts than at any time since 1945 (Wintour, 2025). Added to this, there are widespread concerns that in many countries democracy is severely at risk. At the same time there is a growing global climate emergency of momentous proportions. Mixed into this dangerous scenario, governments and people everywhere are dealing with the outcomes of the unpredictable, unorthodox, authoritarian approach of the world's most powerful elected politician, Donald Trump, the president of the United States.

Almost daily, in the UK, we are confronted with seeing or hearing about the growing real-life difficulties facing millions of people living in poverty and unable to properly feed themselves and their children while struggling to pay for the heating and lighting of their home (JRF, 2024). According to a report from the independent Social Metrics Commission (2024), 24 per cent of the UK population is judged to be in poverty, with more than a third of all children (36 per cent) in poverty in 2022/2023. This is an almost five percentage point increase since 2019/2020.

Meanwhile, globally, millions more are caught up in vicious and seemingly unresolvable, precarious and dangerous armed conflicts, whether as major wars, minor conflicts, or skirmishes and clashes. Others are victims of horrendous humanitarian crises which shatter lives and livelihoods and where the large-scale displacement of people is routine. As a result, people are living without clean, uncontaminated drinking water, nourishing food, proper sanitation, or without shelter from the often-extreme elements, and without access to education and healthcare. Others may be living in less dangerous regions and countries and are in employment but are often receiving inadequate pay for tedious work in unhealthy conditions, and if they are in receipt of welfare benefits, find their income failing to adequately cover their daily living expenses. Research from the World Bank Group (2024), among many other international organizations, confirms that globally poverty is ever-present and increasing in a world of extreme inequality.

At the same time, cherished and vital health resources globally, including in the UK the National Health Service (NHS), are constantly teetering under the pressure of insufficient resources due to years of chronic underfunding and increasing patient demand. Between 2010 and 2024 the NHS patient waiting list for treatment tripled in England, with an increasing number waiting between 18 and 52 weeks for treatment, and a small but significant number waiting more than 52 weeks (Krugman, 2024). The outcome is the development of a thriving private healthcare sector, which caters for patients not based on need but rather on the ability of individuals and families to pay for their care and treatment (Campbell, 2023). The issue of a severely damaged health service is of pressing concern in the UK, where it has been estimated that inequalities have caused one million early deaths since 2014 (Institute of Health Equity, 2024). While there are signs that the Labour government elected in July 2024 is prioritizing tackling the chronic long-term problems in the NHS left by the failure of the previous Conservative government, it could take many years to satisfactorily address the complex issues facing the health service. Alongside this, research in the UK evidences a growing addiction to unhealthy foods that are high in fat, salt and sugar, or have been highly processed, and which are a contributor to heart and kidney diseases and have been linked to the increasing prevalence of type 2 diabetes and obesity. The impact of the addiction to the consumption of unhealthy food is a 'staggering £268bn a year' (Campbell, 2024). Further, against a backdrop of a growing ageing population there is no nationally agreed UK social care policy, which has created serious problems for local authorities, families and individuals. All these developments have been exacerbated by what has been often termed the 'cost of living crisis'. This is the short-hand term for when the cost of essential items like food, energy, transport and accommodation increases more quickly than average household income. Basically, it means legions of people have insufficient income to pay for basic items while over many decades UK governments have failed to raise sufficient funds to pay for critical public services.

Millions of people in the UK, and billions internationally, feel that while they may not be destitute or poor, they do consider themselves to be powerless against economic and political forces far greater than themselves (Amnesty International, 2024). These forces dictate food and energy supplies and prices, as well as the availability of decent paid employment. Simultaneously, the UK housing market discriminates against those on low or insufficient income, making it difficult or even impossible for them to rent or purchase adequate accommodation at a price they can afford.[1]

Many of the problems referred to are interlinked and have been brought about internationally by governments transferring services and industries from the public sector to the private sector. Here, accountability and transparency are usually opaque, often totally inadequate, or non-existent, and the drive to make increasing profits is paramount and often comes before providing much-needed investment. The transfer from the public to the private sector has furthered corporate interests, damaged democracy and reduced our freedoms (Rhodes, 2022). Meanwhile, the increasing numbers of the super-rich, many of whom are company owners or senior executives of large corporations, and who have profited from the present situation, flaunt their increasing wealth and economic power, apparently blissfully unaware, or not appearing to care, that others do not enjoy such income, wealth or lifestyles (Hildyard, 2024; Robeyns, 2024).

Details of the wealth of the richest people in the UK are published annually in the *Sunday Times Rich List*. In the 2024 *Sunday Times Rich List* 165 UK billionaires were named, whereas 14 years earlier in 2010 there were 29 in that category. The richest in the 2024 list is Gopi Hinduja and family, whose empire operates in 48 countries in sectors including oil, chemicals, automotives, finance, IT, energy, healthcare, media and real estate. Their collective fortune amounts to £37.196 billion. Other billionaires in the list include the British entrepreneurs Sir Jim Ratcliffe with a wealth of £23.519 billion, and Sir James Dyson and family with a marginally smaller but still enormous wealth of £20.8 billion. In 2016 both Ratcliffe and Dyson advocated the UK leaving the European Union (EU) and interestingly have, since then, seen their wealth grow, whereas according to a report from the Centre for European Reform, Britain's economy is 5.5 per cent smaller than it would have been if the country had remained within the EU. The Centre for European Reform shows that the UK's trade is 7 per cent lower, and investment is 11 per cent lower, than if we had voted to remain in the EU (Forrest, 2022). Dyson has attracted criticism and claims of hypocrisy by opening a new global HQ in Singapore since the Brexit vote (*Sunday Times*, 2024). It is suggested this does not sit comfortably with his support for Brexit, which Dyson argued would give the UK a newfound 'freedom of spirit'. Clearly a 'benefit' that has yet to reach most UK residents at a time when poverty is rising and rough sleeping is increasing (*The Observer*, 2024).

While there is evidence indicating an increase in the wealth of the very richest, most people are not benefiting from the present economic system. This has led to growing criticism that mainstream economics is failing to consider their needs when providing answers to important questions such as how to address the 2007/2008 global financial crisis, to effectively deal with the COVID-19 pandemic and its aftermath, to satisfactorily minimize the impact of inflation, and what some claim is the elephant in the room, the UK leaving the EU (Toynbee and Walker, 2024). Instead, mainstream economics works in the interests of the elite, who are pushing to deregulate services and industries, while advocating paying fewer taxes, keeping wages low and reducing public spending (Abell, 2019; *The Guardian*, 2024).

To better understand this progressively deepening crisis that is affecting countries everywhere, we need to delve deeper into the ideology and practice that has created and continues to perpetuate the circumstances that impact detrimentally on countless communities, neighbourhoods and individuals both in the UK and globally.

We start here by defining and analysing the major economic, social and political force that since the late 1970s has pervaded all our lives and in turn has shaped a 'common sense' or 'natural' way of viewing, understanding and operating in the world. This dominant force is neoliberalism. In political and sociological terms its dominance legitimates certain norms and ideas, which the state and civil society disseminates through a range of devices such as education, the media, the political structure and the law. This domination is often expressed as hegemony or hegemonic power (Gramsci, 1971; Joseph, 2002; Anderson, 2017). We will return later in this chapter to consider the work of Antonio Gramsci and his writing on hegemony.

We will see how the all-encompassing political, social and economic project of neoliberalism has, through this hegemony, shifted the focus from community and collective wellbeing to individual responsibility, and to corporate acquisitiveness and greed. This shift has severely damaged the complex and often fragile fabric of our world, enriched the already wealthy, and driven down the living standards of millions in the UK, and billions more worldwide.

The second section of the chapter considers the increase of inequality and poverty, which is a constituent and important factor in the theory and practice that underpins the sustaining of neoliberalism. As the book progresses, we will be considering how neoliberalism, and the attendant inequality, has impacted on communities, neighbourhoods and individuals, specifically those living in London.

In the third section we consider the remarkable work of the Italian theorist and activist Antonio Gramsci (1891–1937) in understanding neoliberalism as a form of hegemony.

How and why neoliberalism emerged

It is well documented that as a political, social and economic project, neoliberalism emerged during the late 1970s, first under the military dictatorship in Chile, then internationally by democratic governments, such as those in the UK, led by Prime Minister Margaret Thatcher, and in the United States, led by President Ronald Reagan. These influential right-wing populist governments pioneered shifts in their policies and practices to greater emphasize the free market. The project was first termed monetarism, while in the United States it was labelled as neoconservatism, later recognized globally as neoliberalism (Bullock and Trombley, 1999; Piketty, 2014, 2020; Monbiot and Hutchison, 2024).

The central premise of neoliberalism, which is now recognized as the dominant political and economic ideology in most developed and developing countries, is that the free market is more effective than the state in dealing with persistent economic problems. This dominant narrative was created and fashioned over several years by leading right-wing politicians and economists, such as Milton Friedman (1962, 1993; Friedman and Friedman, 1980) and Friedrich von Hayek (1944, 1948, 1978), who railed against what they considered was the over-reliance on state-funded and state-supported economic activity. Their radical views stood in opposition to Keynesian social economic policies, which were developed during the late 1930s by the influential British economist John Maynard Keynes, and whose most significant thesis is considered a classic of economic scholarship (Keynes, 1936).

Keynesian economic policies get kicked into touch

Keynesian economic policies were introduced by numerous governments after the Second World War, who, dominated by the influence and economic power of the United States, linked their countries' currencies with a fixed rate to the dollar. This enabled them to make strategic borrowing decisions to introduce progressive tax regimes on individuals and companies to help fund and develop their ambitious and much-needed public and social policy programmes. These forms of direct state intervention helped to successfully kick-start and sustain economies around the world: economies and countries that had been shattered by an expensive and destructive war. The central plank of the Keynesian approach was for an active market sector supported by state ownership of core industries: usually termed the mixed economy.

Right-wing academics such as Friedman and von Hayek, together with several key political and economic commentators, had for many years argued that Keynesian economic policies were no longer relevant. They pointed to a crisis of simultaneous inflation and unemployment known as stagflation.

Instead, these academics and commentators, together with the policies and statements emanating from right-wing 'think tanks' such as in the UK the Institute for Economic Affairs, the Centre for Policy Studies and the Adam Smith Institute, claimed that by shifting the emphasis from the state to the market, national economies, and in turn the global economy, would grow more successfully, prosperity would rise, unemployment would be reduced, and taxes would be contained to 'more manageable' levels. Their view was that by giving even greater wealth, and therefore greater economic power, to corporations and the already well-off, the less wealthy including the poor would gain through the 'trickle-down' effect and they would in time become better-off. Monbiot and Hutchison (2024: 18) make a telling comment about these right-wing 'think tanks' that influenced governments, corporations, the media and the public: 'While they presented themselves as independent bodies offering dispassionate opinions on public affairs, in reality they behaved more like corporate lobbyists, working on behalf of their funders.'

What the neoliberals also wanted was to reduce the power of the trade union movement, which they saw as a barrier to the private sector, driving down wage rates and ensuring company shareholders received substantial profits for their investment. During the 1970s prominent advocates of neoliberalism were becoming increasingly aware that there was a declining rate of profitability, due mainly to underinvestment, and therefore a threat to their economic interests.

Thatcher and the Conservatives champion neoliberalism policies

It was no surprise, therefore, that on becoming prime minister in 1979, Margaret Thatcher set her sights on rolling out neoliberalism, including attacks on the trade union movement, which in her view was 'the enemy'. As a result of the Conservative government's neoliberal economic and social policies, large-scale redundancies in major manufacturing industries became commonplace, with unemployment reaching double figures for the first time since the interwar depression years. The Conservative government significantly reduced trade union and organized labour influence and power, and undertook a major reorganization of the welfare system, with increased surveillance of benefit recipients. At the same time, the government encouraged people to become entrepreneurs and to actively consider private education for their children and private healthcare for themselves and their families.

A vivid example of Thatcher's repression of trade union activity, which was one of her core policies, was the harassment of, and brutal and violent attacks on, picketing coal miners by the police. A few months into the 1984–1985 miners' strike, a pivotal event took place which was to shock the British public and observers globally. On 18 June 1984, a terrifying clash between police and miners occurred in Rotherham, South Yorkshire, an event which became known as the 'Battle of Orgreave'. The event, which involved the police on horseback charging at miners, was one of the most violent in British industrial history and has been described by the historian Tristian Hunt (2006) as 'a brutal example of legalised state violence'. Thatcher's success over the miners, who returned to work after a year-long strike, was thought by many as a victory of neoliberalism over labourism. Importantly, commentators such as Mansfield (2009) and Milne (2014) point not only to the impact of violence by the police, but also the increased surveillance by state agencies, which did much to intimidate miners and their families and led to dividing mining communities as well as proving to be a divisive wedge within British society. As a footnote to this event, on being elected to government in 1979, and before the miners' strike, the Conservatives awarded the police a 45 per cent pay rise. Like all authoritarian leaders, Thatcher knew she needed a reliant police force who were on her side as her government implemented what came to be realized as a divisive form of economic policy and practice, neoliberalism (Hall and Jacques, 1983).

To achieve electoral success in 1979, the Conservatives had packaged the radical neoliberal economic policies in the language of traditional conservatism that pivoted on tropes claiming they would 'restore the health of British economic and social life', 'ensure hard work paid' and 'help people buy their own homes'. As Blakeley (2019: 59) has commented, to achieve electoral success Thatcher built an alliance between the 'international capitalist class' centred in the City of London and 'middle earners in the south of England'. In Blakeley's view, Thatcher turned middle earners into mini capitalists through extending property ownership and the privatization of their pension funds.

As a result of Thatcher's electoral success, neoliberalism became embedded in the UK with the privatization of public bodies, the deregulation of capital markets, the introduction of private sector managerialism into the public sector, and significant reductions in government spending. The Conservatives' argument was it would free up resources for creating a private sector that would be efficient in the production and distribution of goods and services, thus driving growth and expansion from which everyone would gain (Cahill, 2012). At the same time, competitive markets were extended into politics and society including the public sector (Springer et al, 2016).

Cracks emerge in the neoliberal project

Just over 25 years into the global neoliberal project, it became clear that it was failing to deliver what the advocates had promised. The global financial crisis in 2007/2008 was a major blow to the perception that neoliberalism and, in particular, financialization, were providing benefits to everyone. Monbiot and Hutchison (2024: 116) argue that the crisis was 'a clear and indisputable refutation of both neoliberal theory and neoliberal practice'. The crisis, which was the worst since the Wall Street Crash of 1929 that had led to the Great Depression of the 1930s, was brought about by lightly regulated financial markets and banks worldwide being allowed to pursue excessive, often reckless, risk taking. In brief, financial institutions were making vast amounts of money out of enormous amounts of money.

The 21st-century crisis not only exposed the fundamental weaknesses of neoliberalism but also permitted financial institutions, which were at the root of the crisis, and had engaged in risky schemes, to be bailed out by governments. For example, at the height of the crisis, the UK government recompensed banks to the sum of £137 billion in the form of loans and new capital. The Chancellor of the Exchequer at the time, Alistair Darling, claimed the UK was hours away from a breakdown of law and order, saying that if the government had not intervened in supporting the financial institutions millions of people would not have been able to access their money (Darling, 2012).

Instead of abandoning or reducing the scope of neoliberalism, the global financial crisis gave governments everywhere an opportunity to impose wide-ranging austerity measures, resulting in further significant reductions in public sector spending, therefore penalizing the poorest sections of society and increasing the reach of the tentacles of the neoliberal project. In the UK, austerity enhanced the neoliberal project, with the 2010–2015 Conservative and Liberal Democratic coalition government arguing that the public spending cuts were needed to meet the obligations accrued from bailing out the financial institutions.

Meanwhile, in low-income countries, the International Monetary Fund also demanded austerity measures, including cutting state spending on public services such as health and education, while requiring governments to accept deregulation, privatization and trade liberalization in return for financial assistance. These came as part of Structural Adjustment Programmes, which provided countries with debt relief or loans. The impact of austerity led to millions globally experiencing stagnant wages, job insecurity and rising living costs. The reductions and in some cases dismantling of welfare systems and public services by governments was to place individuals, families and communities under further serious pressure (Babb and Kentikelenis, 2018).

Austerity comes under attack

Leading economic and political commentators have argued that the austerity measures introduced by governments globally was driven by political rather than economic considerations. For example, the eminent American economist and Nobel Prize winner Paul Krugman (2012) argues that after the financial crisis neoliberal governments took the opportunity to further reduce state spending and activity, particularly in social welfare, to maintain the power and wealth of dominant classes and groups. Meanwhile, the Scottish-American political scientist Mark Blyth (2014) argues that government debt was borne mainly by the poorest in society, and the British scholar of politics Andrew Gamble (2015) states that austerity is a form of statecraft that emerged from a right-wing political ideology and not economic requirements.

COVID-19 pandemic: governments change direction (slightly and not for long)

During the first two years of the COVID-19 pandemic, and to save lives and protect vulnerable health care systems, there was a clear change of direction by governments. Prior to the pandemic, the UK NHS had suffered several years of drastic and damaging financial cuts through the imposition of austerity measures. However, during 2020 and 2021 governments made strategic and large-scale interventions with massive financial borrowing from the international money markets to vastly increase spending on health services, employment schemes and on income support uplifts for the poorest, all of which was aimed at protecting individuals, businesses and national economies. During the 2019/2020 period, prior to the COVID-19 pandemic, the UK government spent £148.9 billion on the NHS. However, in the first year of the pandemic this jumped to £191 billion and in 2021/2022 it was £190.03 billion (Kings Fund, 2022). It is projected that in future years, Labour government spending on healthcare will increase, although with people living longer, the demand for health services is similarly likely to increase. Whatever happens in the UK regarding public spending over the coming years, the continuing domination and influence of the rich and economically powerful means that the government, whether it's the present Labour administration or that of a centre-right political party such as the Conservative Party, or even a far-right party such as Reform UK, is likely to maintain its clear adherence to neoliberalism and restrict spending on welfare, health and education.

What's wrong with neoliberalism?

A finely tuned, impressive critique of neoliberalism has come from a considerable body of progressive and radical commentators. For example, Gilbert (2020) has evidenced that liberalism has over many years taken different forms, but at its heart it has meant putting the rights of individuals ahead of the needs of community, tradition or state. To quote Gilbert:

> [N]eo-liberalism is the most explicitly and aggressively pro-capitalist version of liberalism ever formulated. Where liberals tend to assume that being a self-interested, competitive entrepreneur is the state for human beings, neoliberals know that it isn't. But that's still how they want people to behave. So they want to use both the state and corporate power to force us to behave like that, whether we like it or not. (Gilbert, 2020: 27–28)

Similarly, McChesney (2011: 8) has called neoliberalism 'capitalism with the gloves off', while in the words of Monbiot and Hutchison (2024: 3) it is 'an ideology whose central belief is that competition is the defining feature of humankind'.

In short, while neoliberalism is presented as innate, and governed by nature or in this case the market, it is a powerful and aggressive ideology and practice which has been politically constructed to celebrate and further self-interest and unrestricted competition. Where neoliberalism has been most fiercely applied, such as in the UK and the United States, social mobility has declined, as the new elite has established a hegemony of economic power and influence that involves spending its money on high-end conspicuous luxury consumption; purchasing the 'best', and usually the most expensive, private education for its children; by developing valuable networks and connections (often termed social capital) to protect and further their own and their family's interests; while insulating their children from financial penury with the benefits of tax-break inheritance (Harvey, 2005; Klein, 2007; Venugopal, 2015).

Finally, the author and environmental campaigner George Monbiot has constantly alerted us to the impact of neoliberalism. He has described neoliberalism as dominated by 'powerful agents – corporations and oligarchs – who use their position to demand special treatment: contracts, handouts, tax breaks, treaties, the crushing of resistance and other political favours. They extend their power beyond their trading relationships through their ownership of the media and their funding and control of political parties' (Monbiot, 2017b: 3–4). It is these 'powerful agents' that have done much to shape and determine how we live our lives; where we reside, what schools our children attend, what health and social care services we access, and what employment opportunities are available. Under neoliberalism some people have prospered and grown wealthy, enjoying well-above-average incomes, and a small minority of these have established themselves as the super-rich with what many consider to be obscene levels of affluence. However, the majority have not benefited, and in fact millions of people in the UK and internationally now reside in poverty and many of those have increasingly been dependent on food banks for emergency assistance.

Globalization

The concept of globalization is important here as it operates hand-in-glove with neoliberalism. Since the end of the Second World War, we have witnessed the rapid expansion of a transnational or global economy, where markets and enterprises operate internationally in a 'borderless world' with cross-border production being driven by the need for economies of scale. At the same time there has been a disconnection between the democratic systems of nations and states and large-scale foreign investment which is underpinned and hidden by offshore banking.

Markets have extended their global reach, and in the process have created increasing and deepening interconnectiveness between and across different national and regional economies. Huge transnational corporations, together with powerful international economic institutions such as the World Bank, the International Monetary Fund, the Organisation for Economic Co-operation and Development and the World Trade Organization, as well as expansive regional trading systems including the EU, have emerged as the major players that determine the global economic order of the 21st century.

In response to globalization and interconnectiveness we are witnessing the rise in nationalism. Such examples include the vote in the UK in 2016 to leave the EU, the support in Scotland for independence from the UK, and the populist desire in the United States 'to make America great again' and introduce trading tariffs. India has seen the rise of right-wing populism and religious nationalism, while in Myanmar, Thailand and Sri Lanka we have seen the results of militant Buddhist nationalism.

Despite the trend towards nationalism in many countries and regions, there are limits to what nation states can achieve individually, and consequently they are reliant on transnational corporations for investment, markets and distribution, further empowering a global capitalist class. This class thrives on expanding across boundaries and furthering their profits. To facilitate this, they often collude and reward national governments and their elected officials and civil servants, while exploiting workers with poor working conditions and low wages, and at the same time demanding the removal or reduction of trade union activity.

Nationalism encourages geopolitical competition, hence the establishment of supra-national and economic forums mentioned earlier which can restrict what nation states can undertake as cooperation with other nations and institutions will determine domestic policy choices.

A key feature of globalization is fast-changing technology, whether it is in the development of microchips or artificial intelligence, high-tech is used to quickly switch capital and structural investment around the globe. It is argued that the powerful mixture of technology and globalization breaks down traditional cultures and encourages developing countries to adopt

Westernized and usually Americanized ways of life. This is often termed the 'Washington Consensus', with the deregulation of domestic markets, the privatization of public companies, and the liberalization of trade and finance (Babb and Kentikelenis, 2021). In more recent years, the 'Washington Consensus' has been challenged by the increasing influence of Chinese economic and political power in parts of Africa, Asia and the Middle East, as well as in Europe. This 'Belt and Road Initiative', or the 'Beijing Consensus', is a global development strategy adopted by the Chinese government and involves infrastructure development and investments in over 150 countries and international organizations. The purpose of the 'Beijing Consensus' is to control capitalism through a strong state, and in place of political liberalism that is prominent in the Western model, the Chinese model rewards those supporting the major and influential role played by the ruling political party (Chen, 2017).

Summarizing neoliberalism

As we have outlined, neoliberalism is an ideology that claims that free markets are the most efficient means of allocating resources. It advocates minimal state intervention in economic and social matters and believes in the freedom of trade and capital. Neoliberalism has created a powerful hegemony that benefits states, corporations and influential super-rich individuals. This hegemony encourages beliefs and ideas which serve to justify the interests of the dominant groups and resists any suggestion of policies which would significantly increase taxation on massive corporations and the super-rich. At the same time, attempts to make any meaningful redistribution of wealth and opportunities as well as any moves to increase regulation on the activities of major businesses are thwarted. Neoliberalism has determined policy and practice in all areas of our lives, which over many decades has resulted in greater inequality and poverty in urban and rural communities in all countries. It is to this matter that we now turn our attention.

Increasing inequality and poverty

One of the clearest outcomes of neoliberalism, and which those advocating the ideology claim is beneficial, is growing inequality and poverty. Internationally, inequality has resulted in the concentration of enormous income and wealth into the hands of a few strategically placed individuals, such as Elon Musk, Jeff Bezos, Bill Gates, Mark Zuckerberg, Bernard Arnault and the British billionaire and founder of one of world's largest online gambling companies, bet365, Denise Coates. At the same time, many massive powerful international corporations have wealth greater than some developing nations. Of considerable concern is research linking increasing income inequality with worsening political polarization and disenchantment with political systems (Rostboll, 2024).

The Washington, DC based Institute for Policy Studies demonstrate that, unsurprisingly, neoliberalism has contributed to rising inequality in almost every country in the world. Further, Inequality.org, which is located at the Institute for Policy Studies, reports that the United States exhibits wider disparities of wealth between rich and poor than any other major developed nation. For example, a 2013 UNICEF report ranked the United States as having the second highest relative child poverty rates in the developed world (Fisher, 2013).[2]

The global charity Oxfam has been at the forefront of researching and reporting inequality throughout the world. Its report, *Survival of the Richest* (Oxfam, 2023), makes for alarming reading tracking how the richest in the world have become dramatically richer, while corporate profits have reached record highs. This comprehensively researched report provides evidence that:

- Since 2020, globally, the richest 1 per cent have captured nearly two-thirds of all new wealth, which is nearly twice as much as money as those in the remaining 99 per cent.
- Billionaire fortunes are increasing by US$2.7 billion a day. This is happening while inflation is outpacing the wages of 1.7 billion workers.
- Food and energy companies more than doubled their profits in 2022, paying out US$257 billion to wealthy shareholders.

As Danny Sriskandarajah, Oxfam's chief executive in Great Britain, comments:

> The explosion in billionaire's fortunes at a time when poverty is increasing lays bare the fundamental flaws in our economies. Even during a global crisis our unfair economic systems manage to deliver eye-watering windfalls for the wealthiest but fail to protect the poorest ... they (world leaders) can start to right these wrongs by implementing progressive taxes on capital and wealth and deploying that revenue to save lives and invest in our future. (Quoted in Elliott, 2022)

As Shah (2022) has commentated, wealth is a key determinant of whether households can weather unexpected major shocks such as the COVID-19 pandemic, because such shocks directly affect people's living standards.

To understand the impact and extent of inequality we need to ask why equality is important.

Why is equality important?

This is a contentious area of political, economic and social debate that divides people, with usually conservative-minded people arguing inequality is 'normal' and necessary as it encourages people to work harder and is a valuable spur to economic activity. Others, usually progressives and left radicals, argue that however hard and diligent those from certain backgrounds work, the odds of them gaining significant wealth and income is negligible. This is where a complex combination of class, with the benefits of inherited wealth, together with race and gender, leads to discrimination operating in overt and covert ways. If, against the odds, those from working-class backgrounds secure prestigious jobs, it has been found they earn, on average, 16 per cent less than colleagues from privileged backgrounds (Freidman and Laurison, 2020). While there is evidence of some limited social mobility in the UK due mainly to the expansion of higher education, the development of professions with accessible qualifications, and the increased use of the internet and the 'new economy', there is clear data showing the increasing concentration of wealth and therefore power at the pinnacle of the social hierarchy. It remains therefore that neoliberalism has widened the inequality gap between the rich and the poorest in societies everywhere.

Social scientists have long recognized the phenomenon of inequality. For example, Dorling (2015, 2018, 2019, 2023, 2024), Wilkinson and Pickett (2010, 2018) and Wilkinson (2005) all present irrefutable evidence that the more equal a country is, the more its infants survive childhood, crime is lower, and the population enjoys better health and is consequently happier. These researchers argue that narrowing the disparities between income and wealth among the population benefits all in society. To quote Dorling:

> Inequalities harm the rich as well as the poor. The rich are not necessarily especially hard working, well behaved, happy or creative. Some are obsessed with making money and can be driven by that. Most behave much better when they are more like the rest of us. They can have appalling social skills while believing that they are 'phenomenally bright'. Many don't understand that it is questionable why the poor should work hard for a pittance, obey the law, or any other conventions, when the poor are members of a group being treated unfairly. (Dorling, 2012: 13–14)

As well as being one of the most economically unequal countries of all large European countries (Dorling, 2018), evidence shows that inequality in the UK has increased considerably since 1979, the year neoliberal policies were first introduced by the newly elected Thatcher-led Conservative government. In fact, in more recent times the gap between the richest and poorest in the UK has widened further and, in 2022, the incomes of the poorest 14 million fell by 7.5 per cent while the incomes of the richest fifth saw a 7.8 per cent increase (ONS, 2023).

Turning to wealth in Great Britain, we note an even greater unequal disparity than between incomes. The work of Byrne (2024) is valuable here as he shows that:

- Between 2010 and 2021 the average wealth in the top 1 per cent of the richest in Britain rose by £1,670,121, which is 31 times the increase in the average wealth of the bottom 99 per cent, which rose by just £53,409.
- Overall wealth in the UK increased by more than £4 trillion between 2020 and 2021. Twenty-three per cent of this total went to the top 1 per cent.

Further, research by Advani et al (2020) found that the richest 1 per cent of households had almost £800 billion more wealth than suggested by official statistics, which reflects the view that inequality is far higher than previously thought. These researchers argue that around 5 per cent of the total wealth held by the very richest has been missed by official measures. They show that almost 25 per cent of all household wealth is held by the richest 1 per cent of the population.

Although the wealth of the richest in the UK has grown at tremendous speed, the tax take from this group has failed to keep pace. A key reason for this is that there have been large increases in the value of main residences which remain untaxed. In their defence, Patriotic Millionaires, a nonpartisan network of British millionaires, has called for the introduction of permanent wealth taxes on themselves and other super-rich people to reduce extreme inequality and raise revenue for sustained increases in public services including healthcare (Neate, 2022a).

While the rich have gained increasing income and wealth, the poor in the UK have become further dependent on welfare benefits and food banks (Toynbee and Walker, 2020, 2024). British government statistics report that as of 2022, around 11 million were in relative poverty, with that number increasing to 14.4 million (or 21 per cent of the UK population) when housing costs are considered (JRF, 2024).

The UK non-governmental organization and charity the Trussell Trust states that by February 2023 it was supporting the work of over 1,400 UK food banks, which provide emergency food and compassionate, practical support to people in crisis. Food banks in the Trussell Trust network distributed nearly three million food parcels from April 2022 to March 2023, an increase of 37 per cent compared to the same period in the previous year. This is in addition to food parcels provided by at least 1,172 independent food banks. The fact that one of the richest countries in the world has nearly a quarter of its population living in poverty, together with clear evidence of growing food bank use, is a serious indictment of its neoliberal economic and social policies.[3]

Researchers such as Danny Dorling, Richard Wilkinson and Kate Pickett, as well as the Equality Trust, have undertaken extensive research to inform us how social and economic inequality persists and why societies with less equality have greater social problems than those with a narrower gap between the rich and the poor. Basically, these researchers evidence the damage wreaked by neoliberalism on societies everywhere. They highlight the unsustainability of a divisive economic system that encourages and rewards self-interest while arguing for the move to a fairer world which is driven by values, policies and politics that reject the present unjust approach and, in its place, situate a more socially and economically equal and sustainable future.

As mentioned earlier, the income and wealth inequality that the UK now experiences is a deliberate consequence of neoliberal policies can be traced back to Margaret Thatcher's radical populist political programme dating from her government's election in 1979. As I have written elsewhere, creating greater inequality and disadvantage was a defining feature of what became known as Thatcherism (Popple, 2021a). It provided the Conservative government with the means to encourage and create the divisive environment where British people were divided against each other: miners against the police, property owners against those who paid rent for their accommodation, the employed against the unemployed, those living in the north of the country against those residing in the south, those working in heavy industry against the new technological-based industries, the public sector against the private sector, white people against the BAME population, and the middle class against the working class.

Thatcher's response to those unable or unprepared to associate themselves with the new world of neoliberalism was to label them as 'moaning minnies [sic]', scroungers and lazy (Young, 2013). In short, Thatcher was undoubtedly the most divisive and polarizing prime minister of the 20th century (Hall and Jacques, 1983). During her 11-and-a-half years as Prime Minister, Thatcher was both popular and unpopular in relatively equal amounts. The outcome of the changes the Conservative governments made to British life in that period was due to Thatcher's unwavering support in furthering neoliberalism. These changes were to leave deep scars in tens of thousands of communities throughout the country and created the conditions that continue to exist (Evans, 2013). It is against this background that we can now consider inequality in London, where so many of its population are extremely poor while a few have accumulated massive wealth and power.

London and increasing inequality

As a 'world city' (Forrest et al, 2017), London is a capital city that can be described in several different ways. It is the home of the financial centre of the UK; the most popular city for tourists in the country; home to the UK Parliament and the principal offices of state; a major hub for national and international media outlets; and contains the country's legal focal point with the Central Criminal Court. London is served by five major airports (City, Gatwick, Heathrow, Luton and Stansted), with Heathrow considered to be one of the world's busiest flight hubs, and the main gateway into the UK for non-European visitors. It has been estimated London is the home to a third of the country's wealth, is the playground for the super-rich enjoying conspicuous luxury consumption, while having more people living in poverty than other Western cities. London is, then, increasingly becoming polarized, with a population of the extraordinarily rich and the extremely poor, with areas and communities in-between these two groups.

According to research by Multilingual Capital based in the Department of Linguistics, Queen Mary University of London, London is also the most ethnically diverse city in the UK and one of the most ethnically diverse in the world, with over 300 languages spoken in Greater London. Multilingual Capital also discovered that over 20 per cent of Londoners use a main language other than English. Further, the 2021 Census shows that London is the most ethnically diverse region in England, with 46 per cent of its residents identified with Asian, Black, mixed or 'other' ethnic groups and a further 17 per cent with white ethnic minorities.

While there remain poor communities in the very centre of London, the overall trend is it becoming a segregated city where both the poorest members of society, as well as many from the middle classes, are being pushed to the outer suburbs. Large swathes of inner London are now being taken over by the super-wealthiest, who are engaged in hyper-consumption and hyper-gentrification. Neoliberal advocates argue that this wealth will 'trickle down' to the rest of the city and benefit the country. There is little evidence of this, and although the City of London, as the financial centre of the UK, provides around 11 per cent of all the country's tax receipts (H. Jones, 2017), it is also a fact that London as a capital city has the largest number of wealthy people per head of population, greater than in New York and Tokyo which are also 'world cities' (Forrest et al, 2017), while the poorest have also grown in number. London has been described in the following way:

> This is a city increasingly for money, not for people. It is here that capital, capitalism and the capitalist elite come together. In doing so, these combined forces have torn up the mission statement of the city as a place for all. Now, perhaps more than ever before, it is a playground for the wealthy and a hothouse in which to grow capital under hydroponic conditions, carefully tended by the city's politicians and financial institutions. (Atkinson, 2020: 9–10)

It is generally agreed that the UK's relatively liberal but secure financial practices have attracted the world's mobile hot money into London:

> The international rich come to the city in search of prime assets to buy and sell, to take advantage of house prices cheapened by strong foreign currencies, to escape the insecurities or dangers presented by their own governments, or to offload bundles of criminally sourced cash, laundered through London's real estate. Some even come to the city to live. (Atkinson, 2020: 11)

In 2020 it was estimated that around 5 per cent of Central London homes were empty, with one third of luxury flats in the area being bought by overseas buyers. All of which has led to the comment that the 'London property market ... is now chaotic, massively distorted by money laundering and its status as depository for the world's spare cash' (Jenkins, 2020: 4). Similarly, Hyde has vividly described London in the following manner:

> A huge part of Britian's post-imperial decline has been the breathlessly enthusiastic capitulation to foreign money – from Russia, China, the Middle east and beyond. London has sold off its landmarks to the money, built luxury properties to stand empty while helping the money offshore itself, and worked ingeniously to launder the money. A vast and well-renumerated service class exists to ease all this along, from lawyers to accountants to reputation managers to advise the money on how to get its children into the right schools, with the corruption expert Oliver Bullough memorably describing our new status as 'butler of the world'. (Hyde, 2024: 14)

In summary, while London has Europe's wealthiest region (the inner west of the city) it also has the highest child poverty rate of any region in England with two of the most deprived local authorities in the country (The Childhood Trust, 2021). In Chapter 3 we will be examining in more detail London as a city of inequality and how the capital city is being reimagined by developers with working-class housing estates being demolished while long-standing diverse communities are undergoing displacement to make way for new urban neighbourhoods.

Antonio Gramsci

One of the recurring themes in this chapter, and in the book overall, is the concept of hegemony, in particular cultural hegemony. A major writer in this area has been the Italian neo-Marxist intellectual and political activist

Antonio Gramsci (1891–1937), who offered us a valuable original view of how a ruling elite shape and maintain a society to their benefit.

First, a few details about Gramsci. An Italian born in Sardinia in 1891 his family was considered middle class but had fallen on hard times. While being brought up in Sardinia Gramsci witnessed and experienced at first-hand poverty, famine, disease and illiteracy among the islanders. He saw for himself that elections were fixed by local landlords to benefit themselves while any form of rebellion or resistance by islanders was put down by those in power. He also witnessed his father being jailed on false charges (Bambery, 2006). These experiences radicalized Gramsci and, although disabled and sickly from labouring jobs, he won a scholarship to the University of Turin. It was here that Gramsci became further radicalized with his involvement in the struggles with Turin workers both during and after the First World War. Gramsci's participation in these struggles and his political action in opposition to the fascist government of Bennito Mussolini led to him being jailed for ten years. It was while in jail, and despite suffering from chronic ill health, that Gramsci wrote a compendium of work which from the late 20th century onwards has become increasingly influential. Gramsci's written work was scrutinized and censored by prison authorities so that it came to the public often in a fragmentary, cryptic and disjointed form. However, scholars have worked diligently to faithfully construct Gramsci's ideas and thinking so that we now have an accessible body of knowledge that is both original and wide-ranging. While Gramsci was a polemic thinker, and tentative and undogmatic in his approach, he has brought to us an understanding of what has been described as 'the profound transformation which is under way in Western liberal-bourgeois societies under the aegis of the "new Right"' (Hall, 1982: 10).

Probably one of the most important aspects of Gramsci's approach to politics, which was formed in the context of anti-capitalist and anti-fascist struggles, is his rejection of Marxist thinking that emphasized determinism and economic reductionism. For this reason, Gramsci is sometimes described as a neo-Marxist as he also drew from a range of other writers, including Niccolo Machiavelli, Vilfredo Pareto and Benedetto Croce. Gramsci is best known for his theory of cultural hegemony, which he used to explain the social-control structures of society. What is important for our work here is Gramsci's theory that the dominant ideology projects the view that the social, political and economic status quo is natural and innate. The argument goes that the dominant ideology benefits all. Gramsci comments that to maintain this dominant ideology the ruling elite, sometimes described as the capitalist class with all the power that comes with it, deploy a combination of force, including the armed forces, the police, the law courts and the prisons, and consent through the political, moral and intellectual leadership within society (Gramsci, 1971, 1975, 1977, 1978). The domination by means of hegemony has been described as 'the relation between classes and other social forces. A hegemonic class, or part of a class, is one which gains the consent of other classes and social forces thorough creating and maintaining a system of alliance by means of a political struggle' (Simon, 1982: 22).

For our purposes we need to note that consent is gained through a plethora of apparatus including the media, and education, as well as elements of civil society including churches, charitable and community groups, political parties, and trade unions.

> To achieve an effective hegemony, Gramsci argued, there must be a number of beliefs or ideas which are generally accepted by all but which serve to justify the interests of the dominant groups. These images, concepts and ideas which 'make sense' of everyday experiences are collectively known as an 'ideology'. (Popple, 2015: 76)

In our examination of neoliberalism, we have seen how this has been positioned as 'common sense'. It is the 'natural order' for economic, political and social affairs yet the evidence presented here demonstrates that neoliberalism benefits the ruling elite, the global corporations and the super-rich, and not the majority who are subject to detrimental aspects of neoliberalism including inequality and poverty. The dominant ideology, through a complex web of ideological processes, establishes an agreed understanding of reality that benefits the ruling elite. This understanding of reality 'permeates our principles, social relationships and intellectual and moral positions' (Popple, 2015: 77). We will be considering this concept further in the following chapter when we introduce the notion of 'counter-hegemony'.

Conclusion

This chapter has provided an overview of the forces at play in the crisis that faces us all. We have defined and analysed neoliberalism, and how the underlining political, social and economic ideology has infiltrated all our lives and in turn has become a 'common sense' or 'natural' way of viewing. We have seen how this powerful ideology is now the dominant hegemony which has moved the focus from community and collective wellbeing to individual responsibility, and to corporate acquisitiveness and greed, which in turn has severely damaged the complex fabric of our world.

A useful way of describing neoliberalism is 'socialism for the rich and capitalism for the poor'. This was demonstrated in the aftermath of the 2008 global financial crisis, when the primary financial institutions including banks went into meltdown and had to be bailed out by the governments in most developed countries. These mega banks survived due to the financial bailouts and remedial measures with, for example, the Royal Bank of Scotland receiving a taxpayer bailout of £45 billion from the UK government. However, the outcome for many individuals was devasting, with millions losing their jobs globally and many more being caught in a cycle of debt. In the UK, paying for the economic crisis led to the imposition of austerity by the 2010–2015 Conservative and Liberal Democrat coalition government, with deep cuts in welfare, health and education spending which affected everyone, but hitting the poorest in the country hardest.

However, the neoliberal project is now under pressure, and some would argue is in crisis. We were made aware during the COVID-19 pandemic that governments, despite claiming during austerity that the state should reduce its spending, vastly increased their financial outlay to protect health services and people, and to keep businesses afloat, so that they would maintain their productive levels on returning to full capacity.

The achievement of neoliberal-driven deregulation and free-trade policies has been to increase the wealth of the richest, move national income from labour to capital, and advance corporate profitability. However, it is these very same 'successes' that have heralded a crisis which has destabilized the world economy where the growth of inequality and poverty has become a major political issue with the possibility of social unrest that will require urgent addressing. As we saw earlier, neoliberalism has created a severe disjunction between the rich and privileged, the poorest, and the many in between who live in communities and neighbourhoods throughout London. We will be examining this in more detail in subsequent chapters.

In the final section of this chapter we considered how the thinking of Antonio Gramsci has shaped the understandings we have used to examine neoliberalism and the impact of inequality in the UK and globally.

In the following chapter we discuss that while there is evidence that neoliberalism has damaged democracy, the outcome has led to people engaging in dissent and protest. This is particularly so regarding the global climate crisis which has been stimulated by neoliberalism. The result has been responses from a range of local, national and international environmental groups. We will also consider other strategic and major issues that have become central in UK life, and which have echoes in countries and regions internationally. We will consider how these events have created a toxic culture where democracy is at risk. We will also see how people have agency in confronting these crucial aspects of contemporary life in its broadest sense, both politically and culturally.

2

Challenging the Neoliberal Hegemony

Keith Popple

Introduction

In the previous chapter we examined the centrality of neoliberalism in determining and shaping global and national economic and political affairs and how this powerful regressive hegemonic project creates and sustains growing poverty and inequality. At the same time neoliberalism produces and reproduces massive financial gains for global corporations and the already super-rich.

We considered how these global corporations together with national governments and international financial organizations such as the World Bank and the International Monetary Fund, as well as enormously wealthy individuals, have advocated neoliberal economic and social policies that encourage and reward the privatization of public assets, and the reductions in progressive taxation. This approach goes hand-in-glove with imposing legal restrictions on trade unions and reducing spending on key public services like education and health services.

To further understand the extent of the far-reaching tentacles of neoliberalism we introduced the writings of the neo-Marxist philosopher, writer and political activist Antonio Gramsci, whose erudite work on cultural hegemony demonstrates how the ruling elite shapes culture for its own advantage. This dominant ideology is presented as 'common sense', 'natural' and 'inevitable', which contributes to enabling the powerful and super-rich to subordinate and exploit the majority.

In this chapter, we look at efforts to counter the neoliberal hegemony. We do this by first considering the impact neoliberalism has on democracy, which some consider, in its present form, is not fit for purpose (Lim, 2017).

Further, there is increasing evidence of a lack of trust in UK politicians and political parties that has emerged from numerous scandals and broken promises (Popple, 2021b; Romei, 2024; Jones, 2025).

After interrogating what is meant by democracy and some of the considerable deficiencies as it presently operates, we explore the impact of neoliberalism on recent phenomena and events that have led to a serious questioning, resistance and challenge to the dominant narrative and practice. We will consider significant movements that have emerged as an example of counter-hegemony. We look at this regarding widespread resistance to the climate crisis.

Progressive perspectives and political action that centre on these strategic developments offer us hope for a sustainable, more democratic and equal future than that provided by the present economic and political hegemony. By examining the impact of the climate crisis and the resulting resistance we consider how vested interests in the UK and elsewhere set the agenda that favours powerful elements of the status quo. We examine how human agency and resistance has played an important counter-hegemonic role in confronting the power of political and economic influential groups and individuals and their neoliberal agenda.

Why democracy matters and why it's under strain

It is often stated and widely accepted that most people live in countries that claim to enjoy democracy. At its most basic, democracy means 'rule by the people', that is the people are the highest authority, and in turn the elected representatives are accountable to the people. A central aspect of democracy means actively encouraging citizens to vote and participate in 'free and fair elections' where people cast their vote in private. The result is elected representatives serving in local authorities and national governments which are responsible for the tax-raising regimes that finance the public services that are considered essential in a civilized society. It is agreed that democracy involves ensuring the security and freedom of citizens through the maintenance of law and order and protecting them from external forces. A democracy grants citizens freedom of speech on the understanding that what is said or written is within the parameters of the law. Further, a democratic society is expected to promote political equality and protect human rights (Held, 2006).

The most common form of democracy is representative democracy, where decisions are made by elected representatives. Countries like the UK that have adopted this form of decision making are termed 'liberal democracies'. However, 'liberal democracies' have been described as a sham by some political left commentators and activists, including by the philosophers and political theorists Karl Marx and Friedrich Engels (1848) and the Russian revolutionary, politician and political theorist Vladimir Lenin (Service, 2011). These activists and writers argue that in a capitalist society the privileged elite monopolize power and dominate and rule most people, who are basically passive consumers of capitalist goods and services. In this view the majority or the mass are permitted to express ideals of 'equality' and 'freedom' so long as it does not threaten the status quo who continue to benefit and thrive in a system rigged in favour of the powerful minority. This has led some commentators, such as Ayers and Sadd-Filho (2014), to question whether neoliberalism and democracy are compatible.

It is not possible here to outline the long and turbulent historical development of the UK's democratic structures except to say the modern form of democracy we have now has been hard-won over many centuries, and particularly since the late 1800s. However, there is little doubt that the democratic structures of the 21st century are under considerable pressure. Trust in politics is now at an all-time low. In a UK survey undertaken in 2023, only 9 per cent of the public stated they trust politicians to tell the truth, the lowest since the IPOS annual survey was launched in 1983. In 2022 the figure was 12 per cent. These figures compare with trust in nurses, which registered at 88 per cent, with airline pilots and librarians close behind (Clemance and King, 2023).

There are several reasons why there is a lack of trust in democracy in the UK and around the world. The impact of neoliberalism, with the removal of trade barriers and deregulation of national economies and the resultant increase in inequality in democratic countries, has led to a rise of populist and nationalist politics with the accompanying authoritarian tendencies. These trends, it is argued, are an example of democracy failing (Cooper, 2021).

The rise of populist nationalist politics is particularly noticeable in the United States, which, as we noted in Chapter 1, has serious levels of inequality and poverty. It is in the United States that we can witness the manoeuvring linked with the muscular nationalism of Donald Trump. In his two presidential election campaigns, and then in his time in office as president, Trump has demonstrated narcissistic, socially dominant features coupled with aggressive megalomanic tendencies and a wish to win, at what seems to be any cost, the adoration of others. Trump's grandiose 2016 election campaign message was 'Make America Great' and then in the 2024 campaign it became 'Make America Great Again'. While enjoying the influence and privilege of being the most powerful elected politician in the world, Trump's closest associates and advisers are some of the richest, most powerful individuals and represent the most dominant corporations on the planet. At the same time, Trump claims to represent a considerably less wealthy white working class against the 'corrupt' Washington establishment. During his bruising 2016 election campaign, Trump threatened to 'lock up' his Democratic Party opponent, Hillary Clinton, and during his similarly aggressive 2024 campaign he launched unsubstantiated personal attacks on his Democratic rival Kamala Harris. This, plus Trump's role in the 6 January 2021 violent mob attack on the US Capitol in Washington, DC was to seriously damage the image of, and trust in, democracy in the United States (Brady and Kent, 2022).

Sleaze, scandal and corruption

In the UK, one of the reasons for a lack of trust in democracy is the parliamentary sleaze, scandals and corruption that have been regularly exposed during the last few years (*The Independent*, 2024). The sleaze and scandals range from sexual misdemeanours, the breaking of ministerial codes and, during the Boris Johnson premiership (2019–2022), the behaviour by Johnson, and the Chancellor of the Exchequer, Rishi Sunak, who attended drinks parties that were held by government and Conservative Party staff in 10 Downing Street and other government buildings during the COVID-19 pandemic in 2020 and 2021. This was at a time when public health restrictions prohibited most gatherings. After numerous strong denials by Johnson that he and others attended these social gatherings, it was revealed they had been participating in what was termed 'Partygate' and for which they received Metropolitan Police fixed penalty fines. Johnson's wife, Carrie, who participated in social gatherings also received a fixed penalty fine.

The Partygate incident was part of an observable disintegration of standards in public life during the Conservative government's time in office (Addley, 2024), and this, together with their overall mismanagement of the economy, was to lead to their spectacular downfall in the 2024 general election (Murphy and Baker, 2024; M. Smith, 2024). The failure to properly manage the economy was particularly clear under the tenure of Johnson's successor, Liz Truss, who held the position for 49 days in September and October 2022, making her the shortest-serving prime minister in British history. During her short, disastrous period in office, Truss oversaw a controversial mini-budget delivered by her Chancellor of the Exchequer, Kwasi Kwarteng. The mini-budget was badly received by the financial markets primarily for its proposal for unfunded tax cuts and, as a result, the pound sterling fell to its lowest level against the US dollar, mortgage interest rates and property rents increased, while the Bank of England was driven to engage in buying government bonds (Helm and Inman, 2022). After initially strongly defending the mini-budget, Truss removed Kwarteng, replacing him with another cabinet minister, Jeremy Hunt, who reversed many of the policies outlined in the min-budget, leading to further financial instability (Bogdanor, 2022). Under pressure from her party, Truss resigned, making way for Rishi Sunak, who *The Economist* (2023) described as 'the most right-wing Conservative prime minister since Margaret Thatcher'.

Attempting to defend the Conservative government's chequered time in power, Sunak called an election for 4 July 2024. The government's inability to provide the population with a feel-good factor after years of declining living standards, due mainly to mismanaging the economy, plus overseeing underfunded and overstretched public services, together with the public's reaction to the shenanigans described earlier, led to the loss of people's trust and ended with the electorate comprehensively rejecting them at the ballot box. The outcome for the Conservatives was a catastrophic loss of parliamentary seats and the installing of a Labour government which at the time of writing has a 156-vote working majority. The message from the voters was enough is enough (Romain, 2024).

Cronyism

Another reason for the lack of trust in the democratic system was the Conservative government's response to the COVID-19 pandemic in which cronyism was operating. During 2020, Chancellor of the Exchequer Rishi Sunak made public funds available to deal with the pandemic. In tandem with this development, the neoliberal-driven government reverted to type and began to place contracts for much-needed medical and health equipment and key related jobs with personal contacts, an approach commonly known as cronyism.

In short, cronyism is the practice of awarding benefits, such as jobs or contracts, to friends or colleagues. For example, appointing 'cronies' to influential positions, although they are not qualified or experienced enough to effectively undertake the responsibilities involved in the role. Cronyism has existed in different forms since people exercised power, however it was a source of concern during the COVID-19 pandemic when so many people fell ill and died while health workers and key workers were risking their health and ultimately their lives.

Geoghegan (2021) has provided us with a vivid and detailed account of how the government outsourced much of the pandemic response in England to companies with strong links to Conservative politicians but had little obvious relevant experience. One example of the many that Geoghegan outlines is that of Ayanda Capital, a London-based investment company which, despite having no known experience in the health equipment field, was awarded a £252 million contract to provide face masks, 50 million of which were never used due to concerns about them fitting properly around the face. The deal was brokered by an adviser to the Board of Trade – which prior to her time as prime minister was chaired by Liz Truss MP, who was then a member of the UK government's cabinet, and the President of the Board of Trade and Secretary of International Trade, who as Geoghegan says 'just happened to be a senior board adviser' (2021: 310).

The Good Law Project (www.goodlawproject.org), a UK-based not-for-profit campaign organization that uses the law to protect the interests of the public, has done much to reveal the cronyism inherent during the Conservative Party's time in government. For example, in June 2021 the High Court in London ruled that a government cabinet minister, Michael Gove, broke the law by awarding a contract to a communications agency run by long-time associates of himself and Dominic Cummings, who served as chief adviser to British Prime Minister Boris Johnson until November 2020. The Court found that the decision to award the £560,000 contract to Public First was tainted by 'apparent bias' and was unlawful.

During the COVID-19 pandemic the National Audit Office found that business owners with close links to the Conservative government were given high-priority status for COVID-19 contracts. Meanwhile, during the same period the Commissioner for Public Appointments, Peter Riddell, who rarely spoke in public, expressed his disquiet that appointment panels were filled with Conservative Party supporters. He also spoke out against what he termed 'unregulated appointments' such as that of the Conservative peer, Baroness Dido Harding, who without open competition was appointed to lead the National Health Service Test and Trace programme that proved an unmitigated disaster and a waste of public money (Toynbee, 2021). It was later found by the High Court that the former Secretary of State for Health, Matt Hancock, did not comply with a public sector equality duty when appointing Dido Harding, who had neither medical training nor sufficient experience in public administration, as interim executive chair of the National Institute for Health Protection in May 2020. Harding's previous experience had been as chief executive officer of the British telecommunications company TalkTalk.

Dido Harding, who was praised by Matt Hancock for her 'brilliant' work on the COVID-19 pandemic, as well as by Prime Minster Boris Johnson, who said she oversaw a 'world beating' organization, failed dismally in her role running the Test and Trace programme. The House of Commons Committee of Public Accounts (2021) reported on the Test and Trace programme and stated that it failed in its main objective of cutting infection levels and helping the UK return to normal. This was despite spending a massive £37 billion of taxpayers' money. To quote Dame Meg Hillier, chair of the committee:

> The test and trace programme was allocated eye-watering sums of taxpayers' money in the midst of a global health and economic crisis. It set out bold ambitions but failed to achieve them. Only 14% of 691 million lateral flow tests sent out had results reported. The continued reliance on over-priced consultants … will by itself cost the taxpayers hundreds of millions of pounds. (Quoted in Gregory, 2021: 15)

This is yet another example of cronyism, with a well-paid, high-profile role being given to an insider who was not competent to undertake the duties required, rather than the position going to someone with the skills and ability to lead a complex public health programme where millions of people's lives were at risk.

As we have seen, advocates of neoliberalism claim that private is far more efficient than public. This leads to the creation of space for cronyism, and those with the business or political connections, or ability to generously donate to a political party's fund, receiving public works contracts, rather than work being awarded to those best qualified. This seriously dents confidence in democracy and is a poor return for the citizens who pay the taxes these 'chums' benefit from.

Cronyism is reproduced globally (Alonson, 2016) and has contributed to the sharp increase in social and economic inequalities that we are now seeing. The concentration of wealth and income into the hands of a few is both increasing inequality and decreasing class mobility. The effect of the COVID-19 pandemic has been to increase these negative consequences.

Alongside the UK government engaging in cronyism, and arguably because of it, the percentage of deaths per head of the population was one of the highest in the G7 countries and larger than some countries outside the G7 (Statista, 2024). Over the three years to February 2023, the UK death rate went up by more than 5 per cent, which was more than France, Germany and Spain which saw increases between 3 per cent and 4.5 per cent. The death rate in Italy, however, was 6 per cent higher, and in the United States and Eastern European countries, the rate was 10 per cent above pre-pandemic levels.

Brexit fails to deliver Leave-backing politicians' promises

Another key reason for the lack of trust in politicians was the disagreements and squabbles before, during and after the 2016 national referendum on whether the UK should remain a member of the European Union (EU). The outcome, Brexit, which is an amalgam of the words 'British' and 'exit', was the result of a slender majority voting in favour to leave the EU.

Brexit reflects the very essence of neoliberalism, with the main driving force for the UK leaving the EU coming from those in the Conservative Party, who with far-right groups and wealthy individuals such as Nigel Farage, argued that neoliberalism, with its attendant ideology of deregulated markets and the small state, would be the answer to the nation's problems that they claimed were created by the EU. During the referendum campaign these pro-Brexiteers, supported by Leave-backing mega-rich individuals, combined to create a powerful vociferous group that argued that the UK was held back by the bureaucracy, often referred to as 'red tape', of the EU. The message the pro-Brexiteers presented to the British public was that by leaving the EU the UK could control its immigration, regain its sovereignty and increase the nation's wealth. Their campaigning slogan embodied this central aim to 'Take back control'.

Many that voted Leave saw the referendum as an opportunity to protest against the political establishment, who they considered had, for many years, ignored their needs. Millions of voters living in northern deindustrialized areas had seen their livelihoods and opportunities decline and were rightly angry and frustrated by the situation, especially as those living in the south appeared to have benefited from growth in the economy. Their feeling was one of powerlessness, so the binary nature of the poll gave these voters a platform to express their anger and distrust in the political elite. These voters wanted change and they wanted something better (Powell, 2017). It didn't take much, therefore, for Leave campaigners such as the multi-millionaire and right-wing populist and political disruptor Nigel Farage, together with senior, similarly wealthy Tory MPs such as Boris Johnson, Jacob Rees-Mogg and Michael Gove on the right wing of the Conservative Party, to encourage these voters to believe that leaving the EU was in their best interest. Especially as most national newspapers were also presenting a positive picture of what leaving the EU would look like. These newspapers, and particularly the tabloids, gave the impression that migrants were to blame for workers' job insecurity and the fall in their living standards. The Leave campaign's message that exiting the EU would mean the UK could control immigration had considerable purchase (Loussouarn, 2022).

However, the outcome of leaving the EU has proved rather different. Coles (2016) argues that, by moving away from the EU, the UK has increased and deepened the roots of neoliberalism in the economy and political life. To quote Coles:

> The people advancing the global policy of neoliberalism wanted Brexit. They want more deregulation, more privatization and more internationalism at the expense of domestic investment and production. Most of the working and unemployed persons who voted for Brexit did so for the opposite reason: they want *less* neoliberalism. By funding the Leave campaign, the pro-Brexit elite not only made Brexit happen, they made it look as though they shared the interests of ordinary working people on vague notions of sovereignty. (Coles, 2016: 1, emphasis in original)

In the years since the referendum there are clear signs that it is not the rosy picture painted by the Brexiteers in the period up to the 2016 vote. Since the EU referendum was announced, the Office for Budget Responsibility has been analysing data and presenting research on the potential effects of Brexit on the economy and public finances. The report of 1 May 2024 indicates that the post-Brexit trading relationship between the UK and EU will reduce long-run productivity by 4 per cent relative to remaining in the EU. Both imports and exports will be around 15 per cent lower in the long run than if the UK had remained in the EU, and new trade deals with non-EU countries will not have a material impact, and any effect will be gradual (OBR, 2024).

It can be claimed that what is emerging in the UK is a scenario where the country has been delivered up to the altar of neoliberalism with all the attendant problems of job insecurity, the likelihood of greater not less immigration, and workers being placed in direct competition with countries where labour costs and employment rights are lower (Jessop, 2018). It is little wonder, therefore, that although the Labour Party had a landslide victory with 412 seats at the July 2024 general election it was a government elected with just 35 per cent of the popular vote. In fact, overall, the voter turnout was alarmingly low, with a turnout of only 52 per cent of the electorate compared with 67 per cent in 2019. According to Phipps (2024), millions decided not to vote because the 'entire political class was untrustworthy and even indistinguishable'. Many areas that had voted for the Conservative Party to 'Get Brexit Done' in the 2019 election returned to Labour partly as many of the electorate experienced that they had not benefited from Brexit. The case for leaving the EU was rumbled as communities felt the continuing impact of neoliberal inequality, of reduced state welfare and health interventions, and the fantasy promise of 'sunlit uplands'. Whether the Labour government's managerial pragmatic approach to economic and social policy delivery can satisfactorily address these voters' concerns remains to be seen when, according to Malik (2024), 'a political caste system' is emerging, 'with a policy base fashioned in the interests of a certain cohort' with the 'left behind' being replaced by the 'well ahead' in terms of political significance.

The hegemonic power of the establishment

A further reason for questioning whether democracy really serves the people comes from the recognition by many that a powerful hegemony of vested interests has concentrated power, influence and money in the hands of the few. In the UK this is often termed as the establishment, who are an integral element of the nation's hegemony and represent the interests of the status quo.

During the 2016 EU referendum campaign, Leave supporters argued that Europe was organized and managed to benefit the establishment and the Remain supporters. In fact, as noted earlier, well placed members of the establishment including senior Conservative Party MPs as well as wealthy demagogues and disruptors were leaders of the anti-EU brigade.

There is some debate as to what and who compromises the British establishment but most commentators would say this amorphous, shapeless but nonetheless powerful entity includes the royal family, the aristocracy, the landed gentry, prestigious public schools like Eton College, Harrow School and Westminster School, the Privy Council, top echelons of the Conservative Party and the Labour Party, senior civil servants, KCs, certain academics, writers, journalists and broadcasters, the Church of England, financiers, industrialists, right-wing media and newspaper owners, the armed services and other senior professionals who benefit from a situation that subtly, and not so subtly, excludes the majority (Hennessy, 1986; Jones, 2015; Abell, 2019). The groups and individuals that make up the establishment have, over an extended period, held on to and wielded concentrated social, political and economic power in the UK, that is hegemonic power.

However, not all the groups or individuals that are part of the hegemony are wealthy. For example, although most Church of England clergy are arguably poorly renumerated, they do exercise significant influence in the eyes of many. We note, for instance, that elements of Christianity and other religions preach a range of different values. In Christianity these values include compassion, forgiveness, humility, honesty, integrity and faithfulness. Arguably, adherence to these values helps some followers deal with the alienation and drudgery of often tedious, pressurized lives where they may be undertaking stressful, poorly paid work and/or living in conditions that are unnecessarily unhealthy. It could be argued here that sport and cultural events have a similar role in helping people deal with the monotony and tediousness of daily life. Few of the core values of the Christian church focus on social equality or improving the lives of others, although it should be said that some Christians are engaged in progressive transformative work with the poorest and most disadvantaged people in society. Nevertheless, the Church of England is presented as central in the lives of the privileged, wealthy, state-funded royal family, as it is in churches, chapels and grand cathedrals and abbeys where their children are baptized, where they are married, and where they are committed when dead. These ceremonies are often broadcast and recorded for both British and global consumption, confirming their place among the powerful, influential national and international elite (Baker, 2020; G. Smith, 2024). In fact, King Charles III is the head of the Church of England, which is the official Christian English national church. Therefore, while we live in a 'liberal democracy' it is far from equal, with powerful groups and establishment institutions setting the agenda on the material and cultural conditions that legitimate what is considered the 'normal' order of society.

In his highly readable book on the subject, Owen Jones (2015), the British journalist, political activist and author, has provided us with an insightful analysis of the workings of the unaccountable, often secret network that supports the establishment. Jones argues that the ever-increasing wealthy establishment members claim or imply the status quo works for everyone. However, as we have seen, outside a tiny, very wealthy influential group who are the main beneficiaries of neoliberalism, many millions in recent years have been at the receiving end of falling living standards and feel 'left behind'.

The outcome is therefore that for millions of people, politics can seem an irrelevance. To quote Jones:

> Voting, to many seems futile. In cities and towns across the country, people offered me strikingly similar reasons for not voting: 'nothing ever changes', 'politicians are all in it for themselves', 'politicians are lining their pockets', 'politicians are all the same', 'they always break their promises', and so on. Unskilled workers are now nearly 20 percentage points less likely to make their way to the ballot box than middle-class professionals. (Jones, 2015: 299–300)

In later work, Jones (2025) focuses on the lives of young people in the UK, writing that 'a toxic combination of neoliberal economic policies and austerity have battered the young'. Jones continues:

> Thatcherism promised freedom and delivered insecurity. Secure jobs have evaporated, rents have escalated, wages have fallen, youth services have been decimated and graduates face punishing debts for attending university. Younger Britons have suffered the brunt of policies most never voted for. It's no wonder democracy seems increasingly unappealing to them and their peers in other countries who have suffered at the sharp end of neoliberalism. (Jones, 2025: 1)

There is then a disjunction or crisis between people's wish for a society that better meets their needs and the powerful forces of the establishment that are operating to a different set of values where their vested interests are supreme. An example of the establishment working to the benefit of the few was the revelation that companies donating large sums of money to the Conservative Party received, between 2016 and 2024, £8.4 billion pounds in public contracts. There was no suggestion that the law had been broken or individuals and companies had committed any wrongdoing (Goodier and Aguilar Garcia, 2024). What it does show, however, is that massive amounts of public money have moved to those who handsomely donated funds to the ruling political party.

Russian influence in British life

Before moving to consider the role of counter-hegemonic groups and action, it is important to consider the role of Russia has had, over several years, on the British establishment and the impact on democracy and furthering the neoliberal project.

On 24 February 2022, President Vladimir Putin's Russian military invaded the sovereign country of Ukraine, leading to thousands of citizens in the country being brutally killed by the invading troops, many of whom were tortured before being executed. The outcome has been the largest refugee crisis since the Second World War, with the UN refugee agency stating that around six million Ukrainians have left the country, and something like a third of the population have been displaced (www.unhcr.org/uk). The international response to the invasion was swift and substantial, with world leaders voicing strong and angry condemnation towards Russia, and governments providing significant material support for Ukraine, including supplying military hardware, while large-scale humanitarian aid was brought in from a multitude of governments, aid agencies and concerned citizens everywhere.

Other forms of direct action by Western countries involved coordinating a raft of powerful economic and political sanctions, including freezing Russian assets held abroad, and economically targeting Russian businesses, banks and individuals, causing a slew of problems for the Russian economy. Alongside this, numerous major Western companies, such as Ikea, Nestle, British American Tobacco, Unilever, Starbucks and Adidas, exited the country.

In sum, the war was to have a major influence on global politics and a direct impact on numerous localities and communities, particularly those in Europe which experienced major increases in energy prices as countries attempted to wean themselves off importing Russian oil, gas and coal. Further, Ukraine had annually provided many nations with valuable raw materials, including wheat and sunflower oil, which its war-ravaged countryside could no longer provide.

Significantly for our examination of democracy, the invasion of Ukraine was to reveal the degree to which the British establishment and in particular the Conservative government had over many years colluded with Russian oligarchs and their families who were encouraged to invest in the UK, and which gave them rights to live in Britain. To keep in lockstep with other Western governments, and in the wake of the invasion of Ukraine, the UK imposed sanctions on oligarchs with property and businesses interests in its jurisdiction. Some of these oligarchs were Kremlin spokespeople and members of Putin's elite inner circle. The question is how did Britain become such an attractive place for Russian oligarchs to spend and invest their money?

The answer lies in the catastrophic political crisis in the Soviet Union during the late 1990s, which eventually led in 1991 to the dissolution of the USSR and the creation of 15 independent republics. The largest and most powerful of these republics, Russia, swiftly adopted a capitalist market economy, with the Russian government selling off large sectors of the economy through auctions, which it is generally believed were rigged and largely benefited government-favoured insiders with political connections (Freeland, 2000). The outcome was that many wealthy Russian oligarchs suddenly became even richer and decided to move their newfound wealth to what they considered were politically and financially safe countries, with the UK and in particular London being the main target. As a result, 'Londongrad' and 'Moscow-on-Thames' became concepts commonly deployed for describing the influx of money and Russians to the UK's capital city. A central reason that the UK, and London, was in the sights of the wealthy Russians was its reputation, stretching back decades, for financial skulduggery operating as 'a gigantic loophole, undercutting other countries' rules, massaging down tax rates, neutering regulations, laundering foreign criminals' money' (Bullough, 2022: 4). Moreover, according to Bullough (2022: 4), the UK is considered by oligarchs to be an excellent country for educating their children, 'solving their legal disputes, easing their passage into global high society, hiding their crimes and generally letting them dodge the consequences of their action'.

In fact, from the early 1990s onwards, the British government encouraged wealthy foreigners to each 'invest' over £2 million or more in the UK economy and in exchange offered them entitlement to reside in the country. It is estimated that around 200 of these government light-touch regulation 'golden visas' went to Russians (Bagehot, 2022). There is little evidence, however, that the scheme, which was scrapped in February 2022, led to significant investment in companies that produced goods and services needed by the British public. Similarly, there is imperceptible evidence that much-needed investment from this source went into the UK's manufacturing sector. Rather their investment went through a growth industry of 'enablers' in the legal, financial, property and PR sectors into high-end services for the rich, such as exclusive gym chains and expensive gentlemen's outfitters, and into capital and private equity firms intended to assist the already super-rich make even greater wealth.

A major concern is that much of the money coming into the UK from Russia had been from illicit sources. Transparency International (www.transparency.org.uk) identified that at least £1.5 billion of the UK property market was owned by Russians accused of financial crime or who had links with Putin's government. The organization considers this figure to be an underestimate, with most of these properties held via secretive offshore companies based in tax havens in countries such as the British Virgin Islands and the Cayman Islands. High-value London property owned by Russians is presented in research undertaken by Henderson and Mendick (2024).

Interference in British politics by Russia has long been considered a problem. The Intelligence and Security Committee's Russia report

(2020), published after a nine-month delay ordered by Prime Minister Boris Johnson, and only available to the public in redacted form, found there was substantial evidence that Russian interference in British politics was becoming commonplace and 'the new normal'. Moreover, there was 'credible open-source commentary' suggesting Russia sought to influence the 2014 Scottish independence referendum. This interference is, according to the report, a reflection of Russia's actively hostile approach to the UK and the West and its 'unwillingness to adhere to international laws and norms'.

One of the strategies deployed by wealthy Russians, many with direct links to Putin, has been to cosy up to the Conservative Party. In 2020, Russians living in the UK donated something in the region of £3.5 million to the Conservative Party or their constituency associations (Bullough, 2022). One view is that while in government the Conservative Party could have benefited from corrupt financial sources that have utilized money laundering systems. What we do know is that the outcome is a web of connections between wealthy Russians residing in the UK and the Conservative Party.

One controversial connection that attracted attention is that of Evgeny Lebedev, who derives his wealth from his father, Alexander Lebedev, a Russian banker, oligarch and former senior KGB officer. Evgeny Lebedev is typical of extremely wealthy Russians who have close links with the British establishment, and particularly the Conservative Party. Lebedev has taken advantage of the UK's 'open door' approach to attracting wealthy foreigners wanting to reside in the country by 'investing' in the economy. Now a dual national (Russian and British) he has strategically invested in the UK, including in a national newspaper, *The Independent*, a London evening newspaper, a TV channel, and part-ownership in a riverside London pub, as well as owning high-value London properties.

Perhaps more importantly, in the early 2000s Evgeny Lebedev and Boris Johnson formed a close friendship which was to prove to be mutually beneficial. Lebedev used his London newspaper, *The Evening Standard*, to support Johnson's successful bid to become mayor of London in 2008, and again in his bid to become re-elected in 2012. When Johnson became prime minister in 2019, the favour was returned, and despite the British Security Services assessing Lebedev as a security risk (Yorke et al, 2022), Lebedev was created a life peer and now sits in the House of Lords. Landler and Castle (2022) claim that Lebedev's elevation to the House of Lords is a clear example of the strong links between the Russian wealthy in London and the British establishment.

The 'open door' approach to Russians and other wealthy foreigners is part and parcel of the ideology and practice of neoliberalism. The UK's economy is dominated by its service sector (Elliott, 2014), including a strong London based financial sector which has included asset managers, equity firms, insurance and reinsurance, pension companies and hedge funds. Attracting foreign investment was a key drive of the previous Conservative government, and while the investment by Russians has not been translated into serious investment in the UK manufacturing sector, it has brought money into a host of service-based industries/professions, mainly located in London and the southeast of England. The outcome is an increasing divide between the wealthy, middle income earners and the poor, both within the capital city, regionally and nationally. This has taken place while the Russia state is reported to have attempted to tamper with the UK's electoral system and engaged in activities that compromise national security, while wealthy Russians have donated large sums of money to the Conservative Party and cosied up to members of the British establishment.

Counter-hegemonic practices and visions

We have seen that democracy in the conventional interpretation of local and national government, as commented on by Jones (2015), can fail to meet the needs of the many. This a trend reflected globally, with citizens often cynical or indifferent about democracy, questioning whether it continues to have value. Growing economic insecurity in a world that looks increasingly less safe gives people the feeling that the democratic processes are not giving them a satisfactory platform to express their discontent. As a result, people are looking for alternative platforms to express their grievances. Some have simply resorted to social media posts, while many have turned to regressive populist nationalist ideas and movements, while others have become involved in what can be termed counter-hegemonic practices and visions which are often global in their outlook. Those engaged in progressive counter-hegemonic activity and the accompanying thinking are calling into question the structures, beliefs and norms of the present hegemony, as well as focusing on the contradictions inherent in hegemonic power. Their goal is to attempt to present alternatives to the status quo while offering a vision of what is required and what can be achieved. Counter-hegemony, then, is both an alternative ethical view of society while posing a challenge to the status quo (Cohn and Hira, 2020).

We now look at how hegemonic power is being challenged by considering the existential global climate crisis which has confronted governments and populations throughout the world, and the movements that have brought a fresh understanding to the problem.

'It's now or never': the global climate crisis

There is clear and mounting evidence that neoliberalism has been a major factor in severely damaging the global environment and creating a serious climate crisis, such that it determines the direction of travel for us all now, and in the years to come. The terrifying catastrophe presently facing the globe is rooted in a social, political and economic system that is unjust, unequal and discriminatory. However, thankfully, there is increased critical analysis and concerted action on several fronts to challenge and reverse the forces that are creating this daily devastation.

The scale of the impact of accelerated climate change has been discussed in different international forums for several years. The increased seriousness of the problem is further tracked and reported on by the Intergovernmental Panel on Climate Change (IPCC). Their sixth assessment report (IPCC, 2023), written by the world's leading climate scientists and drawing on the work of hundreds of contributing authors, presents irrefutable scientific evidence confirming that the cumulative impact of human activity is causing rapid and potentially catastrophic changes to the climate. The influential IPCC report states that without an accelerated reduction in greenhouse gases in the coming years the world is vulnerable to the irreversible and exponential effects of global heating, with more frequent serious and life-threatening flooding than experienced previously, and more frequent terrible heatwaves and devastating and repeated droughts.

Further, the IPCC report makes clear that instead of governments keeping to climate pledges we have seen greenhouse gases rising. As a result, in the coming decades large swathes of the globe will be too hot to work in, while harvest failures will be commonplace, and disappearing ice caps will submerge major cities. If the conclusions of the IPCC report prove correct, we are on course for a climate disaster.

The United Nations Climate Change Conference (commonly referred to as CO29) held in Baku, Azerbaijan in 2024 ended with countries making several major agreements. The most important decision made was to uphold the commitment to 'transition away' from fossil fuels, which with the assistance of the Loss and Damage Fund is intended to help countries to protect their people and economies against continuing climate disasters. One major agreement has been to share in the benefits of clean energy. However, the commitments are not legally binding, and the fear is that countries have still not taken the climate crisis seriously. In fact, many of the agreements remain general and unspecific in nature.

Therefore, the overriding concern is whether there is sufficient and meaningful political will and ambition by governments and at major corporation board level to act upon these agreements and implement the IPCC findings. The lack of meaningful action together with inadequate attention and funding from governments on this exceptionally dangerous situation has led to a growth of active and vociferous campaigners and environmental social movements such as Extinction Rebellion (often termed XR) and Just Stop Oil (JSO). Through civil resistance, nonviolent direct action, demonstrations and education these groups and campaigns with and by other large and small organizations are demanding that governments, corporations and public bodies work to reduce and eventually halt climate change to avoid the potentially irreversible environmental damage that results from it.

Environmental social movements

Environmental social movements and campaigners point to the power of the fossil fuel industry and its relationship with capitalism. It is well known that the rapid growth in economic growth and mass consumption from the end of the Second World War onwards was greatly assisted by our reliance on fossil fuels, which includes coal, natural gasses and oils. The powerful hegemony here is the fossil fuel lobby that not only includes the fuel industry just mentioned but also related major industries such as plastics, chemicals and aviation. These industries are strategic to national and international economies and have over many years blocked policy decisions on environmental protection and instead lobbied governments to roll back regulations or, as was seen during the Conservative Party's time in office, justify new drilling of oil in the North Sea. It is estimated that 80 per cent of the world's primary energy consumption, and over 60 per cent of its electricity, comes from fossil fuels (UNEP, 2024).

XR, JSO and other campaign groups are a counter to this hegemony with their key messages that governments need to halt biodiversity loss and ecological collapse, and to reduce greenhouse emissions to net-zero by 2050. To do this effectively, they argue that taxes will need to rise to further fund the growth of offshore wind farms, as well as increasing investments in new technology such as hydrogen and sustainable aviation fuel. They maintain that serious consideration also needs to be given to the continuance of nuclear power as fossil fuel usage is reduced. Meanwhile, the Green Party, among others in the UK, has called for no further developments of the nuclear power industry, arguing that other sources of energy can provide sufficient power for the UK. The dependency of Western European countries on oil and gas supplies from Russia was highlighted in the war with Ukraine and further emphasizes the need to look elsewhere for energy needs, and there is a continuing debate as to whether nuclear power will be needed in the short term.

There is little doubt that neoliberalism has at its core the strong drive for private, often short-term, profit and the marginalization of state involvement, which has had a severe detrimental impact on the environment, which is now threatening to lead to irretrievable damage to our planet and to severely endanger the livelihoods of billions of people.

A key component of neoliberalism is based on aggressive economic growth and the mass consumption of goods and services. The result of the drive to meet and stimulate demand to make financial gains leads to natural resources being consumed quicker than they can be replaced. As the author and environmental and political activist George Monbiot has commented on many occasions, every part of the globe is considered fair game in the race to possess unexploited wealth, whether it is in the Amazon rainforest, the oil and diamonds to be found in West Africa, or the rich natural resources such as gold and copper discovered in West Papua. As Monbiot comments, when these resources run out there are many areas of the deep oceans to exploit, together with the possibility of finding and recovering valuable materials from other planets in our solar system (Monbiot, 2014, 2017a, 2022).

At the same time, the prevalence globally of high polluting industries, and the destruction of natural habitats, has caused a decline in biodiversity. Advocates of neoliberalism have been shown to arrogantly ignore the harmful consequences of rampant production and consumption, meaning that many corporations and businesses are prepared to damage the environment to secure large profits. Interestingly, in the case of China, the ruling Communist Party is aware of the risks of climate change and has a programme of investing heavily in renewables. Simultaneously, however, it has launched a massive programme of building new coal-fired power plants, while 'it is home to nearly half the world's electric passenger vehicles and one in three of the globe's solar panels' (Elliott, 2021).

Fortunately, as noted earlier, campaigners, environmental groups and social movements such as XR and JSO, together with progressive engaged politicians and political parties, have joined forces to promote alternative approaches. These groupings and pressure points are likely to increase and become more vociferous as environmental damage and global warming becomes more obvious. As the market comes under increasing strain from the negative impact of environmental damage, the more likely it is that individuals and corporations will seek opportunities to invest in different ways of operating so as to profit from the changing circumstances. We are already seeing the increased production and introduction of electric cars with plans for a network of charging points; increased renewable energy sources such as solar, wind and tidal; and pressure to reduce the use of personal transport (except for bicycles) and increase sustainable public transport; and, where possible, work from home. Similarly, households in the UK are being encouraged and, in some cases, offered inducements with grants to install low-carbon heat pumps as part of a plan for decarbonizing heat and buildings.

The case for political party and environmental group cooperation

In the UK, progressive political parties such as the Green Party, and to a lesser extent elements in the Labour Party and Liberal Democrats, have been at the forefront of advocating policies to limit the power of corporations, increasing taxation on the richest, and supporting local trade and economies. All UK left-of-centre political groupings believe the main solution is for the state to increase its interventions and create a more equal and greener economy. One key way forward therefore appears to be for progressive political parties to cooperate to gain sufficient public support for effective, meaningful environmental policies. This coalition of progressive political parties and environmental groupings will need to reconcile the loss of tens of billions in revenues from fossil fuel taxes while supporting the move to an environmentally sustainable future. This should also include the need to help support and boost nature by restoring hundreds of thousands of hectares of peatland and massively expanding woodlands while encouraging much more tree planting by individuals, public and civic bodies and groups (Pettifor, 2020; Kaplinsky, 2022). On a further positive note, there has been an increasing demand for diets high in plant protein and low in meat and dairy, which are associated with lower greenhouse gas emissions (Safran Foer, 2018, 2019).

Local environmental campaigns

Living in the English south coast seaside town of Seaford, East Sussex, I have observed small-scale action to clean the local beaches, something that is being regularly undertaken all along the UK's coastline. In this case as part of the Surfers Against Sewage, the objective is to persuade the town of Seaford to become plastic free while providing information on sustainable alternatives and encouraging businesses to reduce the amount of throw-away plastic by making alternatives available. As well as regular organized beach cleaning, a good deal of educational work has been undertaken with school students. Much of this drive to counter the effects of the global emergency came from the late Claire Sumners, a young local organizer and a south coast representative of Surfers Against Sewage who lived in Seaford. Claire commented, 'I care about the planet my children live on and will inherit when I'm not here … ecology and our environment we need to cherish, nurture and respect' (Summers, 2021). Another positive move locally is the Seaford Environmental Alliance, which has a base in the town centre and organizes events, talks, activities, education and projects in the local area to promote sustainability and help build a resilient community.[1]

A short way east along the Sussex coast from Seaford is the world-famous bay of Cuckmere Haven, with its iconic Coastguard Cottages and Cable Hut (a cable station for telegraph lines to France in the early 1900s), and the location for numerous major motion films, TV shows and commercials, including *Atonement, Harry Potter, Robin Hood: Prince of Thieves* and the BBC drama *Luther*. Every year over 400,000 people from across the globe visit to see for themselves the stunning cliffs of the Seven Sisters and the picturesque Cuckmere Coastguard Cottages they recognize from film, TV and guidebooks.

However, increasing severe storms due to climate change have resulted in the serious destruction and erosion of the original coastal defences built in 1947. Over one third of the land area below the Coastguard Cottages has been swept away and the campaign group Cuckmere Haven SOS argues the next major storm could see this iconic view lost forever, together with wildlife, and specialized chalk loving plants, and different species of birds that call the area their home. The Cuckmere Haven campaign group is not only raising awareness of the destruction and erosion, it is also raising major funding to undertake work to stem the damage.

While these examples in Seaford and Cuckmere Haven demonstrate small but important ways in which communities are addressing the climate crisis, much more needs to be done everywhere to confront the problems of climate change at the local level. These initiatives need to be taken alongside pressure nationally and internationally to increase sustainability in our wider economic and social life. For example, maintaining pressure on the fossil fuel industry which contributes massively to air pollution, making it a much greater killer of people than smoking, vehicle crashes or HIV/Aids. Cutting air pollution would increase life expectancy. To quote Professor Michael Greenstone from the University of Chicago: 'Air pollution is the greatest external threat to human health on the planet, and that is not widely recognised with the force and vigour that one might expect' (quoted in Cameron, 2021).

Still much to be done

According to Lewis (2021), the world's most influential lobbyists have been engaged by the fossil fuel industry. As Lewis (2021) argues, massive changes need to take place to hasten the end of the fossil fuel era that presently heats our homes and powers our transport. This change of policy and action must ultimately come from government regulation, which until now has been slow. Therefore, if we are serious about addressing the climate crisis, we need as citizens to demonstrate our real and urgent desire for positive change while engaging our friends, family and colleagues in this action. Similarly, schools and education generally can join in local and national campaigns and publicize and explain the crisis facing all the world's inhabitants.

We also need to recognize a degree of public hostility and indifference to the need to respond to what is arguably the greatest emergency humanity has ever faced. Much of this attitude is encouraged by legacy industries, such as those involved in producing and selling meat, those advocating the continued use of fossil fuels, and elements within political parties and the media.

Further, there is a need to address concerns that the environmental movement and particularly the Green Party is not reflecting the ethnic diversity and class dimension of the UK population, and for green politics generally to gain a greater profile than the niche position it presently holds (Steerpike, 2023). One way forward could be to advocate policies which sufficiently incentivize bank and building society savers by offering an attractive interest paying 'green deal premium' to help fund green policies and practice. There also needs to be consideration and action on creative ways of compensating the poorest for the transition to more expensive, more sustainable food, including less meat and dairy consumption, and energy supplies that people can afford. There are many in society whose main worry is not about the end of the world but the end of the week or the end of the month. The measures suggested here make a strong case for much more rigorous progressive taxation together with encouraging and rewarding personal savings that are linked to green developments.

London's changing climate

The changing climate in London is particularly concerning as increasing urban development and densification is leading to the city getting hotter. London is now experiencing hotter and drier summers than previously, which are further impacted by the Urban Heat Island effect, which has led to the city being up to 10'C warmer than neighbouring rural areas. In large cities like London the sun's rays are being absorbed by its many hard surfaces, whereas in less densely built areas the rays would be taken in by trees, plants and grass. In London, the radiation from the hard surfaces is released into the air as heat. This makes it crucial that all strategic planning and development in London takes account of global warming (Howard Boyd et al, 2024).

The result is that a fifth of London's schools are susceptible to flooding, and millions of those living in the capital are at 'high risk' of suffering from the effects of climate change. During 2021, the mayor of London, Sadiq Khan, announced his commitment to the capital becoming a zero-carbon city by 2030. This followed reports that 200,000 homes and workplaces, together with 25 per cent of rail stations in the capital and 10 per cent of the network, are at high risk of extreme temperatures and even worse flooding (Allegretti, 2021).

Why counter-hegemony is needed

Finally, clearly the present economic and political system has been found wanting in tackling the climate crisis. In fact, the present system has created the emergency we are now having to deal with. The climate and environmental crisis affects everyone, and in particular the poorest, which means that we must work together to stop far greater catastrophic impacts.

The action detailed in this chapter is an example of counter-hegemony and is part of a wider struggle that critiques and confronts the present hegemonic power. In the case of opposing the deterioration of the beautiful planet we live on we have seen an alternative ethical view of society and how we can live in a more harmonious, less ruinous manner.

As we have discussed, hegemony is a complex notion that rests on the view that people internalize the 'common sense' 'natural' understanding that capitalism, in this case neoliberalism, is the best, and perhaps the only, way of organizing economic and social relationships. As we have also noted, the contradictions of neoliberalism, with its baked-in inequality and injustices, have led to pressure on democracy and democratic structures. People are undoubtedly questioning the present system and the response by way of rising populism internationally, as well as distrust in political structures, often fed by malign social media postings, has created a vacuum that is being filled by progressive counter-hegemonic movements and campaigns. These counter-hegemonic movements carry with them views on alternative ways of organizing society.

There is little doubt that protests as part of a counter-hegemony are beginning to be a thorn in the side of the British government. In July 2024 five supporters of JSO received lengthy jail terms, believed to be the longest in the UK for non-violent protest. Their punishment was due to being found guilty of planning disruptive protests on the M25. The protesters, who were focused on highlighting the damage done to the environment by the fossil fuel industry, were prevented from explaining their motives to the jury. To quote Monbiot (2024: 16) they were tried 'as though they were mindless vandals, inconveniencing people for kicks, rather than seeking to prevent, at great cost to themselves, the greatest crisis humankind has ever faced'. The environmental activists were convicted under section 70 of the Police, Crime, Sentencing and Courts Act 2022 which, together with the Public Order Act 2023, was passed by the Conservative government to counter protests of this kind. However, Chris Packham, the British naturalist, nature photographer and broadcaster, speaking after the court judgement, stated:

> Be clear, be very, very, clear, this is not just about climate activism. The laws that have been drafted, the injustices that are being wrought, threaten all rights of free speech. We stand here today because our future security may be compromised by the reckless and irresponsible erosion of our human rights, of our fundamental freedoms. (Gayle and Horton, 2024: 21)

JSO and XR are decentralized direct action environmental movements whose actions have been met with force, arrests and prosecutions. Similar environmental protest movements can be traced back to the formation of

'Earth First' in 1991 who opposed further developments of nuclear power in the UK. During the 1990s 'Earth First' groups grew in number and were primarily focused on controversial road building projects that they argued damage the environment. This use of the coercive powers of the state to suppress protests and campaigns is, as Gramsci has commented, to be expected when the hegemony is threatened.

What unites all these autonomous social movements is their desire to subvert and challenge hegemonic power. Importantly, they offer alternative prefigurative practices that anticipate the ideal they are aspiring to. The social movements that make up a counter-hegemonic approach tend to stress forming networks that are horizontal, while prioritizing self-organization, democracy and direct action. At a time when democracy is considered under pressure from numerous negative and often powerful sources, we have much to learn and appreciate from these approaches that are helping us redefine participation. The key for the counter-hegemonic movements is to continue to make the link between the serious failures of aggressive profit-driven neoliberalism, which rewards the few, while damaging countless numbers of communities and people globally. There is a role here for these counter-hegemonic movements, whether global, national or local, to demand a shift to a more economically and ecological sustainable world.

Conclusion

There is little doubt that liberal democracy in most countries is under strain, which in turn has implications for us all. Attention was drawn to this by US President Joe Biden in his final Presidential Address in January 2025. To quote Biden: 'Today, an oligarchy is taking shape in America of extreme wealth, power and influence that really threatens our entire democracy, our basic rights and freedom' (quoted in Davies, 2025). In the case of the UK there is a noticeable reduction in trust in the political processes and the politicians that are expected to represent us and to carry out their role without fear or favour. However, we have noted numerous consequential times when this has not happened, with politicians abusing the electorate's trust and operating in their own self-interest and in the interest of the hegemony they are part of.

Nevertheless, protest is the cornerstone of democracy, and in the UK as in other countries this has been particularly so in the case of action related to the climate crisis. This crisis is a direct result of neoliberalism which has driven rapid, mainly unrestrained, economic growth and mass consumption with the result of drastic negative impact on the global environment. Local, national and global autonomous social movements have emerged to challenge the present hegemony and have offered an approach that is counter-hegemonic.

The most important lesson that can be drawn here is that protest is crucial to hold our elected representatives to account and to challenge the abuse of power, particularly when it subordinates public interest to global corporations, and the super-rich whose neoliberal economic and social policies have done so much damage. We will see in later chapters how local campaigns have sought to broaden democracy and to draw attention to issues that affect neighbourhoods and communities in London. What we have recorded here is that these struggles are part of a wider movement to defy those who have a vested interest in the status quo. Those who benefit from the present hegemony.

3

'Cranes in the Sky': The Remaking of London

Roger Green, with Malcolm Cadman, Andy Turner, Marion Briggs and Tony Nickson

Background

Keith Popple has clearly outlined in Chapters 1 and 2 how the impact of neoliberalism is destroying the notion of democracy and representation, and has created severe inequality and social and economic injustice for communities. How global investment in London is remaking this capital city for profit while badly distorting the housing market in favour of the wealthy. It is a view of neoliberalism that Cedric Johnson, writing in the *Jacobin* magazine, concurs with, adding that '[t]he experience of neo-liberalization ... has left joblessness, a crisis of affordable housing, economic insecurity and social precarity in its wake' (2020: 132). Monbiot and Hutchison are clear that it is an ideology that has seen the rich becoming richer and more powerful with the rest of us becoming poorer and no longer 'citizens' but 'consumers' (2024). It is a process occurring in other major cities around the world, whereby investment seeking profits via property development and rental value is displacing existing communities and their livelihoods. However, as Lee and Edwards argue, what is happening across London is uniquely different:

> [I]t is a huge, unequal and expensive city to live in and it has a strong heritage of council housing. As the largest city in Europe, the capital of one of Europe's most unequal nations, London has a housing market with very high rents and prices compared with incomes. It is often referred to simultaneously as a wealth machine and a poverty machine. (Lee and Edwards, 2020: xiii)

This chapter will discuss how this capitalist-driven ideological venture, a corporate takeover of cities, is bringing about an increasingly segregated London. Where, under the guise of either redevelopment, regeneration or gentrification, existing local authority housing estates are being demolished and brownfield sites built on for expensive high-rise apartments, with new neighbourhoods and urban 'villages' rapidly appearing.

It will show how London's skyline and its communities are being reshaped and reimagined by global developers, absentee foreign investors, 'dirty money', secretive shell companies in offshore tax havens, and the super-rich with their high-density and high-rise formula for investor profit (Ferguson, 2022). This reconfiguration of the urban landscape across all of London's communities is resulting in:

- The demolition and displacement of long-standing, diverse working-class communities.
- Genuinely affordable socially rented housing being absent in new developments.
- New urban villages being created for wealthy incomers.
- Collusion between local authorities and developers.
- A consultation process and involvement of communities that is rudimentary and 'top-down', with community voices too often muted and largely ignored by developers, local authority politicians and planners.

Remaking London's communities

Background

Walk the streets of Central London or venture beyond into the surrounding London boroughs and you will see that it is undergoing a massive urban structural transformation, with construction sites and cranes everywhere, reaching to the sky and visible from every direction, topped with their red lights to warn off private helicopters, conveying the wealthy in and out of London. What McFadyen aptly calls 'a building site [that] changes before your eyes' (2022: 2), and about which Back et al comment, '[t]oday's skyline bears the visual signature of London's place in the world in the branded monikers of the skyscrapers like the Cheese Grater, the Gherkin, the Walkie Talkie and the Shard' (2018: 1).

Surrounded by glossy, colourful hoardings advertising forthcoming expensive, fashionable places to live, they enclose deep construction sites awaiting new high-end, high-rise apartment blocks. With some 500 plus new skyscrapers expected, financed by overseas investors (Scanlon et al, 2017), some from illegal criminal activities and money laundering, it is a changing skyline (Block, 2019). One that sees high-rise apartments being created, seemingly appearing overnight, for a growing urban elite while at the same time largely neglecting the existing residents, their homes, communities and the histories they are displacing.

All of this has been well documented (for example, Waights, 2014; Watt and Minton, 2016; Lees and Ferreri, 2016; Lees et al, 2017; Watt, 2017; Minton, 2017a; Atkinson, 2020; Knowles, 2022; Tweneboa, 2024). It is what Cochrane and Jonas have called, in relation to globalization and urban areas, 'reimagining the city' (1991: 1), and Campkin, the 'remaking of London' (2013: 23).

This transformation ignores the history of London that has always been a place for work, commercial, creative and industrial innovation, both locally across all its 32 boroughs and, at its centre, the City of London. The consequence of 'land for housing' has squeezed out these places to work, to live nearby, to move through childhood to adulthood in one neighbourhood, and to allow your children to be in within walking distance of the local school. Land previously designated and protected as 'employment land' has been calculatingly and deliberately changed into mixed use redevelopment of employment sites (Ferm and Jones, 2016). The latter has then been predominantly used as a vehicle to build luxury apartments in high-density configurations.

Across London this is now a reality, as we see developers remaking the city in front of our eyes with their promises of supplying much-needed new additional housing for London's growing population and offering local community infrastructure improvements.

However, in reality, if we look closer, what they are really doing is literally uprooting and destroying many of London's long established communities. It's what Sinclair has aptly labelled the 'strategic destruction of the local' (2017: 14) and as John Betjeman, the English poet, writer and broadcaster, remarked many years ago, and which still holds true today, 'the speculators have thought of their money before other people's health and happiness: they have crowded the houses onto sites, and they have spent money on outward show instead of internal good arrangement. They have thought of themselves before the town as a whole – as speculative builders do' (Betjeman, 1937: 69).

The destruction and 'weathering' away of council estates and their communities

Housing estates under siege

If you live on a council housing estate in London, be careful, as it may not be there tomorrow. As Thoburn states:

> Tens of thousands of council homes have been demolished in recent decades, and around 100 London estates are currently under threat of destruction. ... Estate demolition is a tremendously damaging process – both socially for the displaced communities, and environmentally due to the carbon emissions created by demolition and rebuilding. It is

driven not by need — as is often claimed — but simply by a booming construction and housing industry that reaps vast rewards from soaring land values and house prices. (in Stafford, 2023: 32)

We are seeing long established communities previously living out their lives on local authority council estates (known as public housing in the United States, and social housing in many European countries) now being displaced to make way for new developments that offer virtually no socially rented or genuinely affordable housing (Corporate Watch, 2018a; Shelter, 2022).

These estates are being increasingly disinvested in, neglected and run down during recent years despite many previously being subject to the UK's 'Decent Homes Standard' of 1997. This ensured these homes, for example, had adequate bathroom and kitchen facilities, and were in a reasonable 'state of repair'. However they are now becoming but community memories (Centre for Ageing Better, 2021; Wilmore, 2021a). This is primarily due to the previous UK Conservative government's economically destructive austerity programme from 2010 to its demise in 2024. When elected, its continuing financial cuts to local councils' budgets ensured their inability to maintain their housing stock (Gray and Barford, 2018; Local Government Association, 2018; Centre for Cities, 2019).

One of the other consequences of this is the increasing number of newly created islands of expensive high-rise flats for newcomers and the impact it has on the nearby remaining council housing estates that have largely been ignored and left behind. Many of these estates have unfairly been characterized as being tired and monochrome 'sink estates' that are being allowed to slowly deteriorate as local councils were starved of central government financial resources by the then Conservative Party in government. The result is the inability to keep pace with much-needed repairs, maintenance and refurbishment work, and, crucially, housing people from their council housing waiting lists.

With local authorities currently trying to avoid financially going bust, many are responding by raising revenues by either selling off their housing estates and decanting the residents or other publicly owned land through doing 'deals' with profit-hungry developers. These include agreeing to the infilling and privatizing of previously open, and green public spaces, or giving planning permission for private developments on empty brownfield sites across their London borough.

This transformation is now almost routine, with, for example, Estate Watch (2021), a jointly run resource between a coalition of the London Tenants Federation and Just Space, a network of community groups, activists and non-governmental organizations, and Lawrence (2022) highlighting over 122 of London's council housing estates under threat of regeneration. Housing some 30,000 plus residents, these estates are now facing redevelopment rather than refurbishment by the coalitions of developers, local authority planners and politicians agreeing new so-called estate regeneration schemes. This figure is coupled with the net loss of well over 6,000 social and council homes in London due to demolition for housing developments along with almost 200 estates in London torn down since the late 1990s (Wilson, 2022).

It also highlights a grim future for increasing numbers of working-class residents, many with young children, on waiting lists for London local authority housing who are currently placed in inadequate costly privately rented accommodation that ignores their housing needs (Harris, 2016; Boughton, 2018; Berry, 2021; Tweneboa, 2024). It is an issue that the popular UK television soap, the BBC's *EastEnders*, highlighted some years ago with 'incomers' changing the demography of the fictional East London working-class Albert Square in Walford (Martin, 2017).

What we are witnessing here is yesterday's post-Second World War vision of socially rented council housing, 'Homes for Heroes' for all, gradually being swept away, and along with it the familiar community 'cultural landmarks' and important parts of local economies. These include the small, all-purpose corner shops selling everything from newspapers to sweet potatoes; the local 'boozers' (pubs) with their unique community histories and focus as 'community hubs'; the Chinese and kebab takeaways; the local cafe with its 'full English breakfast fry up'; and ever hopeful small entrepreneurs with their small car repair garage woven into the urban backstreets under the Victorian railway arches. Not only physical space acquired for development, but as Budden and Caless argue, 'history, culture and memory also' (2012: 2).

All replaced by a Tesco Express or one other of the supermarket giants' 'little outlets', the ubiquitous residents-only private gym, and gated gardens with no access to non-residents and no play facilities for local children, especially the over-fives and teenagers. Along with new 'all-in-one' private developments, flats offering high priced rented accommodation for singles and friends sharing, particularly for those aged 'Millennials' earning above average salaries. With assorted in-house amenities such as a gym, cafes, bar and general spaces for collective social interaction for residents, 'hermetically sealed playgrounds' as Chatterton calls such places (2019: 92). These simply compound this transition. Collectively they contribute to primarily 'top-down' redevelopments and regeneration that is becoming synonymous with the displacement, fragmentation and the 'social cleansing' of working-class housing estate based neighbourhoods across London (Lees and White, 2019; Romyn, 2020; Pearson-Jones, 2021).

It is a narrative that Thoburn captures succinctly in his interviews with the ex-residents of the Robin Hood Estate in East London, an example of modernist social housing, showing that their views never informed the decision to demolish the estate nor its replacement. That, when asked, unsurprisingly they enjoyed living on the estate, contrary to the local authority's public announcements as they proceeded to empty and displace its rooted working-class residents (Thoburn, 2022).

There is additionally, from tabloid sections of the UK newspapers, a stigma attached to renting a home from a social landlord, a housing association or a local authority. Somehow you are viewed negatively as a 'second class' citizen, who, because you do not own your accommodation, is seen as a failure. A welfare benefits scrounger, a social malingerer who should be thankful for whatever the state provides for you, including the destruction of your home, community and displacement (Ejiogu and Denedo, 2022).

Goodbye Heygate Estate

There are many examples of this transformation, one of which is the Elephant and Castle's 'Heygate Estate'. A South London landmark built in the early 1970s as a local authority council estate with over 1,200 homes and 3,000 residents. It was sold off in 2010 to a global development company, Lendlease, an Australian multinational construction, property and infrastructure company, and subsequently demolished with many residents conveniently 'displaced' (GEOGRAFREEDRISCOLL, 2018; Researchgate, 2021). A euphemism for being forcibly scattered around London to neighbourhoods which they did not know, where they had no social networks or family, away from their place of employment and with the need to find school places for their children in already overcrowded local schools.

Despite promises that many of the residents could return to the new affordable socially rented housing (yet offered at a much higher rent) that would be part of the redevelopment of the site. The outcome to date has seen only 82 units of housing promised by the developer (H. Jones, 2017; Lees and White, 2019; Wilmore, 2021b).

What Robbins called an 'ill-conceived model of urban regeneration' (2022: 31) has now been repackaged as 'Elephant Park'. A £2.5 billion regeneration programme of over 28 acres promoted by Lendlease on its website as one of London's 'most exciting places to live, work and visit … attracting the now familiar high earning professionals to this new very trendy place to be!' (Lendlease, 2021).

Providing non-affordable housing

There are currently estimated to be over 240,000 households on London boroughs' housing waiting lists (Greater London Authority, 2021), excluding those 'sofa surfing' with friends or family, rough sleepers and the homeless. All with little hope of ever getting rehoused in local authority council accommodation and paying a social rent. In some London boroughs a wait of five years or beyond is not unusual and for a number of people the wait is too long, with death happening while waiting year after year on the housing waiting list (Williams, 2022).

While at the same time the existing council housing stock is gradually reducing as council houses and flats are still being continually sold off under Prime Minister Margaret Thatcher's Conservative government's 1980 'Right to Buy' policy that promoted the Conservative Party's dream of a 'property owning democracy'. These properties, under the 'great council sell-off', have been purchased by many existing council residents at heavily discounted prices, however it has also allowed other individuals to build 'housing portfolios' by simply buying up the 'sold off' ex-council accommodation, along with prying property speculators snapping up cheap properties for renting privately or as Airbnb lets.

The result is that, increasingly, real affordable socially rented housing has become almost non-existent for many Londoners on low and middle incomes or in receipt of welfare benefits. 'Affordable housing' as promoted by developers and many local councils is now a confusing array of definitions, such as 80 per cent of market rent and a mix of 'London affordable rent', London living rent and London shared ownership (London Tenants Federation, 2020). Only the 'social rent' relating to local authority council and housing associations, typically 50 per cent or lower of market rent, allows realistically affordable and secure homes for people desperately seeking accommodation.

However local authorities in London and indeed across many parts of the UK are signing off planning agreements to developers with little or no truly affordable socially rented housing being included. One example, among many, is the Bermondsey ex-Biscuit Factory redevelopment in South London. The proposal by the Grosvenor Group, an international property company, and headed up by the billionaire Duke of Westminster, an aristocrat who owns swathes of the City of London, is to redevelop this site.

It was originally rejected by the local authority's planning committee on the grounds of a lack of genuinely affordable homes for local people but reinstated by the Labour Party Mayor of London, Sadiq Khan, in 2019, on the basis that it provided over 1,500 new homes despite only including a miserly 100-plus homes at a questionable social rent level. As a local councillor remarked: 'While we all recognise the housing crisis and the need to build homes, that cannot be pursued at the expense of building the homes that people can actually afford to live in … who will these "affordable" properties be "affordable" to – because it certainly won't be my constituents?' (Salisbury, 2020: 8).

Affordable homes are not affordable

Similar stories litter London's community of local online not-for-profit newspapers and social media, all highlighting how so-called affordable homes are too expensive and out of the reach of many local people. The South

London's online *News Shopper* newspaper, for example, highlighted a story about the London Borough of Lewisham aiming to provide 'affordable' housing on approved private-led developments with no definition of what 'affordable' meant for those thousands on the council's housing waiting list. As one resident commented, 'By the time they are ready it will be 0% affordable homes. On top of that they are not really affordable' (Cuffe, 2020a: 2).

A London-based blogger, Murky Depths, continually reports stories of local authority untruths concerning so-called 'affordable' housing, for example, the Morris Walk Estate development in the London Borough of Greenwich, a borough with over 20,000 people on the housing waiting list. It has questioned what is 'affordable' housing, with some rents shown to be up to '80% of market rates (which in parts of London is still extremely expensive) and shared ownership can include a myriad of fees and charges'. Beyond the financial means for most people on the housing waiting list! (Murky Depths, 2021).

The net result of this chronic under-supply of genuinely affordable socially rented homes for people in housing need is that individuals and families, many with small children, retreat to the largely unregulated private rented sector, which now accounts for a third of Londoners, and this is increasing following the COVID-19 pandemic (Jayanetti, 2021; Generation Rent, 2023). Too often this accommodation is in small, overcrowded bedsits, houses of multiple occupancy (HMOs), and other assorted substandard accommodation offering little tenant security, which impacts on renters' health and wellbeing, particularly babies and young children (Minton, 2017b; Whitehead et al, 2020; Hilber and Schoni, 2021; Shelter, 2021c).

Scanning London's free daily paper, the *Evening Standard*, in its 'homes and property' section you will see houses and flats for rent for anything from £16,000 per week for a house to cheaper properties, such as flats over a shop, at just under £2,000 a week, hardly suitable for single people and families in need of secure, affordable housing (*Evening Standard*, 2022, 2024).

This is a situation becoming increasing more problematic when, for example, developers attempt to revise their commitment to affordable homes by instead offering a financial settlement to a local authority. A developer in South London, for example, reputably offered the local authority that gave planning permission for the development almost £6 million to reduce the number of affordable homes, thereby allowing the developer to sell or rent flats on the open market and thus increasing its profit margin (Russell, 2023).

This is quite simply a case of developers undertaking a financial viability assessment. Whereby they report that their profit margin has slipped, and despite London's local authorities planning rules requiring a percentage, for example, 50 per cent of new builds to contain 'affordable housing', not social rent, the developer will state that it is no longer financially feasible to build the number of affordable homes originally promised.

The outcome, for example, as the former Conservative Party run London Borough of Westminster showed, is to make a payment to the council's 'affordable housing fund', as in the case of the Hinduja brothers. One of the wealthiest families in the UK, their development of the historic Old War Office near to the prime minister's residence in Downing Street proposed 85 luxury flats and a 120-room five-star Raffles hotel along with 'affordable housing'. However following a financial viability assessment the outcome was a loss of the initially proposed affordable housing for those waiting patiently for years on the council's housing waiting list. Instead some £10 million were paid into the council's coffers. This perhaps illustrates a bending of the rules (Neate, 2022).

Elsewhere in North London a developer has played the system by informing the local authority, the London Borough of Enfield, that its initial promise of providing 46 homes out of 148 at genuinely affordable social rent and receiving planning approval for this is now not possible. Following a financial viability assessment, the local authority planning committee was informed by the developer that they would now not be able to afford to deliver any such housing. Profit over housing need! (Better Homes Enfield, 2023).

Similarly, housing associations, a key provider of housing at social rent levels alongside local authorities, witnessed a reduction in the number of homes completed during the COVID-19 pandemic (Clark, 2021). Many switched to tackling other important priorities, with Clarion Housing, for example, the largest provider of 'affordable housing' at social rent levels in the UK, diverting funding from building homes to ensuring fire risk defects are minimized and replacing external combustible cladding on its buildings. This follows the Grenfell high-rise fire in London in 2017 in the Kensington & Chelsea Tenant Management Organisation's tower that killed 72 of its social housing residents with more than 70 others injured and with 223 people escaping (Booth, 2021).

New expensive housing for the few

New communities

Across London the professional high-earning middle-class, often from the 'super-rich' and the upwardly mobile Millennial generation, are colonizing newly created urban neighbourhoods. Promoted by colourful glossy property magazines, they offer '[n]ewly fashionable areas [that] are often pioneered by the "creative classes" … and if you're brave, these new areas could give you a great return on your investment' (*The Resident*, 2016: 1).

Developments with quaint 'Old English country' names criss-cross London, such as the 'East Village London20' development, which promises 'country air' on the site of the 2012 Olympic village in once inner-city working-class Stratford, East London. Another is the 'Kidbrooke Village', in South London, previously the now demolished working-class council Ferrier Estate, described by the developer 'as a place to grow'. New luxury apartment buildings, what Atkinson and Mingay refer to as 'ultraland' blocks separated from the surrounding urban spaces, with discreet entry points for both residents and their vehicles, offer privacy and security, not conviviality and encounter with others outside (2024: 1).

Such new self-selecting 'intended communities' or 'new communities', as the construction company Redrow has interestingly named them (2017), for those with the financial means, are being built and planned across London with enticing promotional advertisements to shape perceptions for not only living somewhere but also as investment opportunities (Neate, 2018). Chinese families, for example, purchasing expensive flats for their children studying at London's universities (Yu and Kantor, 2022; Viet Nam News, 2024).

New regeneration projects such as the 'Nine Elms' development highlight this trend. Aptly named 'Dubai-on-Thames' and the new 'Belgravia' (Sampson, 2022), the site in and around the old Battersea Power Station site in Southeast London epitomizes how global capital flaunts its wealth. Superstars such as Sting have purchased apartments there, all under the watchful eye of the King of Malaysia and the consortium of Malaysian investors who financed the 42-acre project.

Nine Elms is exclusively comprised of highly expensive flats and requisite amenities, including the much ridiculed 'Sky Pool'. Located over 30 metres above the ground and wedged between two high apartment blocks, its see-through glass bottom swimming pool, for the exclusive use of flat owners, allows its residents to literally swim above the proletarian streets far below (Gregory, 2022b). Built in what was previously a predominately working-class district of London, the development had, by the end of 2023, still only sold around one-third of the apartments.

Unsurprisingly this is not a new phenomenon, indeed the journalist Simon Jenkins, writing in the London-based *Evening Standard* newspaper, highlighted this some years ago. He has described this as the 'emptying' of London as wealthy overseas investors compete in a 'land grab' to buy up and keep empty new apartments and houses in some of London's richest boroughs, particularly in Kensington and Chelsea (Jenkins, 2017).

With these new neighbourhoods and communities being created, as a Transparency International report highlighted, the 'London property market is highly vulnerable to corrupt wealth', fuelled by Russian oligarchs and others laundering and investing stolen money, pushing up property prices and shutting domestic London buyers and renters out (Martini, 2017; Boffey, 2022).

These new housing estates for 'incomers' are high-priced and, for them, affordable homes (Gurran and Whitehead, 2011), while other buyers seek to establish Airbnb rentals (Shabrina et al, 2021). Not only does this 'hollow out' the capital's housing, with over 86,000 properties available for short-term holiday lets with Airbnb alone during a three-month period in 2023 (Benham and Reeves, 2023), but it further exacerbates the process of excluding local people in need of low-priced housing for social rent or even to buy.

At the same time it is increasingly producing silent and empty new housing developments, with many of the flats within 'ghost towers' remaining unoccupied, despite this taking place against the backdrop of London's severe housing crisis, for example, in London's smallest yet richest borough, the Royal Borough of Kensington and Chelsea (Watt and Minton, 2016; Neate, 2018; Coad, 2020; Green, 2021). As a CIA Landlords report (2022), which surveyed vacant homes in London, noted, the capital had almost 100,000 empty properties, adding to London's severe housing crisis.

Brownfield sites

A number of the sites of these new housing developments are also on brownfield sites, estimated to be over 2,000 in 2018 (Greater London Authority, 2018) and close to 3,000 in 2020 (Keyte, 2020). These sites, empty and long deserted, previously industrial and often contaminated derelict areas, litter London's urban landscape as Hersh et al (2012) has noted. With many having shipbuilding histories, they are now available for post-industrial redevelopment as prime locations with access to water. It is becoming a common phenomenon worldwide, not just in London (Hersh et al, 2012). As Parker shows, these new London development opportunities are seductive in what they promise: '[D]efunct industrial sites along the Thames and the city's hundred-mile network of canals are being reinvented as new neighbourhoods ... and pricey waterfront real estate featuring pedestrian friendly public spaces and retail shops that favour local entrepreneurs over chain outlets' (Parker, 2019: 4). The regeneration of London's Docklands in the 1970s is but one early example of brownfield site redevelopment. Along with others, we see new expensive apartments crowding along the River Thames, from wealthy Richmond in the west to poorer Rotherhithe in Southeast London.

However, as to whether such developments actually benefit existing communities surrounding such sites, is a moot point, for, as Dixon and Adams note in a critique of brownfield regeneration, the provision of genuinely affordable homes on such sites impacts on the profitability of a development and therefore is problematic (2008). Therefore, the key rationale is that the economic rewards to developers outweigh not only local housing needs, appropriate design and historic preservation, but also any other relevance to neighbouring contexts and sensitivities.

Indeed as Atkinson et al (2019) question, does any partnership between developers and local authorities building on brownfield sites actually benefit communities at all? Taken with the lure of profit margins for developers from new builds, whether for the wealthy to buy, rent or invest in, and supported by filling the financial holes of compliant local authorities, it would appear profit is a much more attractive proposition than providing opportunities for creating much-needed socially rented affordable accommodation on these sites.

In whose interests? The corrupt planning process

Planners: whose side are they on?

Local authority planning departments have the job of negotiating between their political masters (local authority councillors), developers, their consultants and lobbyists, and local communities affected by any proposed development, along with any campaign against such plans.

Key to this role is their relationship with the local authority councillors responsible for planning decisions and the latter's relationship with developers. With the latter aiming to regenerate a geographical area, usually with promises, for example, of either providing new affordable housing, creating employment opportunities or improvements in the public realm all within the local authority borough's boundaries.

With these promises, unless on a brownfield site, often comes the destruction of existing homes, small businesses and local amenities, all seemingly viewed as collateral damage irrespective of the emotional and physical impact on people, their families and their livelihoods. What the American travel writer Jonathan Raban described, in another context, as he was travelling though the Florida Keys area in the United States during the early 1990s and viewing the physical changes he witnessed, as being 'developed with the licence and ebullient energy that goes with greed' (1991: 383).

The financing of these new developments of high-cost housing for sale cannot occur without the tacit support of the planning officers and local politicians. So, on one side, we see contested public space between developers, global investors, such as the Australian developer Lendlease, who have bought up vast swathes of London for redevelopment (Corporate Watch, 2017), while, on the other side, local authorities which need financial gains and to fulfil ideological promises of more local housing, versus local community action and campaigns to either stop a development or offer an alternative proposal or plan. The result, too often, sees the latter pushed to one side as planning decisions are decided upon the financial rewards to the local authority and not, unfortunately, the often negative impact on a community, and any recognition of its real housing needs.

Politicians and decision making

These close seductive links between developers, local politicians and planning officers in London are long-standing and undoubtably affect how planning decisions are made. One clear example of this is that, during Boris Johnson's tenure as mayor of London.

Various property speculators donated money to the Conservative Party, Johnson's party (Inman, 2021). Not illegal, but when these donors were awarded planning permission on a proposed development then the question of favouritism and bias arises.

Indeed, during his tenure as London mayor, Johnson called in 17 planning applications from London's local authorities (Branson, 2019; Deloitte, 2021) that subsequently resulted in the majority being given approval. The Convoys Wharf development in Deptford, Lewisham, Southeast London, discussed in a following chapter, was one of these.

Then in 2020, for example, the then Conservative Party's Secretary of State for Housing, Robert Jenrick, came under fire for initially approving a £1 billion property scheme for 1,500 new homes in East London. This was following a donation to the Conservative Party and him meeting up with the property developer, Richard Desmond, at a Conservative Party fundraiser event. Fortunately, however, following a successful legal challenge, Jenrick was forced to withdraw his approval for the scheme, which has now subsequently seen the proposed development rejected on appeal (Gelder, 2021).

Other similar questionable or 'dodgy' deals between London local authority councillors, planning officers and developers are in the public domain. These result in the local authority, for example, receiving a financial award that allows the developer to fund 'planning briefs' or 'supplementary planning documents' for the local authority, thereby easing the planning application through the relevant council planning committee. Examples of this include the destruction of a Victorian gas-holder in South London to create a pathway for the developer's proposal (Chamberlain, 2020) and a West London local authority looking to build up to 1,000 new homes on Ministry of Defence land (Booth, 2020). As Wehner commented, 'planning departments have been accused of conflicts after it was revealed that a number of supplementary planning documents had been paid for by the developers of the sites they were intended to protect' (2020: 3).

Supporting the local infrastructure?

Such planning decisions for developers are also helped by the complicated world of 'section 106 agreements' (s106) arising from the Town and Country Planning Act, 1990 (UK Government, 1990) and the newer Community Infrastructure Levy (CIL).

The former is specific to the site or land where there is a proposal to develop. It, for example, can require a developer to include 'affordable housing' (often not qualified as to its actual definition) on the site that was primarily intended for private sale on the market. Whereas the CIL provides local authorities with the ability to charge a general levy on all new developments for local infrastructure needs across its geographical area (GOV.UK, 2024).

The s106 in particular acts as an agreement between local authorities and developers linked to the latter gaining planning permission and/or easing the path for a proposed development. For example, in the case of a proposed residential development that might bring new residents to an area, possibly placing massive pressure on existing community infrastructure, such as the availability of school places, green and open spaces, and areas for children to play. The s106 agreement would aim to require the developer to rectify this, with local infrastructure proposals in conjunction with the local authority.

In theory, s106 payments should aim to make acceptable a development that would otherwise be unacceptable in planning terms. However, these agreements and obligations are normally thrashed out behind closed doors, hidden away from the general public and any local community groups protesting against a proposed development. Only seeing the light of day when they appear on a local authority website as part of a planning proposal prior to being heard at a local authority planning committee.

This is despite planning officers having a public duty to reflect the concerns and interests of the local community. In the absence of this, it is very difficult for campaigners and the general public, usually as volunteers from a community group with no resources, to navigate the highly complex planning system.

How and what appears at the end of this process is often the result of negotiations between the developer, local authority councillors and their planning officers. Often, the community that might be impacted on by a development is 'left out', with the financial viability of a development, that is, the profit from the new build, paramount. In reality, communities affected by a development with promises of new infrastructure facilities and services as part of the s106 agreement often end up with little or no local improvements, with their local expressed needs not listened to.

Similarly, the CIL collected centrally by a local authority is not always evenly distributed across its locality to support infrastructure needs. In addition, substantial amounts, 'millions of pounds' (MacFarlane, 2021: 29), of both s106 'community money' and CIL often go unspent by UK local authorities both in and around the proposed development site and more widely across the local authority's area and, in some instances, are returned to the developer (Tarver, 2014; Lanktree, 2019).

Across London, in particular, this figure of unspent s106 and CIL payments is colossal and challenges the view that these developers' payments support local communities. Labiak, for example, notes these amounts to be 'at least £1.288bn unspent as of 30 March 2020, around £914m is from Section 106 contributions and nearly £374m from CIL payments' (2021: 3). As Nicola Gooch, planning partner at Irwin Mitchell, said in relation to CIL: '[T]he London authorities failure to spend the £1.29bn showed CIL is not achieving what it was intended to achieve' (Labiak, 2021: 5). In London's wealthiest borough, the Royal Borough of Kensington and Chelsea, these monies have been spent on expensive sculptures and security patrols in the richest southern part of the borough with its multi-million-pound houses. Not in the northern part of the borough where there is severe housing need and where the Grenfell Tower stands in the poorer working-class Lancaster Housing Estate (Booth, 2023).

Malcolm Cadman, chair of the Voice4Deptford campaign, in Southeast London, commenting on s106 and CIL, sums up this situation: 'No benefit to a local area, and often money is held centrally by councils or can be spent elsewhere outside of the area where the development is taking place' (2024). The question has to be asked as to what might effectively tackle this situation and indeed make the planning process more democratic? A recent Centre for London report, for example, put forward suggestions for improved community involvement in local planning decisions to democratize the decision-making process. These included 'street votes' for residents, increased resources, including additional staff for local authority planning departments to speed up the planning process and to provide for effective scrutiny of planning applications, and improvement in the 'right of appeal' by affected local communities (Harding et al, 2023).

This is promising, however two of the UK's most prolific property development and investment companies, Landsec and British Land, both active across London, have argued the opposite. That with larger development applications they should perhaps avoid what they see as the cumbersome local authority planning route with its community objections and instead go directly to the overall strategic authority, such as the Labour Party controlled Greater London Authority. One might say, hoping for the previous favourable response they received from Boris Johnson when mayor of London previously? (Hill, 2023).

The community consultation cul-de-sac

In the midst of communities challenging 'top-down' redevelopment, the consultation process regarding any proposed new development that impacts on local residents and their communities is inadequate. Whether it be, for example, the demolition of an existing housing estate or the redevelopment of a brownfield site, it is highly problematic and contested. Leeson summed this up: 'Large-scale re-development of post-industrial sites can easily railroad over the needs or wishes of its existing inhabitants, or at best involve them in peripheral consultation' (2019: 1). Indeed, it is questionable as to whether urban redevelopment and regeneration, in whatever guise, with its often subsequent promised wider regeneration and gentrification, rarely, if ever, brings so-called benefits to existing communities, particularly in working-class, socially and economically deprived areas (Cooper et al, 2020).

Similarly, it has to asked why it is that publicly owned land of mainly social housing on council estates is being actively given over by local authorities to the private sector to redevelop? Not, it has to be said, private houses and streets owned by the very wealthy and professional middle classes living in the more expensive parts of London, such as Chelsea, unless, of course, a Compulsory Purchase Order is issued, which would be doubtful, as these are usually for large-scale infrastructure projects such as the HS2 high speed rail link between London and Birmingham.

So, given consultations are primarily delivered as top-down developments with usually not a whiff of real public participation or co-design with local communities, one would have to be an extreme optimistic to believe that any meaningful engagement with local residents would be the norm. Brown highlights this in the review of the Centre for London conference that brought together activists and community representatives, local authority planners and officers, and developers (2019).

Don't talk to the residents

Lees et al (2013) highlights the fact that with council estates under threat of demolition, the last people to hear about plans for this are the residents themselves, apart from leaseholders, who have a legal right to be informed via a different process of such a decision. With key decisions already been taken before coming to any affected community and the public's attention or scrutiny it is already too late to have any real influence on the outcome, which has to be reactive and objections-focused, with community social space becoming a highly contentious issue.

Unfortunately there is a long history of this occurring. For example, Carpenter's (2014) excellent review of regeneration and the Urban Development Corporations, established during Margaret Thatcher's Conservative government in the 1980s, shows that the internal evaluation of their work highlighted this disregard for consultation, and they were 'strongly criticised on a number of counts: for their failure to engage with local communities, their disregard for the social impact of their activities, and their lack of concern for local accountability, marginalising local authorities from development planning' (Carpenter, 2014: 3).

This absence and marginalization of community voices by developers has been further highlighted by Steele, for example, in her brilliant historical reflections of Deptford, South London. She underlined the virtual total absence of community consultation and participation in the public monies channelled into the regeneration of Deptford from the 1960s onwards via government initiatives such as City Challenge and the Single Regeneration Budget (Steele, 1993).

Phoney consultation?

Even when consultation is offered to communities the reality is that it is often skilfully manipulated by developers who can hire expensive City-based consultancy firms from outside of communities to favourably massage a proposed development. An example of this is the colourful information material promoting the developer's plans and their offer of attending consultation events to inform the community of the benefits to them. Quietly pushed through the letter boxes of the homes of intended community victims, these notices of 'community re-development or regeneration' compete with other letter box flyers, for example, offering pizzas from local takeaways at reduced prices.

So often the message doesn't get through and the subsequent attendance at a consultation event is minimal, what has been called the 'gap between the rhetoric of community empowerment and communities' experience of trying to influence the planning system' (Yellow book ltd, 2017: 27).

This is not helped by these events frequently being held at times of the day and at locations that residents cannot easily attend, for example, due to work commitments, childcare responsibilities, the lack of a creche or that evening events are inconvenient.

An example of this was during the COVID-19 pandemic of 2020 onwards when webinars became the favoured communication tool for hired consultancies leading these community consultations. These were conveniently set up, with one-way presentations by the consultants and the developers along with, for example, their architects, ensuring they were given priority in presenting the planning proposal, followed by selected questions, only allowed via the 'chat box', from residents and other objectors.

The 'good' and the 'bad' community

It is not unusual for developers and their consultants to view the affected community as being either for or against their development. Developers view consultations with local communities, in whatever form they take, as a process whereby they target and 'socially construct' any potentially 'supportive' section of the residents, the community and/or other key local stakeholders, such as local councillors and other potentially malleable local groups.

The aim here is to engage with whichever individuals and groups they consider to be beneficial to achieving their desired outcome, that is, to obtain planning approval for their proposed development (Ingram and Schneider, 1991; Schneider and Ingram, 1993). This allows them a mechanism for managing their agenda, usually led by a consultancy outfit from outside of the community, in how their development might impact on a community. But, more importantly for them, to reduce a community's ability to participate in the consultation engagement processes and defuse any community redress or campaign against their proposed development.

So, for example, those labelled as being 'negative' towards their plans, such as residents' campaigns, community 'activists' working with them and general objectors, are separated from what they view as the 'real community'. This latter group, having been positively constructed, can then be offered incentives or inducements such as opportunities to submit proposals for short-term 'meanwhile use', on say a brownfield site, prior to the commencement of building on a site that has been given planning permission.

Another ploy is to award one-off small funding to a local community group or school. These arrangements, aimed at gaining the trust and support of local communities, may last weeks, months or even years, with examples including commercial pop-up shops or cinemas, exhibition space and temporary music venues. Indeed, the ARUP (2020) report for the Greater London Authority highlighted the positive benefits of such arrangements to local communities and their social value, particularly in the context of post-COVID-19 recovery.

However, those within a community raising objections to a proposed development, either at the planning application stage or once planning permission has been granted, may be viewed 'negatively'. The result is to be kept at arm's length and marginalized by the developer and their consultants and typically denied such 'meanwhile use' or other opportunities.

Similarly, as with some local authority planning officers, elected local councillors, if they are seen as supportive or non-committal (not taking sides) to a development, could be viewed as often siding with this questionable process by responding slowly to objectors' questions or simply ignoring them, to outright opposing their constituents concerns (Barnes et al, 2003; Newman et al, 2004; Brown, 2019).

Apart from local residents, community campaigns and objectors within communities that have been labelled 'negative', there are also other groups who have been traditionally excluded from involvement in the consultation process. Children, young people and older people, among others. Wood argues that this is because the focus is on 'economic considerations' only. Children's and young people's views are paramount for small urban spaces on new-build sites, even to the extent of designing their play spaces with them within any proposed new development (Wood, 2020).

Invisible communities: children and young people

There would generally seem to be an increasing intolerance of children and young people, especially in the group of people developers aim their marketing at. Some developers even, directly or by implication, promote their property by reassuring potential buyers there will be no children to disturb their peace, with children considered as noisy and a potential nuisance, and promoting the view that people – adults – would generally be fearful of young people gathering near their homes. Children are therefore seen as not directly bringing any profit for the developers.

Marion Briggs, from the Alliance for Childhood, an international network of people and organizations, and a former member of the Voice4Deptford campaign in Southeast London is an advocate for 'child friendly cities' and the involvement of children and young people in decisions that affect their communities. She has argued that children and young people are not only not consulted but have also been designed out of new developments across London. Particularly after the COVID-19 pandemic, when children's mental health is such a concern, it is more necessary than ever to give children spaces to play, to be heard and taken seriously. Marion contributed the following commentary:

> In the 1950s and 60s, there was an attempt to create homes for people 'from the cradle to the grave' in communities. The dominant trend in architecture at the time was the Corbusian concept, inspired by the garden city movement, of high rise building, with streets in the sky. Building upwards allowed a quality of space which included plenty of shared green surroundings. The Pepys estate in Deptford, South East London, is an example of this.
>
> Gradually, as market economics took over and land values rose, buildings became taller, with improved building techniques, and more densely placed together. The garden city element was squeezed out, along with children's play space. The 'Right to Buy' introduced by Margaret Thatcher depleted affordable housing stock. Councils adopted a market approach to housing and government policy pushed more responsibility on to developers to provide social housing. Cuts in public funding brought about an unhealthy reliance by councils on developers' infrastructure levies. In the process, children began to drop out of developers' awareness.
>
> Their focus turned to high-earning couples and single people in one- or two-bedroom flats, who would buy, but more likely, rent property from owners who are foreign or institutional investors. In

many cases, the mainly City companies who employed them owned the flats they lived in. These businesses acquired the property for workers who came on short-term contracts and moved on after a year or two. Couples who had young children also moved on when they needed larger, longer-term housing.

As can be seen from the Convoys Wharf development, Southeast London, the approach taken is to provide minimal facilities for children. The 2016 London Structural Plan Special Policy Guidance on Children and Young People's Play and Informal Recreation stipulates that larger developments with more than ten residential units should allow an area of 10m^2 minimum play space for children of all ages on site. In the 2021 London plan this guidance became policy in an attempt to stop developers finding ways round it to the detriment of children and young people. The London Plan focuses on the under-fives and say that older children can go elsewhere, using local play areas. The policy allows this for smaller developments in return for a payment to the local authority to upgrade surrounding play areas, but larger developments should provide for children of all ages on site. Not doing this has the consequence that children who use the surrounding spaces can be crowded out by the incoming children.

This is another situation where cash-strapped councils see an opportunity to raise funding from developers at the expense of local residents, in this case children and young people. They invariably have no say in these decisions. This is an erosion of their rights under the UN Convention on the Rights of the Child, for example, article 12 (respect for the views of the child). Every child has the right to express their views, feelings and wishes in all matters affecting them, and to have their views considered and taken seriously. This right applies at all times, for example 'during immigration proceedings, housing decisions or the child's day-to-day home life'. (Interview, Marion Briggs, 2020)

Whether this situation is improved with the Mayor of London's current 'London Plan', only time will tell. Certainly its aims of 'instructing' the 32 London Boroughs to be generally more aware of the needs of families with children, to consult with children and young people as to their play needs, particularly their need for safe, adventurous and secure play, and informal spaces near to their homes, are laudable (Greater London Authority, 2021).

However, maybe what influences developers primarily is their pursuit of profit and not their concerns about who they should consult. Again, as Briggs has commented:

> Planning Authorities appear to have little say in this, despite their policies and guidance. It's not clear, in the experience of the Voice4Deptford

campaign, whether planners are even aware of what their own policies are. If they do know, they may choose to ignore them. Planning authorities are understaffed, and local authorities underfunded so the issue of financial contributions and dependence on section 106 money will always be a temptation. (Interview, Marion Briggs, 2020)

Excluding children and young people and other groups within communities from having any real involvement in how their estates and communities are remade by developers is now commonplace. The pursuit of profit along with both overt and covert collusion by many local authorities in London lie behind this. This is counterproductive in that approaching any development from a child-centred viewpoint might lead to far better and more attractive places for people to live, that is, it adds value. However, the emphasis on finance for profit makes this an unattractive approach for developers. Perhaps they just don't get it?

Conclusion

This chapter has highlighted how the financial capital of the world, London, is undergoing a process of remaking and reimagining by 'outsiders'. What Madden and Marcuse have called '[t]he neoliberal transformation of the city initially spurred two trends in housing: gentrification and abandonment' (2016: 31). How its housing market and its associated infrastructure, its communities, are being remade by profit-driven developers creating vistas of glass and steel in their own image. In doing so it is driving a housing crisis across London for those families, ordinary Londoners, particularly with children, on low incomes seeking secure and safe housing at low social rent levels. This, Ringrose argues, is fuelled by developers who view house building as about profit margins and investment potential, not social need (2021).

This is a stark reminder of Jane Jacobs, the writer and activist, and her critique of urban planning policy in the 1950s in her book, *The Death and Life of Great American Cities*, in which she argued that 'urban renewal' and 'slum clearance' did not respect the needs of city-dwellers (1961). This is still relevant, as we have highlighted how the eviction and destruction caused to once settled communities, predominately working class, with their deep historical roots to a geographical area of London, are being displaced to make way for glossy new urban neighbourhoods. Newly created communities which have 'socially cleansed' existing local authority housing estates in the pursuit of profit and a better class of resident.

There are many new developments with fanciful village-sounding names, as the developers attempt to recreate Gans' (1962) concept of the 'urban village', albeit a distorted version where these new neighbourhoods have the local corner shop, the artificial small outlet of a supermarket chain or similar incarnation, where individuals know each other via the in-house gym, and feel a comfortable attachment to their surroundings, where everyone looks the same and is from a similar socioeconomic background.

We have also highlighted the continuing lack of real housing accommodation at 'social rent' levels, whether it be local authority council housing, housing association or privately rented, that is now a familiar part of new housing developments and which is exacerbating the chronic housing shortage across London. With so-called 'affordable' housing in all its various shades out of the reach of most people in severe housing need, particularly those on local authority housing waiting lists living in precarious housing conditions in often over-priced and inadequate privately rented accommodation.

We have shown how this tyranny of private capital has seen the local authority planning process skewed and corrupted in favour of developers. Often with the direct and indirect collusion of local authority planning officers, and locally elected councillors, politicians who allegedly are expected to represent and serve their constituents at the ward level. A virtual acquiescence to developers' plans and their dubious promises of infrastructure benefits to communities affected by their proposals.

We have seen how planning officers working for London's local authorities and indeed the planning process itself are faced with almost contradictory roles. On the one hand, they supposedly work for the best interests of local residents and their communities while, at the same time, as Stein (2019) argues in relation to New York, but relevant to the 'land-grab' in London, they inflate land values (real estate) on behalf of developers through planning decisions in developers' favour against community objections. Thus, leading to his question: '[T]oday's urban planners face an existential crisis: if the city is an investment strategy, are they just wealth managers?' (Stein, 2019: 6). This undemocratic chaos, along with the lack of consultation and disempowerment brought about by the demolition and displacement of communities by developers with, as we have argued, the collusion of local authority politicians and planners, will not achieve, as Cotton (2021: 36) outlines, '[d]ecent, secure and genuinely affordable housing [which] is about much more than just a roof over your head. It is the platform upon which we build healthy, happy, better lives and communities'. A situation not unfamiliar to Frederick Engels who, writing in his pamphlet the 'Housing Question' in the late 19th century, was clear that for working-class and poor communities, insufficient, inadequate housing was a feature of their daily lives (1887).

This chapter has also shown how the attempted demolition and forcible takeover of homes proceeds with little or no genuine consultation with residents, more often than not resulting in little or no substantial community gains for the surrounding communities. What occurs, we have argued, are manipulative attempts by developers and their consultants to divide and rule community objections. By casting elements of communities that could be encouraged to support a planning proposal into the 'good' and the objectors into the 'bad', with subsequent negative repercussions for the latter.

One key question arises that we need to ask ourselves is whether the chronic housing crisis we face in London today, and indeed in other UK cities, and primarily led by developers, is unique? Perhaps not, for example, the Ladywood Estate, in Birmingham, the UK's second largest city, a community campaign has mobilized against a proposed project whereby almost 2,000 homes are under the threat of demolition in one of Europe's largest single-site estate regenerations (Ladywood Unite, 2024; Murray, 2024).

As we have seen in this chapter, the clear answer in the case of London is that this situation continues in the 21st century. Further afield, across the UK, almost 50 per cent of publicly owned land and spaces have been sold off to private interests for profit since the 1970s. In England alone it has been estimated that over 4,000 public space and buildings are sold off every year (Good Law Project, 2022). Indeed, evidence from recent research at Sheffield Hallam University shows that the seven largest private developers in the UK paid over £15 billion in dividends to shareholders over the past 20 years, with Berkeley Group PLC, who build high value property in London and Southeast England, doing particularly well (Archer and Cole, 2023). The future therefore looks bleak for people and their communities requiring social housing, as Malcolm Cadman commented:

> The problem is this is all about the 'housing market' that the middle classes have already seen so much increase in wealth from over the last 10 to 15 years especially, and more. And have probably been 'boasting' about how much more their properties are now worth, to each other.
>
> Yet, now, the 'other side' is coming out, where younger people – including their own children – are being priced out of this type of housing market. All of the 'solutions' being proposed are just 'moving the deckchairs'.
>
> There is nothing really about real homes, for a lifetime, for ordinary people. Nothing about the devastation to council estates of social rented homes, through demolition by local councils working with private developers, to then be rebuilt with only a few as 'affordable', and mainly to be privatized for profit. The problem is the value of the land, when it is designated for 'housing', and the number of units that can be built on the land by high density and high rise. That has become a market commodity for profits. Not for housing needs as really intended and needed (Cadnam, 2024).

The next chapter follows on from this overview of London by introducing the reader to Deptford, a relatively small geographical community in

Southeast London, less than five miles from the City of London's commercial centre. A community that lies at the heart of the contested battle between developers and the local Deptford community. The voices of Deptford residents graphically highlight the sense of loss and helplessness as the developers move in and reshape their community. However, within this acknowledgement of their powerlessness to stop it happening lies the seed of this being 'wrong' and 'unjust'. A remembrance of the Deptford community's history of reluctance to merely accept and to 'fight back', and, in doing so, provide lessons for themselves and other communities.

4

Deptford: Community and Change

Roger Green, with Marion Briggs, Malcolm Cadman, Warda Farah, Joyce Jacca, Richard Katona, Tony Nickson and Andy Turner

Introduction

We begin, first, by introducing the reader to Deptford, in Southeast London, a relatively small geographically urban community and part of the London Borough of Lewisham. Bordered on the north by the River Thames and squeezed between the London boroughs of Southwark and Greenwich. Less than five miles from the financial capital of the world, the City of London.

We discuss its diverse demographic make-up and, importantly, its significant maritime history, with reference to Convoys Wharf, a large, empty, post-industrial brownfield site facing the River Thames. A site that lies at the heart of the contested battle between a global developer and the local Deptford community. It is this site and its heritage, largely forgotten and ignored by this developer, that epitomizes the rapidly changing face of the Deptford community.

The voices of Deptford residents graphically highlight this transformation, the sense of felt loss as the developers move in and reshape their community. However, within this acknowledgement of their powerlessness to stop it happening lies the seed of 'this is wrong and unjust', a remembrance of the Deptford community's history of their reluctance to merely accept and to challenge injustice.

Deptford

Deptford is in Evelyn Ward, with a population of just over 31,000 and one of 19 wards within the London Borough of Lewisham. An inner South London borough with a population of over 300,000, making it the fourth largest of London's 32 boroughs (Lean, 2019). A borough with a traditional

Labour Party constituency with all of its three Members of Parliament and its 54 elected local authority councillors representing the Labour Party.

As a separate local authority entity, the Metropolitan Borough of Deptford ended in 1965 when it was subsumed into the newly created London Borough of Lewisham under the 1963 London Government Act that came into force in 1965. This Act created the 32 London boroughs and abolished the smaller and more numerous existing local government districts such as Deptford. Along with this, Deptford lost its own grand Grade 2 listed town hall. Opened in 1905, it was converted into the administrative offices of Goldsmiths, University of London. Deptford became simply just another part of a new London borough.

As part of the Evelyn Ward in Deptford it lies in one of the most deprived local authority areas in England, with Lewisham ranked as the 31st most deprived borough (London Borough of Lewisham, 2019). Relative to the rest of the country, Lewisham's deprivation is increasing, for example, the proportion of children in poverty, at 39 per cent, is slightly above the London average of 37 per cent (Trust for London, 2022).

It has high levels of poverty, inequality and deprivation, with affordability an issue across all types of housing tenure (London Borough of Lewisham, 2017). It is also one of the most deprived local authority areas in London (Elvery, 2019; London Councils, 2019).

Deptford also sits in a ward that has the most 'income deprived' children by ward in the borough (London Borough of Lewisham, 2019) and statistically Deptford has a younger age profile as compared to other London boroughs (Belfield, 2015), with over 30 per cent of households with dependent children (Qpzm, 2022).

It is predominately a working class, ethnically mixed neighbourhood, with a white British majority and significant communities of Black British, African and Caribbean heritage. With over 11,000 households, the neighbourhood has mostly people living in rented accommodation, with almost 50 per cent in socially rented local authority council housing or other social housing providers, putting it in the 'top 15 wards in all of London for its proportion of socially rented housing' (Baston, 2019: 10).

At its centre it has Deptford High Street, the location of the well-known street market, with its small independent shops and roadside stalls selling a variety of goods and items, from Vietnamese food to African yam and sweet potato, once described as 'the capital's most diverse and vibrant high street' (Potts, 2008: 41).

A maritime history

Pick up any book relating to Deptford and it will immediately announce its proud naval history and its contribution to the global reach of Britain's imperial expansion. As Mee commented: 'Deptford, its fame is around the World' (1937: 833).

Deptford was the site of the Royal Navy's first dockyard, from King Henry VIII in the 16th century through to the mid 19th century, and its history is littered with famous names (Francis, 2017). Over this almost 300-year period, all manner of maritime history started in Deptford. In 1577, Francis Drake sailed from Deptford to circumnavigate the world, returning to host Queen Elizabeth I on board the *Golden Hinde* at Deptford. He was knighted upon the *Golden Hinde* at Kings Yard, the naval dockyard (The Golden Hinde, 2020). While Sir Walter Raleigh allegedly placed his cloak over a puddle to allow Queen Elizabeth I to step over it, and Peter the Great, Tsar of Russia, came to Britain as a young man, to learn about shipbuilding both at Kings Yard, Deptford, in 1698 (now known as Convoys Wharf) (Mee, 1937; Coats, 2018). The dockyard built and maintained warships for over 300 years, as well as Captain Cook's two ships, setting sail from the dockyard to chart Australia in the *Endeavour*.

Deptford is also the place where Trinity House, the organization that ensures shipping safety around the UK coastline, was founded in the 16th century (South London Club, 2019). While John Evelyn, the famous horticulturalist, diarist and resident, and friend of Samuel Pepys and Sir Christopher Wren, architect of St Paul's Church in central London, had a large 17th-century house and garden by the River Thames, at Sayes Court. This was demolished during the 18th century, and replaced by a workhouse, with only a fragment remaining in the nearby Sayers Court Garden (Thorold, 1999). It is also where Christopher Marlowe, the Elizabethan English playwright and contemporary of William Shakespeare, lived and met his death there in 1593 (Marlowe Society, 2022).

The Deptford Royal Dockyard (now Convoys Wharf), along with Sayers Court Garden, were added to the World Monuments Fund's watch list (Weinreb and Hibbert, 1992).

Convoys Wharf

The dockyard situated in Deptford's Evelyn Ward is the historical centre of Deptford. Richard Katona, the late long-term Deptford resident, local community historian and Voice4Deptford campaign activist, commented, 'scratch anywhere upon the history of Deptford and you will find Convoys Wharf and its earlier incarnations lurking at the bottom of it' (2020).

Occupying most of Deptford's Thameside land, it closed in 1869 and continued in a different form as a foreign cattle market until 1914, when taken over by the Ministry of Defence and used as the Royal Naval Victualling Depot until the early 1980s (Museum of London Archaeology, 2017; Naval Dockyards Society, 2018).

In the 1950s the remaining above ground parts were demolished to make way for new warehouse structures. These lay disused, until purchased by Rupert Murdoch's News International in 1980 as a storage facility for the importation of newsprint, to use across the river at its site in Wapping before finally closing in the late 1990s (Transpontine, 2011).

The Convoys Wharf site had been empty for a number of years following News International's withdrawal from using the site and, despite planning proposals to develop the site coming and going, it has remained a derelict, empty brownfield site since.

However, from 2000 onwards, several planning applications came forward, each led by private developers. In 2005, Cheung Kong Holdings and Hutchison Whampoa (based in Hong Kong) were selected to develop a mixed residential and commercial project of luxury apartments, according to the high-density 'Dubai' style build, of 3,500 flats, with 15 per cent designated 'affordable' but no social rented provision for local people.[1]

Following an intervention by the then mayor of London, Boris Johnson, after returning from a trip to China, in 2013, he 'called in' the planning application following the London Borough of Lewisham's attempts to improve the planning application (Deptford Dame, 2014). *Private Eye* viewed this as 'Boris's Chinese chums have effectively been told they can do what they want' (Piloti, 2013). Outline planning approval was granted by the Greater London Authority in 2014 (Gould, 2014; Greater London Authority, 2014).

Johnson took the following view regarding the Convoys Wharf scheme: 'I think it is odd that people actually try to stop developments going ahead. I think of the amazing development at Deptford (South East London) that's been blocked for twenty years' (Greater London Authority, 2014). Therefore, the Convoys Wharf scheme by Hutchison Property Group Ltd, a subsidiary of the Hong Kong global developer, owned by Li Ka-shing, the world's richest real estate entrepreneur and chairman of CK Hutchison Holdings, came into being (*China Daily*, 2022).

However, since this approval was granted, in the intervening years the planning application has had a tortuous passage through the London Borough of Lewisham's planning committee structure. Residents and local Deptford community groups raised questions concerning the proposed development.

A forgotten history?

Deptford and its dockyard also has another history as well. It was connected to the slave trade, a history that is seemingly forgotten by some accounts of Deptford, the history of the royal dockyard and the archaeological excavations between 2000 and 2012 (Francis, 2017).

As Erasmus noted, 'the Royal Dockyard at Deptford played a significant role in the slave trade' (2002: 23), while the Museum of Slavery and Freedom

(MoSaF), based in Deptford, states that: 'The first ever British slaver, John Hawkins, enriched Elizabeth 1 with profits from slavery. He lived and worked in a naval house in Deptford' (MoSaF, 2020).

A detailed historical blog by the 'unknown' author, Mudlark121 (2020), provides an insightful expose of the importance and extent of the slave trade that involved Deptford and its dockyard. From Captain John Hawkins, described as the first English slave trader (Anim-Addo, 1995), to Caribbean plantation owners setting off from Deptford, and slaves being landed at Deptford, the location played a prominent part in this infamous aspect of British colonial history. As Hefler describes, the East India Company was a

> slave trading company, and that, like the companies trading human cargo, it developed a set of formal policies to reduce the high cost and risk associated with its trade. ... African slaves played a vital role in both the Company's trade and its rise to become a colonial power in the nineteenth century. (Hefler, 2018: 19)

The East India Company leased a yard at Deptford and built its ships there for a number of years in the 17th century (Dalrymple, 2019; Old Royal Naval College, Greenwich, 2022; Royal Museums Greenwich, 2022).

While for Sir Francis Drake, a privateer and compatriot of Hawkins, Deptford was the source for ships leaving and returning with human cargo, with the area rapidly becoming the location for London's global slave trade (Allain et al, 2019). It was also in Deptford, in 1762, that Olaudah Equiano was sold back into slavery, before going on to raise money to buy his release and become Britain's first Black political activist (Anim-Addo, 1995; MoSaF, 2020).

Local groups, such as MoSaF and Deptford People's Heritage Museum have arisen organically in recent years in response to the proposed development of Convoys Wharf. Both critically highlighting this history of the slave trade at Convoys Wharf, then known as the Royal Naval Dockyard, and its importance in contributing, and for many, creating, the personal wealth of some individuals and families in the UK. Its information, news and planned events ensure this Black history is not forgotten, particularly for all young people growing up in Deptford and across London.[2]

Deptford still exists

Jess Steele, in her history of Deptford, highlights the indifference of local politicians and others 'in power' towards what she calls its 'special and spectacular history [that] has been neglected for over a hundred years' (1993: 222). Similarly, listening to residents today, much of the Kings Yard or Convoys Wharf history, and Deptford's generally, remains silent and almost forgotten. Instead, Deptford could be viewed as a liminal space, an 'in-between' place, always somewhere to pass through, on the A220 road through to central London, rather than a destination.

This feeling may be partly rooted in Deptford's own waning, from the late 19th century onwards, along with neighbouring communities, with its hundreds of warehouses, wharves and tanneries becoming lost and derelict as the area became increasingly urbanized and its industries changed (Inwood, 2005). Deptford declined, becoming referred to as quite 'the worst part of the great City's story' with 'the muddy, melancholy banks … the desolation of empty silent yards' (Ackroyd, 2000: 552).

In recent years Deptford as a place and its heritage have been viewed by locals as being forgotten by outsiders, with little or no evidence that it exists within the greater area of the London Borough of Lewisham, for example, street signage has been removed. As one Deptford resident commented in a street interview:

> Talk about Deptford and you immediately get on to Lewisham … 'Lewisham this, Lewisham that'. Lewisham takes everything! People in Deptford even say that they're from Lewisham – when they're in Deptford! What is 'Lewisham'? Deptford has always been an embarrassment. It's a route through … invisible. There isn't even a sign for Deptford!

It is no surprise, then, that residents who know Deptford's history are angry at the London Borough of Lewisham's disinterest in its heritage, the story of Deptford's people and its history, even as nearby Greenwich continues to trade successfully on its own past. According to one Deptford resident of the Pepys housing estate, speaking in 2016, 'Deptford has always played second fiddled to Greenwich – and yet we've got so much more history and significance! And Lewisham just sell us down the river – literally!'.

Despite what has been seen by many residents as the attempt to erase Deptford as a place, its history and rich heritage is relevant to its residents. Livsey and Price's filmed celebration of the local authority council estate, the Pepys Estate in Deptford in 2016, for example, entitled *Reading Pepys*, shows residents' conversations moving across historical time periods, including using archival material relating to Samuel Pepys whom the estate is named after. Similarly *The Secret History of Our Streets* series that examined the history of Deptford High Street from the 19th century to the present captured the voices of shop keepers and residents. The filmed conversations about the place where they lived and worked demonstrated the rich vein of historical memories that permeates Deptford, its residents, and its importance to them (BBC Two, 2018).

Regeneration in Deptford: the developers move in

Deptford, like so many places in London, used to be a place where you lived and worked, knew the neighbours and your family and friends were close by. Now Deptford and the London Borough of Lewisham itself, like so many London boroughs, is experiencing the rapid remaking of its urban and cultural landscape. High-end, high-rise blocks of flats are appearing and changing forever the familiarity of place, neighbourhood and community (Garcia, 2021).

One resident commented:

> I don't think a lot of people know what they're voting for when they tick a box until something like this happens to them, or near them where they have no say, they make you think you have a say but behind the scenes they're already shaken hands done a deal with the developers. (Vickers, 2022)

While another resident remarked during a street interview, '[h]igh rise, high cost that puts the wealthy first … is this the remaking of Deptford?' (Deptford resident, 2023)

Deptford's the place to be, according to London's *Evening Standard* newspaper, with the average rent for a private apartment at £3,000 a month and rising (2024). This 'top-down' regeneration, where locals cannot afford such rents, are being pushed to the very edges or cut out of the picture altogether, and local people are never asked for their views about what is happening, is now the norm. A form of 'social cleansing' brilliantly captured by Stewart Morgan Hajdukiewicz (a Lewisham resident) in his documentary (2021).

It is a regeneration process that has been gaining momentum since Tony Blair's Labour government's 'City Challenge' programme came to Deptford in the 1990s. The redevelopment of one of the high-rise blocks of flats on the working-class Pepys Estate witnessed the decanting of the existing local authority residents, replacing them with private luxury flats for more wealthier incomers (Calafate-Faria, 2014).

It highlights all that is wrong with a process that effectively disenfranchises local people and which creates growing disparities between them, the local authority, planners, developers and 'new' people moving into the area.

As Strasser notes, Deptford has been changing, with its partial River Thames frontage and its historic ex-bustling shipyard seeing post-industrial decline, leading to Deptford slowly being undermined following the slum housing clearance in the 1960s. Replaced by increasingly new, large-scale housing developments for outsiders. Meanwhile, its connections to its riverside and maritime heritage, rich and complex post-industrial and post-colonial histories, are also left behind (Strasser, 2020).

Deptford is emerging as a place of two communities. This can been seen in residents' concerns about increasing inequalities and the growing gap with the new affluent 'incomers' as Deptford competes with other areas of South London experiencing the redevelopment and gentrification process. Nearby Peckham, for example, with working-class residents living in relative poverty, particularly children, on grey, decaying council housing estates and lost forever on housing waiting lists as new expensive flats appear around them.

It is an example that is symptomatic of the remaking of London at the local level, and how these gaps and distances between these different social classes play out in urban planning decisions, the increasing land struggles and the politics of urban regeneration.

In Deptford we now see people moving out and changes to the local Deptford High Street, with the opening of expensive artisan shops and the requisite coffee shops. As *Time Out* magazine described in 2022, 'Deptford High Street in the borough of Lewisham, south-east London, has been named one of the 33 coolest streets in the world, following a vote by Time Out magazine' (Garner, 2022: 4). While one resident interviewed commented:

> We don't actually have a one-off fancy type of coffee shop we will have five! … People are more interested in Deptford; young people or older people who can't afford Hackney or Hackney Wick, Deptford is kind of like zone 2, it is a little bit cheaper and it is on the south end so people feel 'Oh, OK, we will make something here' and so they have come here and they noticed there was no Costa here and now there is one and then they said 'OK, we don't actually have a one-off fancy type of coffee shop we will have five!' There is a Stockton, the Velo, the Waiting Room and I think it's all to do with business owners cause they were all the ones on Deptford Yard. But that is where all the people from Deptford went. But Tony's deli is also losing customers and he was a staple. (Deptford resident, 2022)

Deptford, along with Lewisham generally (Hajdukiewicz, 2021), has in recent years has become the centre of a massive building programme which has alienated and ignored the housing needs of the local, diverse working-class population. Alongside these changes the borough is experiencing a severe housing crisis, with over 10,000 families on the housing waiting list, which has at least a ten-year wait to be awarded local authority social housing (Cuffe, 2020b).

New developments are also springing up both along its River Thames waterfront and inland. Deptford's traditional local services are being recalibrated with, for example, middle-class incomers not requiring face-to-face banking services, leaving local people finding their banks disappearing along Deptford High Street and creating a 'banking desert' (Deptford Dame Blogger, 2020).

This reinforces the approach taken by developers that the 'remaking' of Deptford requires such a shift in services from the much needed face-to-face banking, required by the High Streets stall holders, in favour of online impersonal connections that promotes new 'incomers' to the area. All totally ignoring the socioeconomic and community need for local services that fit with Deptford's existing diverse working-class demographics.

This continuing gentrification of Deptford and its surrounding neighbourhoods has been monitored by 'Corporate Watch', which has collated and highlighted 15 new developments, all of which are investment vehicles for both global and UK developers with no 'social housing' or meaningful infrastructure offers available for local people (Corporate Watch, 2019).

Such changes to residents' lives do not go unnoticed:

> Unless people live with their families they cannot afford to get a property here. … Sometimes you would walk down Deptford High Street and you would bump into lots and lots of your friends but now I don't see that for young people. I don't really see very many young people out that much at all, or if they are out, they are going from point A to point B whereas we used to go out just for the sake of going out bump into our friends, go to the adventure playground. … I think a lot of the people that I grew up with were moved out of the area so they took up houses further away like Thamesmead or Erith or their families were moved out … lots of people due to lots of multi-factual reasons are not in the area anymore. … Unless people live with their families they cannot afford to get a property here unless they got a council property from being on the waiting lists so I think there are a many factors here like that. (Warda Farah, Voice4Deptford member)

Similarly another resident commented:

> The spaces for local people to eat, to meet up with each other is very limited … it is now not recognisable like from both ends like from the beginning and the end. It's not the same with all new shops there is only a bit in the middle that is recognizable, which is the bit of the market or the staple Pound Shop, but the rest of it is the fancy coffee shops, the barbers, the restaurants that none of the local residents go to, so the spaces for local people to eat, to meet up with each other is very limited, it is like limited to the fried chicken. I mean literally outside the fried chicken and there is nothing in the region of people's price range. (Deptford resident, 2022)

In conversation with Deptford resident and Voice4Deptford member Warda Farah, she talks of being born and bred in Deptford. Living close to Deptford

High Street, she has seen Deptford change incrementally and doesn't feel part of her community anymore, instead becoming an outsider. The bustling and diverse Deptford High Street of her youth has changed, with developments across Deptford destroying her identity:

> My parents fled a civil war and found a safe haven in this special part of Southeast London. Every street corner, park and estate stairs holds deep vivid memories of me growing up in a deprived area but not feeling in need. We had a community, friends, support networks, youth clubs. I remember we used to call the Pepys Estate the ghetto, the large grey bricks looked as if they engulfed the sky but for us it was our own world. We would play for hours outside, knock for our friends and stay at the adventure playground till it was dark, or our parents came to find us. It was our Deptford and we made the best out of it, even when people would make derogatory statements of how rough and dangerous it was.
>
> You see I was made in Deptford and now I feel as if the place that defined who I am is dying piece by piece, with each new edgy coffee shop and barber my old stomping ground ceases to be. I never saw the gentrification happening, each new block getting closer and closer to the high street, new facilities for a small portion of the population coming to existence. It's as if it all happened overnight and there I was left out of the process. Now when I walk down the high street I no longer recognize where I am, until I see the few staple shops that are fighting to stay open. I sit in the new coffee shop and as I enter the door it feels as if I am the alien in the room, I no longer belong here. This is incredibly hard for me to reconcile because I along with my family, friends and our community built the tapestry, fibre and flavour of the Deptford you see today. When nobody wanted to live here we took pride and looked after it and now we are being pushed out, discarded and ethnically cleansed.

Talking to another resident, Joyce Jacca, an ex-Labour councillor in Deptford's Evelyn Ward, at the Pepys Resource Centre in Deptford, who has lived in Deptford for over 19 years and works locally as a community health worker, she was both concerned and angry about the future for young people in Deptford and the proposed redevelopment of the Convoys Wharf site:

> Some of the places they are building, built like they are called you are segregated; you know they have built walled gates so you cannot walk through so then it becomes more 'them' and 'us'. What you need to remember is that there will hardly be anyone from here, it will be the people from the outside that will come in here but what you have to remember is that those people they have to join up with the people that are already here.

It looks like poor people live there and people with money are living down there and that is what I don't like. So it is like a class thing. In ten years' time there is going to be no original people here in Deptford not even the young generation because there is not affordable housing. There is affordable housing but not accessible housing, that is what I call it. It is affordable but it is not accessible to us, right, so people will be moving out and, yeah, we might be the new Chelsea. That is how I look at it because I can see all the changes that are here.

Resistance to injustice

These voices of Deptford residents graphically highlight this transformation as the developers move in and reshape their community from the outside. However, within this acknowledgement of a sense of powerlessness to stop it happening there is a remembrance of the Deptford community's history of challenging injustice, and their reluctance to merely accept others' imposed realities when their community is threatened. This history of resistance to perceived and actual injustice has a long tradition, with examples from industrial trade union action to community campaigns.

In the mid 18th century, for example, Deptford shipyard workers took strike action against the stopping of the custom and practice of taking home pieces of broken wood unsuitable for shipbuilding, known as 'chips', as a means of topping up their low wages (London Radical Histories, 2018). Another example is the 1911 school strikes, part of what was known as the 'Great Unrest' when hundreds of strikes took place across Britain, with the *Times* newspaper (12 September 1911) reporting that a number of pupils, boys, at a school in Deptford 'organised a demonstration outside the school, and amused the neighbourhood by shouting "We are on strike". Students chalked demands on the pavement for the abolition of home lessons and the cane, and an extra half-holiday in the week' (Basketter, 2011).

During the same period in 1911, over 500 dock workers in Deptford went on strike over employers breaking an agreement resulting in a large group of strikers marching to the company's London-based headquarters at London Bridge (Transpontine, 2010).

In more recent years, support for the 1970s miners' strike against the Conservative government of Margaret Thatcher witnessed pickets from Betteshanger Colliery, Kent, at Deptford Power Station joined by local residents and community groups (Ingram, 2022). While the 1986 Wapping dispute between Rupert Murdoch's News International and the newspaper print unions (TUC, 1986) saw a warehouse fire that destroyed 20,000 tons of newsprint at the then Rupert Murdoch owned Deptford Convoys Wharf site. An unresolved mystery, with any trade union activism involvement denied by a trade union representative (UPI, 1986). Finally, community and local trade union support for the national ambulance strikes of 1990 through to 2023, with picketing at Deptford ambulance station, shows solidarity across the Deptford community (People's History Museum, 2022; NewsLine, 2023).

Nearby Goldsmiths, University of London, on the border of Deptford and New Cross, with its central administrative centre located in what was once Deptford town hall, has seen recent years of trade union unrest and student protest. From 2016 onwards University College Union members, along with Goldsmiths Student Union members, have taken strike action, supported on the picket line by Deptford-based community groups, such as Voice4Deptford, and the local Member of Parliament for Lewisham Deptford. This has been in support over wages, gender inequality, job insecurity and pension rights (East London Lines, 2016; McCarthy, 2018; Freedman, 2020; Goldsmiths University and College Union, 2024).

Along with this trade union action, community resistance has been against the local authority and developers and has centred on fighting to keep historical and cultural landmarks, such as the 'save the anchor campaign' in 2013.

A cultural symbol that illustrates Deptford residents' desire to preserve its communal heritage and its sense of place was the battle to save the 'anchor', a popular landmark at the bottom of Deptford High Street donated by Chatham Historic Dockyard in the 1990s as a reminder of the area's maritime history. It was unceremoniously removed in 2013 by the local authority, ostensibly to get rid of street drinkers who daily used to congregate around its base. For locals the indignation was in part the absence of any consultation about the anchor's removal. It was also a sense that whatever acknowledgement of local history there was, however modest and discreet, the wider local authority, the London Borough of Lewisham, failed to understand this, or see any significance, and were happy that this symbol of the Deptford story was, according to residents, 'erased'. However a local campaign successfully resulted in its return in 2018 (Waywell, 2018; Strasser, 2020).

A less successful outcome was the bitterly contested 'battle for Deptford' during 2018. The destruction of Tidemill community gardens and the Reginald House estate was resisted by residents and local groups with a vocal campaign against the local authority who were aided by bailiffs and the police. The aim was to save an open public green space, community garden and block of council homes for low-income families from demolition and redevelopment, or 'forced gentrification' as one resident called it (Corporate Watch, 2018b; Strasser, 2020; Worthington, 2020; Vickers, 2022).

Conclusion

In this chapter we have seen a Deptford community, with its maritime history, with a high street and market still trying to retain its small independent traders serving a multi-ethnic community, being overtaken by developers at the expense of local people. How the everyday lives of the people of Deptford, their voices, show the changes that are taking place and which they seemingly have limited power to influence, change or stop.

David Widgery took the following view:

> We need to recover from the developers and the estate agents' thrall different and better possibilities: of low rent housing, small scale manufacture, informal places and unofficial uses. We have to stop showering hardship on the working class of the inner cities and instead respect their ingenuity, their bravery and their beauty. For the true makers of a city are not those who possess its property but those who live there. (Widgery, 1993: 237)

This remaking of Deptford is a microcosm of what is happening within not just London and the UK, but around the world. Large corporate developers finance developments and regeneration projects as they compete for profit. While local planning concerns, objections and regulations are rolled back in their favour.

For Deptford residents experiencing this, the impact on their local area feels drastic and bewildering, a rewriting of skylines with large-scale high-rise blocks, the displacement of sections of the community, and distinctive local amenities and services priced out and swept away, replaced by corporate supermarket chains and 'anywhere' artisan stores.

Despite an undercurrent of seemingly always being 'done to' rather than innovating their own futures Deptford's residents have been remarkably resilient in fighting back, to have a say in how their community is shaped.

The example of the Convoys Wharf historical site typifies this. Following the decision made at the Convoys Wharf public hearing at City Hall, London in 2014 to award outline planning permission, the decision was a catalyst to bring about the 'Convoys Wharf Community Group' and ultimately Voice4Deptford and its campaign to challenge this.

A campaign drawing on Thompson's ideas of 'histories from below' (1974). How ordinary people, residents of Deptford and their supporters, began to take their strength from their collective community experiences and perspectives, that contrasted with the stereotypical view of power being the preserve of only politicians, planners and corporates. It is their campaign, a fight against a corporate developer's 'land-grab' of the Convoys Wharf site, that they tell in the following chapter.

5

Defiance and Resistance: The Voice4Deptford Campaign

Roger Green, with Andy Turner, Malcolm Cadman, Marion Briggs, Vanessa Celosse, Warda Farah, Joyce Jacca, Richard Katona, Tony Nickson, Kenneth M. Thomas and other members and supporters of the campaign

A story worth telling

In this chapter we focus on a unique campaign to resist a proposed massive private housing development facing the River Thames in Deptford, Southeast London. Members of the Voice4Deptford campaign tell the story of resisting the demands of a global developer and working for imaginative community alternatives.

From its beginnings in 2013, the chapter tells of how a group of residents, activists and their supporters succeeded in diverting agency, power and knowledge away from outside holders of power and experts into the orbit of the community. How the campaign has actively encouraged and supported local people, residents, to step forward and incorporate Gramsci's idea of community 'organic intellectuals' based on who they are, their expertise, local knowledge and class heritage (Forgacs, 1988). By doing so, now in its eleventh year, the campaign continues to challenge the developer, local power holders and their entitlement to retain a hegemonic hold over the Deptford community by denying them their voices, their real participation and their plans for the future.

Essentially, how the campaign is at the community level is a key example of developing a counter-hegemonic action that feeds into the wider left and progressive movement against resisting the ruling and accepted political, economic, beliefs and power.

The chapter opens with how the campaign began, the formation of the initial 'Convoys Wharf Community Group', and the trials and tribulations of daily campaign life. This is followed by the campaign's transformation into Voice4Deptford, with its higher profile, its use of community meetings in engaging and working with the local community and other community groups. The approaches and tactics used to retake power and promote the campaign, including the 'pop-up' shop, the judicial review and the community's 'new vision' for the site, are all discussed.

The chapter looks at the deliberate tactic of getting people 'around the table' as an approach to engaging with all the key stakeholders, those with 'power', the developer, politicians, local authority officers. How the campaign developed from growing community voices to its continuing confrontation, resistance and posing alternatives to the developer's vision for the Convoys Wharf site.

The chapter concludes with a discussion of the campaign's eleven years, including what has been achieved and what is still being learnt, the key successes, its setbacks, and its unique, multi-faceted approach that utilized a diverse range of engagement tactics and strategies.

How it all started over a 'cup of tea'

What do you do when a global multinational corporate developer such as Hutchison Property Group Ltd, a company part of CK Asset Holdings Limited, a Hong Kong based global developer, owned by one of the richest people in the world, plans to build more than 3,000 high-rise private luxury apartments outside your front door? In doing so transforming your neighbourhood forever, while ignoring local traditions and history, kinship and social networks, and the existing housing and other priority needs of your community? A scheme that, according to the developer's 'master plan', promised the following:

> I think the people of Deptford and all the people around here are going to rediscover a piece of the Thames, with a great walkway, a great jetty, and a lot of history underneath the surface, and they will own it, have walks, and festivals and markets, this will be their territory. (Farrell, 2012)

In the late summer of 2013, Roger Green, an academic urban community researcher and activist, met up with Malcolm Cadman, a long-standing Deptford resident and community activist. At the time, Green was director of the Centre for Community Engagement Research at nearby Goldsmiths, University of London campus, and Cadman was the chief executive officer of Pepys Community Forum, a well-known community organization based off Deptford High Street.

Over cups of tea, the conversation focused on the changing nature of Deptford, as new housing developments criss-crossed the area in the absence of adequate consultation with residents. One such example being the plan to build on the nearby historic Convoys Wharf site alongside the River Thames. Cadman had been involved in challenging this development over a number of years, along with other activists such as 'Deptford IS', organizing and supporting the voices of the Deptford community to be heard, as different architects and their plans for the site came and went.

One of the last Thames riverside developments in London, Convoys Wharf is a brownfield site with a unique historical maritime heritage and located on the doorstep of several poorly maintained local authority and housing association estates. With only limited community consultation previously undertaken with the local community in recent years, there was a concern that the development would go ahead without any significant input from local residents.

The proposed development was viewed as unaffordable for the majority of people living in the predominately working-class area of Deptford. It did not meet the social housing needs of local residents experiencing life on low wage employment and those surviving on state welfare benefits. While also failing to house any of those thousands of families with children, and others patiently waiting on the London Borough of Lewisham's housing waiting list for accommodation.

Instead it offered a high-rise, bland, out-the-box 'anywhere' design for those with sufficient personal capital, including overseas investors.

As Cadman recalls:

Around 2013 Roger Green and myself first met. Roger was doing a tour of local organizations as part of a research project. We met at the Pepys Community Forum office ... I think we seem to get on personally ... the dynamics just seem to work. He said what he wanted to do and I said what I've been doing ... he wanted to work directly and be involved quite closely. We decided to work together ... we knew there was a need to get the local community involved in getting their voice heard. So after some more meetings between the two of us, we formed the Convoys Wharf Community Group. (Cadman, 2021)

A site visit by Cadman and Green to the Convoys Wharf site followed, part of the annual Open House London event one Saturday morning in late September 2013. With hundreds of other people, they walked around the site, previously closed to the public, and viewed a crude 'matchbox' size model, created by the developers then consultants, of the proposed development that would not have been out of place in a Year 5 primary school class. The consultants were on hand to promote their model, but were not really listening to questions from the public, and instead showing off their proposed development as an inspired cutting-edge architectural design worthy of our praise. Talking to local residents attending the event, it became evident that the needs of the local Deptford community, and what benefits the proposed development might offer them, appeared to be totally absent!

As Cadman remarked in discussion with some local residents:

> A new developer, a Chinese company, now appointed the Sir Terry Farrell Partnership to come forward with another master plan … a bit more dense, high rise blocks and less beauty … just more standardization, but more conformist to what the developer was asking them to do. Which has produced a profit-making site which would benefit the company and not so much encompass what local people were looking to get … they can't see any visible benefit themselves, they can't see any new jobs emerging and new shops emerging, a new playground, access to the river, and so on, they can't see what benefits they can get. (Malcolm Cadman, chair, Voice4Deptford, 2021)

This general feeling of mistrust as to what was being planned for the site was further compounded later that year, following an intervention by the then mayor of London, Boris Johnson, in 2013, after his visit to China. He called in the planning application for what was seen as the Hong Kong developer's impatience with the London Borough of Lewisham for withholding planning permission. At a packed hearing at London City Hall in March 2014, despite Cadman and other community voices speaking out passionately against the development, outline planning approval was granted to the developer by the mayor (London Assembly, 2014).

As reported by some media outlets at the time, the 'whiff' of something untoward about Johnson's intervention and his decision was commented on, for example:

> The Mayor of London, recently back from a business-boosting China trip, has stepped in after Hong Kong-based Hutchison Whampoa became frustrated at 'unrealistic demands' from the council over their Convoys Wharf project and urged him to intervene. (Chandler, 2013: 1)

> [T]he developer Hutchison Whampoa wrote to the mayor last month asking him to intervene after falling out with council over architect Sir Terry Farrell's masterplan. (CITY A.M., 2013)

This was, however, not an unusual outcome at the time, for it was one of a series of controversial planning decisions by Boris Johnson, during his tenure as mayor of London, that cut across local planning procedures and undermined London's democratically elected local authorities. This approval acted as a catalyst for the formation of the 'Convoys Wharf Community Group'. The aim of the newly formed group was to bring together residents and supporters with a shared concern to ensure Deptford's voices were heard in challenging this development, and the wider regeneration of their neighbourhood, in addition to offering alternative suggestions for the site.

Convoys Wharf Community Group
Getting started

By word of mouth, a small group of people came together and plans for a public meeting of this newly formed campaign group was hatched. Prior to the meeting, street interviews were undertaken in Deptford High Street with shoppers, stall holders and shop keepers by students from Goldsmiths' Centre for Community Engagement Research and members of the newly formed community group. The aim was to discover people's knowledge of the proposed development, their views about it and what were their priorities for the Convoys Wharf site and neighbouring area (Green, 2014). As Cadman commented: 'We did street interviews together. We got some students involved from Goldsmiths ... and we had some local people involved as well ... there's a mixture. We were able to get views of the area. ... We concentrated on Deptford High Street.'

The findings unsurprisingly showed that local residents identified a general lack of consultation about the proposed development and the absence of housing for social rent on the site. People also reported anxiety about their grown-up children being forced to move out of the area due to the lack of low-priced housing. People expressed a wish to have a voice in what was going to happen, to be kept informed, and a significant number asked to attend any future public meeting. These street interviews were supported by a follow-up survey undertaken of Deptford's community groups. It similarly highlighted a general lack of knowledge about the proposed development and a wish to be involved in having a voice about the site's future (Green and Ferguson, 2014).

Bringing people together: community meetings

> The first meeting had a very good response ... people just wanted to know what was going on and what progress was happening at this particular time, and how they could influence it and get involved in it ... there were so many good people. There was a good discussion with good outcomes. (Cadman, 2024)

On one evening in June 2014, the fledgling Convoys Wharf Community Group (CWCG) held its first public meeting. Chaired by Andy Turner, now a member of the community group, a community activist known for his pioneering work with residents on the Kingsmead Estate in Hackney (Turner, 2009) and an academic colleague of Green's from Goldsmiths.

The venue, the new Deptford Lounge, the old library in Deptford High Street, was attended by over 50 people who had been encouraged to attend by extensive house to house leafletting and posters distributed by the CWCG around the local housing estates and streets. The agenda brought together residents and people living and working in and around the Convoys Wharf site and the wider Deptford community. It provided the opportunity to bring people together to discuss the proposed development and help make connections between each other. Information about the development was available, along with members of the community group being on hand to listen to and discuss people's questions and concerns.

After a noisy two hours during which individuals voiced their questions, views and objections, ideas and plans emerged to take the campaign forward. A consensus was reached to challenge the lack of affordable housing for local people, the non-existent public consultation by the developer, and the inadequate community benefits outlined in the 'Section 106 agreement' between the Greater London Authority, the London Borough of Lewisham and the developer.

A small working group agreed to meet regularly throughout 2014 and 2015 and further community meetings were held at various local Deptford community venues, including the Methodist Mission, the Noah's Ark pub and the Armada community centre. Again, these were advertised using street posters, flyers and by word of mouth. The agenda included updates on Convoys Wharf, the developers and the council, a continual request from attendees for news, alongside emerging issues, consulting and making decisions about the usefulness of future agenda items.

Such community meetings formed a key part of the campaign, from agreeing objectives to settling on tactics and strategy as to who does what, when and how to grow an effective campaign. Meetings were also an opportunity to share insights and to update everyone.

However, maintaining the group's momentum proved harder. Attendance at community meetings varied, the numbers ranging from ten to 20 people, with turnout wildly inconsistent. This meant meetings might repeat previous discussions, an item requested by late attenders or those who missed a meeting. Inconsistency and infrequency led to repetition of previous discussions in meetings, to update those absent from earlier meetings, which was often frustrating for regular attendees. Reasons for infrequent attendance varied, from 'getting home late' and 'I'm exhausted', to 'no baby-sitter' and 'I'm away'. This inconsistency reflected the real demands on people's lives. Alongside this, at some meetings individuals attempted to control discussions by discrediting the contribution of others, or interrupting, talking over and domineering the discussion. Sometimes contrasting contemporary challenges with abstract historical circumstances from years ago. All of this demanded careful facilitation and management to chair the meetings, nurture participation, promote quieter voices and retain everyone in the group.

Informal planning group

> What I realized when I started to do more community work was that I had a value ... being involved, not just attending meetings but to get involved where I could say something and use my experience and what I was interested in ... that kind of involvement or community work, gave me a lot of confidence. ... It gave me my voice back. (Vanessa Celosse, Voice4Deptford member)

To organize and facilitate these community meetings, the informal planning group of a small number of people, all volunteers, emerged from these community meetings, a recognition that talking the talk was inadequate, that a strategy and actions were needed. Not action for the sake of it, but useful, strategic and progressing work, ensuring momentum.

Early on it was agreed by this group that an effective CWCG would progress the initial objectives, to challenge the lack of public consultation by the developer, and present alternatives to the proposed Section 106 agreement, that is, funding provided by the developer to the local authority to finance local infrastructure such as jobs, social housing, increased transport links and a new school.

Attendance ebbed and flowed at these group meetings, some tasks were followed up inconsistently, depending on the group or individual availability and capacity. For some, the temptation to agree an action in a meeting, and to then, for whatever reason, not follow up, highlighted a mismatch between appetite for change and individual or organizational capacity.

For CWCG, with no funding or paid staff, it required its small group of volunteers to organize themselves, including their own communication, marketing, publicity, paying for venues for some community meetings, and supporting its volunteers. This often resulted in repeating previous mistakes and failings.

To counter this, Cadman and Green prepared an Awards for All funding application to the UK's 'Big Lottery' programme. It successfully raised £10,000 for one year's funding. This enabled the group to resource its focus on outreach work, pay for community meeting venues, employ local residents to offer a creche at these meetings, and for the group to consult further for the 12 months from 2016 onwards.

Setback

As with many community campaigns, sometimes the reality is that to campaign against a global developer with their huge resources, financial 'deep pockets', consultants and legal teams, mistakes are made. So it was that the CWCG, early into the campaign, failed to deliver on a legal challenge.

This involved submitting a challenge to the Greater London Authority (GLA) over a lack of consultation on the Section 106 agreement. Challenging the absence of any consultation over how the Section 106 might be used could, in our view, invalidate the development process and in turn provoke a review of the scheme. This was seen as an essential goal for CWCG.

To help process this legal challenge the group had been fortunate to be joined by an enthusiastic trainee solicitor who volunteered their expertise. The group waited, ready for the opportunity to submit the challenge to the GLA for the absence of, what the group considered, community consultation. In the event, although the deadline to challenge the process came up, CWCG failed to get sufficiently organized enough and construct and submit the legal response against the final Section 106 deadline. The error was a serious blow and a major setback.

The group's lack of success to organize and complete a fundamental and essentially key task such as this highlighted the CWCG's weaknesses. This over-reliance on a solitary expert volunteer, without sufficient support and guidance by the group to complete their task, also resulted in the volunteer's unfortunate withdrawal from the group.

The error was compounded by poor communication between lead members of CWCG and the absence of any back-up plans and was demoralizing for the group. Some volunteers expressed disappointment and anger at others for letting the group down with no explanation. For others it was the moment to walk away and be done with it. Either way, the major setback created an opportunity to review and rethink CWCG's activities, tactics and, with a small core group, including new members, it regrouped in late 2016 to plan ahead.

Regrouping

This regrouping after the 'dust had settled' allowed the group to both review its activities and approach. It also produced a candid reflection and acknowledgement of the further work and growth needed. If anything, the group needed to redouble its efforts, which meant growing its membership, engaging with more residents, recruiting new volunteers and being more focused and professional in confronting the implication of the proposed development.

With this regrouping of CWCG, issues under consideration included the rethinking of its approach, with some arguing for a name change, that the name Convoys Wharf Community Group was perhaps too passive, bland, offering a name as description, when more clarity and propulsion in a name was needed. It was felt that the name needed to indicate purpose, capturing function, in short, the name as verb indicating action! One group member proposed 'One Deptford', with its notions of unity, standing in solidarity with other 'One' community campaign groups in London at the time, such as the 'Our Tottenham' campaign, organizing against proposed regeneration plans for the North London area and challenging inadequate consultation with the residents and the community (Our Tottenham, 2021).

Uneasy at the possible implication of only 'One' Deptford, given the local politics and perhaps the negative perception from other Deptford community groups, the group instead chose 'Voice4Deptford'. The name itself capturing the essence of its approach, Deptford people using their voices for the benefit of their community. Using available funding, the group commissioned an artist, agreed logos, with stickers produced and a website quickly set up. The renamed and 'updated' campaign was up and running.

As Malcolm Cadman, chair of Voice4Deptford, commented at the time:

> We rethought the name of the group. We had a brainstorming session, and some work on it. We employed a local person, a graphic and web designer ... she took forward what we were talking about. It became this phrase 'Voice for Deptford' because we kept saying we need the voices of people. Voice became a strong word, associated with the location. The logo adopted this black and red and white scheme ... like a street sign. We did printed information and we put some stickers up ... people were interested to find out more by coming along to a meeting.

The Voice4Deptford campaign

> It was great when Voice4Deptford was established and I mean we had a really good turn out and it was all organizations that came towards that and I think we needed that voice because if it wasn't for that I think the buildings would have been started by now. (Joyce Jacca, Voice4Deptford member)

Understanding local power and connections

With a new name and the feeling that we had a fresh approach, the focus was on a series of community meetings built on the consultations outreach in Deptford High Street and the wider Deptford area, with local residents, community groups and supporters framing their priorities for the community in relation to the Convoys Wharf site. The focus moved from 'agenda-setting' to articulating our priorities, to 'process' and 'mapping power'. Research by Corry and Reiner (2021) notes the significance of 'protester policy engagement', the processing, production and communication of changes planned by those in communities outside 'established political systems' and identified as part of social movements, where support for radical change is linked to knowledge and interest in policy agendas.

For some, these knowledge networks were important. Here the group evaluated and listed its collective networks and concluded it had lively connections to social actors with responsibility across various sectors, the media, health, politics, law, journalism and universities. Contacts were made with people perceived as 'powerful', and who might help accelerate the emerging campaign. How the group perceived its collective agency, its capacity and power to mobilize skills and connections for our collective agenda was an ongoing concern and discussion. Did we know anyone and could we get 'this' done were key questions. For some, the external power of the local state and corporations felt imposing, distant and intimidating. For others, the group connections and contacts, the 'power mapped', was of distant contacts, so the opportunity to 'work the power network', call in a favour, lobby for change, all seemed unlikely. What was apparent, however, was how the internal power of the group was growing, the energy from collective encouragement, the solidarity, helping to sustain a confidence to 'read the world' (Freire, 2014: 12), defining either what was important or what should happen (Meade et al, 2016). This was about a confidence and clarity to make plans and organize, our right to correct something that was inherently wrong.

Growing the campaign

> What the group was able to do from the beginning was to create an atmosphere, where people felt safe being open and honest, and having open and honest conversation. And even when we had disagreements. … We could go to the pub later or have a tea or coffee or something like that. And I think that was so important. … I think it's equally important in community groups. … Create a space where people who are involved … feel like they can stay involved. (Vanessa Celosse, Voice4Deptford member)

From 2016 onwards, a regular series of open community meetings were held, shifting between the Armada Community Centre in Deptford, to the nearby Deptford High Street Salvation Army Hall. With the funding available, a creche and refreshments were provided, staffed by campaign supporter, Fartuun Shide, and her Muslim sisters. Flip charts, pens and papers were available for ideas and planning. Again, a mix of distributing flyers and putting up posters was used to promote the meetings.

From these meetings new members and supporters joined the campaign and a more organized and diverse planning group emerged, deemed essential to grow and steer the campaign. Key members included Joyce Jacca, local Labour Party councillor, Deptford resident and outspoken activist, and Sue Davies, a former journalist and Deptford resident, who both found out about the campaign and attended after reading a poster, and became drawn into conversation at a community meeting; Marion Briggs, an experienced campaigner for children's rights with the Alliance for Childhood; Vanessa Celosse, with key experience of urban development and architectural design; Warda Farrah, Lecturer/Researcher in Speech and Language Therapy and local resident who grew up in Deptford and a long-standing Deptford youth worker. Later, Tony Nixon, chief executive officer of Lewisham Council Voluntary Service, and Richard Katona, local historian and long-term Deptford resident and community activist, joined. Cadman, Green and Turner were the other planning group members. While these members and others ebbed and flowed depending on their commitment, available time and the occasional 'falling out' with another member, a degree of fluidity familiar to most campaigns was evident.

Planning group action

> There was a sense that the committee was working as one. That people could speak and say what they wanted. ... You brought people in you didn't allow too many people to dominate too much. Some people dominate ... by dint of who they are. As a chair you take account of that. (Voice4Deptford member who chaired some of these meetings)

This new group of people formed the cornerstone of the Voice4Deptford campaign. First, tracking and, to engage in the local authority planning process, attending and speaking at planning meetings, including those during COVID-19 held online. Challenges and objections to the agreement to build on the site, and the next stage from planning consent to permission to start building. This also included engaging in emerging issues such as the planned Cultural Strategy, an aspect of the Section 106 agreement. Second, to campaign for a review of the development and to plan and present an alternative proposal for the site, and, third, to organize and promote community involvement in the campaign. Despite some lobbying of the local authority councillors sitting on the planning committee there was little success.

Meeting venues for the group, as with the community meetings, explored new venues in part to spread the word of the campaign and to draw in new people. Typically these included a mix of informal eating spaces, the local Deli X on Deptford High Street, the Dog and Bell pub, facing the Convoys Wharf site, or a community space, such as the Pepys Resource Centre overlooking the Thames on the Pepys Estate.

As the group grew in number, attracting more local knowledge and expertise, so tactics and plans became more refined, sharp and strategic. Priorities were identified and clear: first, to challenge the bland 'out-the-box', 'anywhere' housing development design proposed, which ignored the local heritage and history of the site. Second, to increase the mix of social housing rented property and family-friendly housing proposed, reducing the amount of unaffordable housing that was too expensive for most Londoners and people living in Deptford. The plan that emerged was focused on meetings with different other local community groups to lobby and persuade, beginning, first, with all the major stakeholders.

Engagement with the powerful

Early on in the campaign, after much discussion and the occasional disagreement between individuals, there was a collective view reached that the campaign should adopt a 'round table' approach to engaging with those holding the power to make decisions as to the future of the Convoys Wharf site.

Traditionally community campaigns have often taken a confrontational, direct action approach to engaging with developers, local politicians and local authority planning officers. What might be called a 'vertical' rather than a 'horizontal' approach. Cadman's view, however, as the Voice4Deptford chairperson, was that we should engage with everyone concerned with the Convoys Wharf site. An almost Gandhian approach to conflict resolution and 'peace', not just with the developer but every key stakeholder.

What followed was, and is still, a unique aspect of the campaign – meetings held with the developer, their consultants, the local Lewisham Member of Parliament, the local mayor and politicians, planning officers from the local authority and the Greater London Council and many other lesser mortals. Meetings held in a 'neutral' space either with everyone attending and/or smaller meetings, with, for example, the Member of Parliament and local councillors. Or individual meetings with a senior planning officer, the Cabinet member for housing or with the local Member of Parliament at their constituency office.

So it became a key principle of Voice4Deptford that all voices needed to be heard across all the contrasting groups, those with the power and others with less power, none were off-limits.

The campaign would meet with the developer and architects, officers in the GLA and the London Borough of Lewisham Planning Department to lobby for change and a review of the proposed development. The point was to confront the more obvious power, from Lewisham Council, elected councillors living locally, or council and GLA officers managing the housing portfolios. This involved working out the party politics and policies, the rhetoric and the realities.

Travelling upriver, the group pressed against powerful political currents, complex dynamics from the GLA, the institution who had, via the previous mayor, undercut the local authority and approved the planning go ahead. Under a new and politically alternative manifesto could they be persuaded to review the scheme? Finally, across the River Thames, on the east bank, stood Canary Wharf and the City of London, the global corporations, consultancy firms, law companies, the headquarters of global banks, some trading real estate and sales of luxury apartments in the Far East, others with direct link to the developer, Hutchison Whampoa, in Hong Kong. Here was a bewildering, intimidating list of circumstance, social actors and institutions, each with connections to the Convoys Wharf development.

Questions were repeatedly asked about how to navigate this and what power did we have to shape change, and, critically, where could we find more? But also, the behaviour of other groups often reluctant to engage, listen, share power or change their position. By focusing its attention squarely on a single issue, Voice4Deptford evolved a translatory role, between various social actors, policy makers, professionals, front-line workers, managers and voluntary groups, among others. The mediation process involved Voice4Deptford members seeking out, exploring and finding solutions for change, a process of interpretation, creativity and judgement, finding ways to translate ideas, the example of Convoys Wharf imposed from above, into a congruent 'local' context (Meade et al, 2016: 37).

This was the beginning of Voice4Deptford's reimagining an alternative use for the site and establishing its priorities and communicating opportunities to planners and policy makers. The point is while feeling 're-empowered' with the process of translating and finding solutions it often felt overwhelming, however despite this the group inched its agenda forward.

Building community alliances

The group met with and worked to build alliances with other local community groups. This was fraught with complexities linking to lively power dynamics, the internal and external experience and ambition of individuals and groups, starting in the neighbourhood and community.

Here individual Voice4Deptford group members worked through their perception of and allegiance to other community groups, and vice versa, including whether they were on side. Their position impacted interpersonal dynamics, particularly those living locally, for example, when confronting a group over local issues or politics. How to be supportive without threatening a group, or being combative while, if possible, maintaining solidarity. There were occasions when this wasn't possible, with group allegiances and personal dynamics stretched to breaking point and impacting individuals. Tension between community groups running organized activities, the politics of personalities jockeying their group or project to grow participation, attract funding, be seen at an event and building public perception.

Here, although group rivalries frequently surfaced, community groups also worked hard, making calls, meeting up to manage and work through disagreements. Despite this, public perceptions of groups squabbling were at times evidenced, individuals expressing frustration, the differences frequently amplified by politicians, officers or policy makers into a convenient narrative of community group division, disorganization and disarray. This was often to discredit rather than validate a group's work, or the campaign. All this Voice4Deptford worked to spot, manage and, where possible, resolve, to build solidarity and alliance. The result was some successes and a few disappointments.

Community meetings

> Thanks it was a well-attended meeting and people are feeling more empowered in terms of how we need to proceed. Today was a great day it proved we can plan ahead for the future and we have a space and place to mobilize from. Let's keep the collective team spirit going and we will never surrender I am honoured to work and interact with you all. (Kenneth M. Thomas, Deptford community activist and Voice4Deptford supporter)

Group members were aware that despite its immediate proximity, many residents, particularly those living in council or social housing flats with balconies overlooking the Convoys Wharf site, had no real idea about the proposed development. The campaign's regular community meetings were essential for anyone to call in, learn more about the plans and ideally to get involved. Power dynamics in the meetings were often lively and a challenge for the chairperson to exercise the group's authority sensitively, reigning in the 'usual suspects' dominating discussion, encouraging quieter voices, closing irrelevant dialogue and spotting useful disruption. Alongside this, powerful forces linked to race, gender, class, sexuality, disability and age were apparent, and shaped behaviour and responses, to be managed, called out and worked through, leading people to make their own choices about whether to attend, speak up, participate and engage, or not.

The campaign 'pop-up shop'

> Coming into the shop … I didn't feel uncomfortable at all. I got a nice welcome from one of the Voice4Deptford people … and just plonked myself down. Somebody offered me a cup of tea which was really nice, and I had a chat with the person I was sitting next to. … People were very open and it was quite easy … she did a hell of a lot of work, she told me a lot about it and then one of the Voice4Deptford people gave a bit of a talk … it was good, it was a warm environment … it was a nice melee of people … milling around talking. … I could see all this stuff about the campaign on the wall … it was important to have the presentation. People were there, talking about a serious issue … many of them talking with a lot of what seemed to me, quite impressive in-depth knowledge. … People knew so much more than I did and I thought, 'I don't know where to hook into this'. … When the discussion started, people were firing off from all over the room. Again some very impressive contributions from people. It was a group of people … who obviously knew a lot about the area, had a deep concern. It seemed to me to be the right people in the room … I joined the group. (Tony Nickson, Voice4Deptford member and chair of many of its meetings)

> You brought this old shop back into life … I've come every day to see what was happening, what you're doing, what's happening round here … thank you … they never tell us anything … me grandson wants to live in Deptford … you tell me where he's gonna get a place … not on Convoys … good luck. (Local resident)

Various ideas had been continually floated to promote the campaign, and one in particular is worth highlighting here, that in practice proved productive for the campaign. This was the idea of a pop-up shop drawing on the work of Davis (2015) regarding the positive community development aspect of 'pop-up' shops and providing visual representations of the campaign by adapting Fredericks et al's 'use of interactive, situated digital technologies deployed within a pop-up style format used for the purpose of community engagement' (2015: 1).

It involved the setting up of a time-limited 'pop-up' project in 2019 following an application to access one of Goldsmiths University's vacant shops on the busy New Cross main road at the front of the university. Here, a three-day drop-in, exhibition and a programme of discussions, revisiting and learning from what the campaign had achieved to date, was hosted by the campaign.

Getting it organized was a challenge. Furnishing the shop, setting up refreshments, booking a programme of contributors, from volunteers and residents to artists and academics. The well-attended event attracted residents and others already involved in the campaign, students and staff from Goldsmiths, passers-by calling in and 'newcomers', residents who wanted to know more.

Voice4Deptford members led discussions on the London housing crisis, play spaces for children and the two proposed heritage projects on the Convoys Wharf site, the Lennox Project and the Sayers Court Garden proposals, part of the Section 106 agreement. Other impromptu sessions evolved during the three days as individuals felt comfortable to raise a topic for discussion.

The focal point provoking discussion and reflection was the 'Voice4Deptford Wall', a visual historical collage of the history of the campaign complete with original early posters, flyers, notes from community meetings, action lists and an assorted collection of other artefacts. Around the wall people debated, argued and noted the distance travelled by the campaign to date, including the setbacks. Discussion allowed feedback supplemented by a daily logbook capturing attendees' comments and recruiting new members. A success!

Raising objections: communication and campaigning

Buoyed by the success of the pop-up shop, two active Voice4Deptford members took a lead in further developing and growing the communication and campaigning, by refreshing the website to promote the campaign along with writing regular press releases and improved social media communication, for example, via Facebook. Reports highlighted campaign updates, news, action and issues that were addressed to the council, politicians, the GLA and the developer. National newspapers felt to be sympathetic to campaigns against developers were also sent campaign updates. The latter resulting in articles in, for example, the *Guardian* newspaper (Grant, 2022). Key to this communications uplift was raising objections and getting support from residents to the developer's planning proposals.

An innovative 'Big Red Button' was set up on the campaign's website, linking to a micro-website and detailing reasons to challenge the planning application to start the first phase of the building. This gathered hundreds of signatures and comments, with views on the planning proposal fed directly through to the London Borough of Lewisham Planning Department. It was a dynamic and effective example of community consultation and action.

Later, at a Voice4Deptford planning group meeting in the Salvation Army Hall off Deptford High Street in 2018, news broke that the planning application had been halted. This interruption was in part the outcome of months of campaigning, updating the website, gathering comments, framing objections, pestering the planning office, meetings, phone calls, emails, and more meetings. One member exclaimed, 'Wow! We do have power! I can feel it. We are powerful! We can do this!'

Here was a collective sense of achievement in the group's dissent, of being an ensemble and together 'winning a skirmish'! Whatever individual effort this involved from the campaign's communication team in leading the action, it was about an outcome from something collective, a group effort. Freire suggests that reflection without action is verbalism, encouraging a passive 'armchair revolution', whereas action without reflection is 'pure activism', that is action for action's sake (2014). These real challenges for the campaign, with its 'organic community coproduction approach' of getting everyone to be involved, have their say, a 'bottom-up' starting point, a collaborative passion for 'we are all in it together' was a realization that communities have power as well (Green and Baker, 2020). It is this process of monitoring and challenging the developer's applications to the local authority planning department and organizing a well-argued community response that is a key aspect of the Voice4Deptford campaign that continues.

Community consultation: the 'battle' of Mary Ann Garden

> There was the awful exhibition ... they were calling them an 'exhibition'. ... Had I known and had the wisdom of hindsight of knowing that they were not listening to anything we'd said in the Salvation Army meeting. By then, I had thought, No. These bastards are not even in the things that they themselves have signed like the Section 106 agreement, were they willing to fulfil their obligations ... I realized then what I know now, which is that it's an extremely hard battle with these people, who feel that they can just speak to, can neuter community groups by simply having an 'exhibition'. They tick a box and say that they've had a few boards up and few people have said a few things. (Voice4Deptford member)

> There was a catastrophic meeting with Convoys in the hall of the Salvation Army and then there was another one. And maybe after they'd gone, I suppose I was a bit cock-a-hoop, the fact that they actually bothered to come again, and to appear to listen. I think, you have to have those things, and sometimes you have to believe them. I suppose I've become more sanguine now. That I don't really think that Hutchison (the developer) is interested in listening at all. (Local resident)

Community consultation is usually top of the list for any proposed new development, the developer hiring expensive suited consultants, sub-contracting to companies who may have expertise in community engagement. Here, the process rather than any outcome is a main determinant of community satisfaction with engagement processes (Cavaye, 2004). Partnership working between local key stakeholders where possible is also significant (Murdoch, 2007). The failure to engage with communities potentially hinders positive regeneration sustainability (Jarvis et al, 2012), it continues to be no different for the Convoys Wharf site. Here, what is being planned had already been decided with the then mayor of London's decision in 2014, leaving very restricted options for any change through a consultation with communities in Deptford.

The developer repeated their approach to 'controlled' community consultation and engagement, not just on the Convoys Wharf site but on another one of their sites, for example, the Lots Road power station waterfront site in Chelsea West London, with its luxury apartments (Passino, 2024).

This lack of real engagement with a community by a developer, about a housing scheme and plans to 'develop' is well illustrated by the Convoys Wharf site developer. Use of various sub-contractors, each referring to the planning decision as an excuse for failing to properly connect, communicate, and engage with or consult the local Deptford community. One example was the now notorious public meeting arranged between Voice4Deptford and the developer Convoys Wharf Property Ltd, the company now responsible for the development and owned by Hutchison Property Group Ltd.

The idea was that a representative from the Convoys Wharf developer would participate in a question-and-answer session with a community audience. In an exchange of emails, Convoys Wharf expressed reluctance to participate, preferring to take questions with members of the public via an exhibition, controlling the questions by individuals speaking one-to-one to architects and Convoys Wharf staff.

In the end the developer's representative initially stayed away from the public meeting arranged by the campaign at the Salvation Army Hall on a hot evening in July 2018. Consultants and architects huddled defiantly around their exhibition display, refusing to go into the auditorium or participate in the question-and-answer session with members of the community. In the end, the 70-plus strong audience that had turned up for the community meeting expecting to question and engage with the developers, the first community meeting of its kind with them, trooped into the lobby, squeezed into the entrance hall, where one-to-one questions could be 'listened in' to by the audience pressed up against the glass.

The chair, Andy Turner, hosted questions from the audience, some indignant and shouting at being compelled to stand to 'take part', while others participating were stunned at the arrogance and bad temper of those representing the developers. Chaos reigned, with some shoving and pushing.

Eventually another member of Convoys Wharf staff turned up, fielded questions and, after 30 minutes of standing huddled together in the hallway, agreed to reconvene in the more convivial seating of the Salvation Army Hall. The aim was to get the consultant and architects to field more questions, and agree to attend a second meeting. Yet the fear, arrogance and absurdity of the developer on display at the 'battle' of the Salvation Army Hall highlighted a profound disconnect from the community and betrayed an alternative agenda. Rather than be with, listening to voices of local people, learning from them, to flex and inform their own agenda, maybe include, or incorporate imaginatively into their ideas, vision and aspirations for the Convoys Wharf site plan, the residents and local community groups were deemed largely irrelevant, to be ignored.

Despite the occasional dropping of 'community' language in their planning documents, with vague references to 'community engagement', Convoys Wharf Property Ltd were, from the get-go, uninterested in the community, instead engaging in only phoney consultation as a means to getting on site and starting building work.

This continued and has done so for the past 11 years. Another example of phoney consultation being the 'Cultural Steering Group' that was established under the Section 106 agreement following Outline Planning Permission for the site in 2014. The 'Cultural Steering Group' has since met a handful of times, with changes in leadership and members, and a lack of clarity or transparency about its function. The group also has no real representation from the Deptford community, yet the area has a rich, eclectic social history and vibrant cultural life. Why is this absent from the Cultural Steering Group? Put 'Deptford' into a search engine and a treasure trove of creative arts, writing, photos and short films will appear, each documenting the voices and life of contemporary Deptford. Here people make the opportunity to come forward with views and experiences about living in Deptford and how they want to see its future for them and their children.

Currently, this phoney consultation or 'community engagement' includes what the developer calls a 'community forum': 'We have established a Convoys Wharf Community Forum to hear the views of those who live and work in Deptford. Representatives from local Deptford groups meet with the project team on a quarterly basis to discuss updates relating to the development' (Convoys Wharf Community Forum, 2022).

Unfortunately this forum does not meet on a regular basis, its agendas are completely 'top-down' despite the campaign offering alternative 'co-produced' examples to them. Minutes of forums are sketchy, totally exclude voices from the Deptford community who attend, and are filtered through the work of their consultants. Attendees' selected quotes, that occasionally turn up on the developer's website, are packaged as colourful community engagement feedback that provides a false image of the forum meetings.

Other examples of this have been the developer's online consultations, attended by members of the Deptford community and Voice4Deptford. They revealed a tightly choreographed, highly controlled format with engagement again via third party, once removed from the developers. This approach, with a consultant acting as a mediator and apologist for the developer, generated frustration, leaving attendees alienated and with more questions than answers. One tactic used by the campaign was to flood the 'question time' allowed with multiple questions, demanding responses direct to the campaign following the event.

For Voice4Deptford members and supporters, the developer's attempts at engaging with the Deptford community have, over the years, been ineffectual, as Joyce Jacca, a Voice4Deptford member, commented;

> I still do not think they [Convoys Wharf Property Ltd] have done consultation properly. I mean I think at the end of the day I mean now there has been no community engagement. They could have gotten residents to sit around the table, given them a blank canvas with just a diagram of the outline of the place and then you could say what you wanted there. They could even employ some local people to be outreach workers and actually and go out and talk to people. You take the time out to do it properly. Community development, community engagement, outreach work – go and talk to people. Have serious workshops with them and actually talk to them so that they feel valued and they feel you care about what they want, and then bring it all back for people to have a look and say, 'Well we had this meeting, and this is what they said.'

The judicial review

> The judicial review process brought us together much more as a group … and it did help to show people the kind of different abilities that people have and what they can do once they are engaged. It helped because we could talk to each other. (Voice4Deptford member)

In late 2020, the campaign decided to take legal action to determine that the developer's outline planning consent had timed out and was no longer valid. We took the view that the developer would have to reapply and come forward with a new, fairer master plan which importantly included the voices of Deptford people. Essentially a development which met the local housing need, respected the historic site and a place the community could be proud of.

This action came about following the London Borough of Lewisham Strategic Planning Committee approving the first Reserved Matters Applications for the Convoys Wharf development. It was the trigger point for launching a judicial review of the outline planning consent. As with previous setbacks and failings, the campaign stubbornly refused to be beaten and regrouped, a process accelerated by the relative ease of meeting online and making plans. While some members were incredulous, fed-up and defeated, peeling away from the group, looking to move on from the campaign, the long-standing key members in the core group, joined by new members, persisted.

The campaign had been discussing and questioning, for some time, the section of the consent which sets out the timing for approval of reserved matters and commencement of construction. Comparing the wording with the wording of the 1990 Town and Country Planning Act, it appeared that the consent had timed out. Campaign members had already held meetings about it with Lewisham council and the GLA, but were getting nowhere, hence the decision for a court ruling. Fortunately, as has happened on many occasions during the history of the Voice4Deptford campaign, a law student and a retired barrister joined the campaign and were both able to advise on navigating the judicial process.

A Voice4Deptford member recalls the outcome:

> We discovered that the law works within very tight parameters and however hard we tried to find a way to make our point, we were prevented at the first hurdle. In an effort to give maximum flexibility and allow improvements to be made to the development plans, the Outline Planning Permission took away the control the planning authority has over the timing of RMAs [Reserved Matters Applications] and allowed for delay and so-called land banking, the very things the planning act sought to avoid. We also discovered the extent that the legal process favour the developer, whether in the parameters of case law or the choice of judge.

So a legal defeat, yet the campaign was a success, raising some £16,000 to pay the costs, as well as generating wider interest and support for the campaign from across London but also further afield. With some reporting on the outcome in a couple of UK national papers and on social media, this interest gave the campaign the basis for moving to a further stage of the campaign, by further expanding its mailing list and contacts, consolidating its monthly newsletter, and expanding coverage across social media.

A new vision

Voice4Deptford has spent many years objecting to the planned development on Convoys Wharf, formerly the Kings Yard and Deptford Docks. The Outline Planning Permission (OPP) is now years out of date. Events have overtaken it. We need to consider the climate emergency, housing crisis, changing lifestyles. Green space and nature and space for children and young people are even more important following the pandemic, not least because of the effects on mental health. All these factors are sadly lacking consideration in this scheme. Our new vision is for Convoys Wharf as a Centre for Innovation, Education and Research. This builds on Deptford's history and culture through Heritage Led Regeneration. It takes into account the views and suggestions of Deptford people. Our aim is to offer it to the Hong Kong owners of the site as a more viable and relevant way forward. (Voice4Deptford Re-Vision)

We don't think it's too late. We hope that our vision might reach the offices in Hong Kong where they are deciding the future of our neighbourhood. (Briggs, quoted in Grant, 2022)

The campaign has continually discussed ways of presenting the developer with different and new alternative views of how the site could be developed in conjunction with the community. How it might be constructed in a manner that offered a celebration of its heritage, provided opportunities for everyone irrespective of who they were, and offered a view of a development that responded to the environment and climate changes. Simply to create something 'special', different to most, if not all, the other now hundreds of similar housing developments across London.

Lengthy meetings and discussions took place at the smaller campaign planning group meetings on constructing an alternative vision for the Convoys Wharf site, focusing on a 'charter' for the site. The Centre for Innovation, Education and Research emerged in 2021 as the central theme of the charter, which included a new design plan for the site.

The plan, or rather the 'New Design Framework', was led and created by a new campaign supporter, Herta Gatter, an accredited town planner, using as its starting point the original master plan and recreating a new plan in line with the community's expressed views.

Workshops and meetings were held to develop the plan alongside the charter. At the same time, and with the help of another academic at Goldsmiths, the campaign brought together Deptford people's stories, 'showing the multicultural origins of Deptford people, telling your stories through a cherished object'. Named 'Deptford Lives', this interactive atlas supported the 'charter' and gave a human face to Deptford people, showing the diversity of lives and talent that was crucial to the developing new vision for the site (Voice4Deptford Re-Vision, 2022).

As a member of the Voice4Deptford campaign explains,

In December 2021 Voice4Deptford (V4D) held a planning workshop over a number of days and set out a new strategy. This was to show what V4D did want to see at Convoys Wharf rather than what they did not like. Through a number of synchronicities, including the launch of Prince Charles Earth Charter, the discovery of the aims of CK Hutchison founder Li Ka-Shing and his charitable Foundation, V4D made the decision to write a Charter setting out a vision of Convoys Wharf as a Centre for Innovation, Education and Research.

The idea behind it was to build on Deptford's heritage as a place of innovation and creativity and its historic place in the world. (Deptford Dockyard is the place where the ships of the British Navy were built and where they set out from to carry out trade, resulting in the British Empire in all its positive and negative aspects.) It would be a modern-day centre for excellence, providing sustainable social rented housing, employment, life-long learning and more.

Voice4Deptford held a series of workshops and meetings to develop the plan alongside the Charter. At the same time, and with the help from colleagues at Goldsmiths, Voice4Deptford brought together stories from Deptford people about an object which showed something of the world they came from, including Deptford. This interactive atlas gave a human face to Deptford people and showed the diversity of lives and talent.

At this stage of the campaign, the objective was to get signatures for the Charter through a petition website to show the support for the re-vision of Convoys Wharf; to meet with stakeholders such as members of the GLA, Lewisham council and parliament; and heritage and other groups which have an interest in what happens at Convoys Wharf. The ultimate aim was to show Li Ka-shing that this was a better way forward than the present plan and that it would provide him with a lasting legacy.

The end result was that the alternative vision had three key sections: the Charter for Convoys Wharf as a Centre for Innovation, Education and Research; a New Design Framework for Convoys Wharf; and an Interactive Atlas. Combined, it offered a grounded approach to the site's heritage and connectiveness with its community and environment, a friendlier and greener community for human habitation for people to engage with, and a celebration of Deptford's multicultural origins and histories.

At a crowded, well-attended community meeting organized in September 2022 at the now familiar Armada Community Centre, the 'New Vision' was launched. Messages of support flowed in and with hundreds of 'like hits' on the Voice4Deptford website the proposal was forwarded to the Hong Kong developer's headquarters and Convoys Wharf Limited office based in South London. It was also circulated widely to local politicians, council planning officers, the GLA and other relevant stakeholders including local and London wide community groups and activists.

While it unfortunately failed to receive a response from the developer's headquarters in Hong Kong and was dismissed as 'not possible' by the Convoys Wharf developer's London office, it did gain traction with a broad cross-section of people and community organizations locally in Deptford and across London. With the campaign's website receiving many 'hits' and requests for more information from other London campaigns and details of future campaign meetings.

It also proved to be a useful in two other ways, first, as a bargaining tool at meetings with the developer and others, particularly concerning, for example, bottom-up and community-led ideas based on their lived experience and future projections rather than outsiders' 'drawing board' designs to maximize profit to the exclusion of a community's changing realities. Second, it raised people's level of understanding, consciousness and learning as to what was possible if they raised their hands, worked together and said this is what we want! Through working on the vision with 'face-to-face' meetings, a form of 'consciousness raising circles' (Duncombe and Lambert, 2021: 121), and what Rowley has called, in relation to community challenging power, 'a permanent transformation in the balance of power in favour of the many not the few' (2017: 240), lessons were learnt for future campaign challenges.

Conclusion: The fightback continues
Some thoughts

The Voice4Deptford campaign continues to shine a light on what can be done when people come together, share their views and begin to organize together, in doing so working for social justice, equality and power against all the odds. The dynamics experienced between people in this process have and continue at times to be isolating, aggravating, alienating, demanding, but also rewarding, affirming and exhilarating. Relationships and interactions have impacted, and continue to do so, on the campaign's work together and their capacity, then playing out in community life, with friends and neighbours, in the workplace and with other groups in the Deptford locality.

The campaign has seen participants focused on organizing tactics, writing on the website, doing the social media, organizing, and facilitating meetings, door knocking, pasting up street posters advertising meetings, running campaign stalls in Deptford High Street, and for some sharing a space to share anxiety and find support. Some passed through, completing a job, then moving on. While others in the group, including some from the original core group, over the years have stopped attending.

The experience of the campaign has been, and is still, seeing those involved being animated, members shifting from feeling hopeless or thrilled, to requiring an extra meeting, or needing a Zen-like capacity to prevent being

Figure 5.1: Aerial view of Deptford Dockyard (Convoys Wharf)

Source: © Historic England Archive; reproduced with permission

Figure 5.2: Convoys Wharf site front gate

Source: Roger Green

Figure 5.3: Convoys Wharf site looking to Canary Wharf

Source: Roger Green

Figure 5.4: Convoys Wharf site from nearby council housing estate

Source: Roger Green

Figure 5.5: Roger Green speaking at the Voice4Deptford 'pop-up shop' meeting

Source: Andy Turner; reproduced with permission

Figure 5.6: Voice4Deptford campaign meeting

Source: Andy Turner; reproduced with permission

knocked sideways. Messy dynamics, complex local politics all take their toll, impacting on members of the group, the meetings of highs and lows, our group process over mugs of tea and biscuits, or a pint of beer at the Dog and Bell pub after a meeting, all collectively flavouring the character of the campaign and our ability to function.

Reflecting on this, and the imaginative tactics and creativity of the campaign, has shown, to date, the ability to proactively engage with everybody around the table and the successes and failures experienced in

Figure 5.7: Voice4Deptford logo

Source: Voice4Deptford; reproduced with permission

Figure 5.8: 'Give Deptford a voice'

Source: Ian Gouldstone; reproduced with permission

doing that; the attention to continually organize and inform the community with updates through community meetings and newsletters; the innovative 'pop-up' shop becoming a supermarket of ideas and action; how despite the disappointment of the 'judicial review' it brought together hundreds of people committed to taking on the powerful and the legality of their argument; creating a masterpiece of ideas for an alternative development and presenting this 'new vision' for the Convoys Wharf site all the way to the developer's board room in Hong Kong.

So not so much lessons learnt but rather collective ideas that have come from group meetings, people talking and listening, being in the same room together but not always agreeing the best way forward. The simplicity of argument, not seeking out differences, instead finding solutions to take the campaign forward to the next challenge.

What is to be done?

Voice4Deptford continues to organize, undertake community re-empowerment work, developing community resilience, working hard for equality and social justice with the Deptford community. It's successes and disappointments in organizing and engaging for real change with a global developer, the local authority, politicians and other key stakeholders highlights profoundly the challenge that all campaigns experience. The struggle continues.

It also shows the inadequacy of local democracy in the UK, and that the extent to which politics at the local level are community-focused is questionable. A need for reform, not only of the planning laws but of these local democratic and political processes. How notions of re-empowerment are understood and supported by both the nation state and the local state, the local authority. Where perhaps groups, campaigns like Voice4Deptford should perhaps be spotted by a local authority, their independence nurtured, their work with the community celebrated and supported, as they work for social justice and change with local residents.

The campaign is now in its eleventh year, with a much smaller 'planning group', with only three of the original members of the CWCG still actively involved, along with a cluster of ever-changing supporters from the Deptford community, students from Goldsmiths and other London universities, interested local residents and people from other parts of London.

However the fighting spirit is still in the air. The developer's 'community engagement' forums continue to be irregular and reporting on its website is cursory, with our response to write up the campaign's interpretation of the forum's meetings and publish them on the campaign's website. Needless to say, they give a more detailed and possibly 'realistic' version of events compared to the developer.

Periodic meetings between the campaign and the developers continue to take place, held at the GLA headquarters building in the London docklands, chaired by a senior Labour Party politician and Member of the London Assembly. These meetings are opportunities to quiz the developer, and their consultants, on, for example, issues relating to both verifying and increasing the numbers of 'real' affordable housing on the site, at 'social rent' levels, questioning them on the current financial viability of the site, and now, post-Brexit, on how the shortage of construction labour, along with the increasing cost of construction materials, is impacting on the development.

Similarly, meetings with the local elected councillors and planning officers focus on the sharing of information, ongoing discussions concerning potential and actual leverage from them and the council. Ensuring the developer keeps to its commitments on community engagement, the Section 106 agreement, the continuing fight for 'social rent' priced housing on the site, public access and community spaces, and whether they will 'build out' the site or sell it.

There is perhaps one important lesson that we understand from the Voice4Deptford campaign and its longevity. The campaign is a pocket of resistance against neoliberalism, along with all the other campaigns that spread, in our view, new understandings of thinking and acting. A Gramscian approach that creates new possibilities, new structures of power and gives a different, alternative view of the reality that is imposed on people, residents of communities who, when presented with a fait accompli by a developer or a local authority, or both at once, have the power to say 'No, this is what we want instead!' That unless we fight back against redevelopment, gentrification, regeneration, or whatever else it is termed as, it will continue to break up and destroy working-class communities and their cultures. Why? Because they do not fit into the imagination, the categories, of the very different world of developers created by these global and national corporates and the rich.

6

Confronting the Developers

Roger Green, with Malcolm Cadman

Introduction

The challenge to top-down 'land grab' urban redevelopment or regeneration across London was extensively explored in the previous chapter with the detailed case study of the unique Voice4Deptford campaign in Southeast London. Community campaigns such as this have a continuing historical lineage in resisting, organizing and 'fighting back' against developers, from the regeneration of the London Docks in the early 1980s up to the numerous active campaigns of the present day by communities under threat of losing their homes, jobs, their sense of community and their 'way of life', which are now part of the changing London urban fabric.

This chapter will discuss this historical lineage, followed by highlighting a number of current community campaigns and action across London's diverse communities. How developers' proposals to displace existing communities by 'social cleansing' are challenged; how 'community plans' by communities themselves provide a community-led alternative to developers' visions; and how the use of differing approaches to tackle 'top-down' regeneration by campaigns offers a range of methodologies in fighting back. How their creativity, the demands for genuine involvement and a say in the future of their communities challenges developers' commercial interests, as Elms remarked: 'You don't want luxury apartments, gymnasiums, concierges and endless poxy coffee shops' (2019: 229).

It concludes with an example of community resistance in the form of highlighting the 'buying-up' of expensive properties and land by the 'super-rich' in London's wealthiest borough.

A historical lineage

A useful starting point are two community campaigns in the late 1970s and 1980s, when London encountered the demise of the London Docks which for centuries had been the capital's centre for shipping trade and commerce, employing thousands of working-class Londoners. A multi-acre site left empty and desolate, apparently with no future. Similarly, a number of Central London locations including deindustrialized Thameside land became deemed ripe for redevelopment by eagle-eyed developers at the expense of the local communities.

First, the Joint Docklands Action Group (2021). This was formed to challenge the massive proposed redevelopment of Docklands in East London in the early 1980s. Described by developers at the time as the 'largest piece of real estate in Europe' and that witnessed the financial City of London expanding into a previously industrial working-class territory (Dench et al, 2006). Then, second, the Coin Street Action Group's campaign in the late 1970s and early 1980s that successfully stopped a high-rise hotel and office space development, instead creating a now much-loved multi-purpose community resource on the banks of the River Thames alongside the National Theatre (Coin Street, 2021).

The Joint Docklands Action Group

This campaign demonstrated the conflict between community voices, local needs and their plans for the area to be seriously considered against commercial market-led imperatives directed by the then Conservative government's London Docklands Development Corporation. As an unelected body the London Docklands Development Corporation successfully leveraged in private capital to invest in the abandoned docks area leading to, for example, the creation of the Canary Wharf financial district (Buildner, 2022).

The Docklands campaign brought together different local community groups who fought the regeneration plans, including the siting of what is now London City Airport (cSPACE, 2021). They organized a series of protest events, including a mock funeral mourning the death of the community at the hands of developers and property speculators by parading a coffin round the Isle of Dogs, which is part of Docklands, and taking a herd of sheep up to Parliament in an armada of boats (Brooke, 2020; Dunn and Leeson, 2022). Pat Hanshaw, chair of the Association of Wapping Organisations, was clear:

> There has been a lot of talk about land, land for this, land for that. But Docklands is not about land, it's about people. And the birth right of the people is being sold off. Although the people have never owned the

land, they've lived on it, worked on it, died on it. It is their heritage –
it should be their future. (Quoted in Leeson, 2019: 3)

As the campaign developed, and lessons were learnt in facing these powerful groups, the campaign took the decision to be less confrontational and instead offered an alternative proposal. This action, among others, resulted in the 'People's Plan for the Royal Docks' in 1983:

As campaigning progressed, people were discovering that proposing alternative strategies was more effective than being oppositional. One example was the People's Plan for the Royal Docks (1983) where people developed their own plan for what should go there rather than the proposed London City Airport. It was far better researched and is still in use today as a model of community planning. It's better to be doing your own thing and recognise your own power than just be oppositional, because that can also confer power onto those who already have it. (Dunn and Leeson, 2022)

As Leeson concludes, the campaigning to save the London Docklands was not overall successful, however it showed that community resistance is possible in a number of ways (2019), for example, using art as an intervention strategy by what Duncombe and Lambert (2021) see as making objective things into subjective forms. Experiences, feelings that people remember. It was allied to offering alternative models, a Freirean analysis in the act of people getting involved, which is itself a 'transformative' act, that people become aware of their power to resist and change the world around them and indeed their own world (Freire and Macedo, 1995).

Coin Street Action Group

This was a campaign led by local people and their supporters in a working-class and increasingly marginalized community alongside the River Thames, in Waterloo, South London. It successfully fought off targeted developers' plans to build hotels and office space over a number of years on a derelict site that was experiencing rapid urban decay (Bibby, 2009; Tuckett, 2021).

The successful high-profile campaign, including attending two public inquiries, resulted in the Group purchasing and redeveloping a 13-acre site in the early 1980s. With the support of other groups and the then Labour Party controlled Greater London Council, which initially was against the campaign and pro-developer, the Group created its own 'community plan', prioritizing the community, its residents, their homes and community resources and facilities:

Walking along the riverside by Oxo Tower Wharf, it's hard to imagine that in the early 1980s the area was bleak and unloved, with few shops and restaurants, a dying residential community and a weak local economy. That all changed thanks to an extraordinary campaign by local residents and supporters, which led to Coin Street's purchase and redevelopment of a 13-acre site. (Coin Street, 2021)

The Coin Street Community Builders, as it became known as, emerged from this and has over the years successfully created its own housing co-operative, a multitude of facilities and services for the local neighbourhood, all on behalf of the community. In addition to various commercial enterprises all on behalf of the community. Now a social enterprise, they proudly state that it is '[a] place for people to live, work and play' (Coin Street, 2024).

Forms of creative resistance

These two earlier examples of community resistance to redevelopment and regeneration are examples of the capacity of London's communities to fight back against developers. This is now a familiar story across London and is gaining momentum with, for example, the Radical Housing Network (2021), a network of groups fighting for housing justice, based in London, estimating that over 49 campaigns were 'fighting for housing justice' across London. While the Runnymead/CLASS report on gentrification across all of London's 32 boroughs highlighted the numerous 'grassroots campaigns' across London for better housing and improved housing conditions (Almeida, 2021).

These campaigns, one would argue, are needed given the most recent figures from Estate Watch (2022a), highlighting over 100 council housing and housing association estates under threat of demolition, the majority with active community campaigns fighting for their homes. The London Tenants Federation estimate that over 35,000 homes are at risk of demolition on these 100 estates (2024).

The resistance takes on various forms, for example, challenging attempts at 'social cleansing' that displace an established and existing primarily working-class community; communities providing alternative plans or visions for where they live than those being offered by developers; campaigning against a specific proposed development; and highlighting how developments and property purchasing are often funded from questionable financial sources. While not all these campaigns have been successful, they do provide examples of community organizing producing an array of different creative approaches that challenge the power and hegemony of developers, and local authorities' decision making.

Fighting social cleansing

Social cleansing, as Lees has noted, is the removal of local authority council housing tenants from their existing homes (Lees and White, 2020). It also includes the shops, small businesses and restaurants that serve them. Within a developer's planning proposal, demolition and replacing them with new-build properties for higher socioeconomic groups. It is arguably a form of what Watt (2021: 25) calls 'dispossession and displacement for the dominated classes'. Indeed, one could argue that it is reminiscent of the Enclosure Acts in the UK from the 17th century onwards. When open fields and common land were taken from the villagers by a combination of those in power, i.e. parliamentarians comprised of property owners and lawyers; what Thompson called an act of 'class robbery' (1974: 237).

The term is elaborated on by Hatherley, writing in the *Guardian* newspaper in 2011, referring to 'class cleansing' in describing the Park Hill council housing estate in Sheffield where residents of this poorly maintained and increasingly unliveable estate found themselves decanted to other areas of the city. Followed by a regeneration of the entire estate for incoming wealthier and professional families (Hatherley, 2011). McKenzie similarly refers to 'class' rather than 'social' cleansing in her study of three London boroughs with middle-class professionals gentrifying parts of London, both council estates and neighbourhoods of older houses, previously occupied by working-class families (2021).

Whichever term we feel is most appropriate, 'social cleansing' or 'class cleansing', the distinction between the two need not detain us here, as they both clearly highlight a practice that destroys long-established working-class communities. It continues across London, eloquently summed up some years ago, but still highly relevant, by an active campaigning group working with tenants' associations and other community activists: 'We are witnessing social cleansing on a mass scale as London is turned into an investment opportunity and playground for the increasing number of the super-rich both home-grown and foreign, with local and national politicians firmly behind them' (London Group of the Anarchist Federation, 2016: 1).

Catford Against Social Cleansing

In Catford, the centre of the London Borough of Lewisham, the 'Catford Against Social Cleansing' campaign organized by local people has come together to raise concerns regarding the regeneration of the town centre. It is arguing the need for more socially rented housing and challenging the proposal to demolish existing homes and buildings in and around the town centre, including 'Milford Towers', a housing estate with over 250 council homes (Against Social Cleansing Catford, 2021).

The campaign has included a range of creative activism events, including 'door knocking' at those homes under threat and asking residents for their views and concerns, their housing needs, attending London Borough of Lewisham council meetings, distributing 'flyers' around the Catford town centre area, and organizing an online petition (Change.org, 2022). The campaign held public meetings with speakers from other London housing campaigns (Catford Struggle, 2022), plus a five-minute YouTube video to promote the campaign along with Twitter/X and Facebook pages.

Despite this campaign, the Lewisham Town Centre Plan has now been accepted, with the existing 1970s shopping centre and council flats making way for 2,000-plus new so-called 'affordable homes', a redeveloped shopping centre and town centre hub (London Borough of Lewisham, 2024). However the campaign's Twitter/X account still hums with messages of resistance to the Catford redevelopment, and other aspects of regeneration and gentrification occurring across the London Borough of Lewisham.

Aylesbury Estate

Campaigns have different outcomes, with a different story emerging from the Aylesbury Estate in Walworth, Southeast London. Built in the late 1960s and into the 1970s, upwards of 10,000 residents living in 2,000-plus flats, the estate was one of the largest in Western Europe. Seen initially, as with many other large council housing estates across London, as a positive response to the housing needs of South London's working class. Later they became viewed by politicians as a failure of providing social housing, architectural deserts full of poverty, crime, drug dealing and community breakdown that needed to be demolished and redeveloped (Baxter, 2013; Beckett, 2016).

Following the London Borough of Southwark's decision in 2005 to demolish and redevelop the estate, a campaign started to stop the regeneration of the estate on the principle that people had a right to stay in their council homes and not be forced out against their wishes by the local authority, the London Borough of Southwark. The campaign had a number of strands. Central to this was the campaigners' view that local authorities across London needed to build more council homes, not destroy them, on the basis that many working-class Londoners, due to their low incomes, could not ever afford private accommodation or to buy a property in London. Security of tenure on where you lived in London in a council property was a key element for residents.

One long-term resident, Aysen Dennis, fought a long battle not to move, at one point opening her flat on the estate as an 'estate exhibition', a place celebrating the 'community resistance' to the social cleansing of the estate (Robson, 2023). As one of the last residents on the estate, the Public Law Interest Centre supported her in a successful judicial review claim in the High

Court against the London Borough of Southwark and the developer, the housing association Notting Hill Genesis. While the resident, as one of last remaining households on the estate, has reluctantly agreed to move out of her flat to a new flat on the redevelopment (Russell, 2023), the High Court victory is an important judgement for community housing campaigners generally. Broadly that when 'outline planning permission' is given to a developer, and a regeneration scheme is proceeding, they should not change or deviate from the proposal that residents voted on, or in the case of the Aylesbury Estate, they were originally promised (Public Law Interest Centre, 2024).

Direct action

Support for explicit direct action to highlight a campaign to hinder and attempt to stop social cleansing can take a number of forms, as the following example graphically highlights.

Further along the River Thames from the Aylesbury Estate in the South London Borough of Wandsworth lies the Winstanley and York Road council estates. Both are now more than 50 years old, neglected, tired and arguably deliberately disinvested awaiting regeneration by the then Conservative-led council (now a Labour Party controlled council since 2022), with both estates being increasingly surrounded by new-build properties with their gated communities and private gardens for the wealthy professional middle class.

This has seen three 'tree protectors' occupy an ageing black poplar tree in the York Gardens part of the estate aimed at forcing the council to review their plans. Marcus, one of the 'tree protectors', came down from living in a tree for ten days to find the area surrounded by a newly erected wire fence and accompanied by stony-faced private security guards. He explained in an interview with one of the authors (Green) the aim of the direct action:

> [I]t's for the bigger cause … we must get on working together … working with nature rather than against it … we want the community to have as many of these mature trees as possible … as I mentioned before as far as we know the way of the planning of this estate has been going has been appalling … they have done very little to include the voices of the people that are actually affected by these changes … 70 per cent of the mature trees in the vicinity are due to be cut down by this development. What for? Mainly profit, flats that, as you know, are luxury flats, something like 90 per cent more and only about 10 per cent of the so much needed of council flats on the estate … it was built in the 1960s and people maybe not having the greatest time living there … and maybe its unsafe in some ways … its true we need to give people a chance to live in better housing … but it's not a solution to build, build and build and then all stand empty and sell them overseas

that should be illegal … the rich get richer … it's just speculation on this vital resource of living space … need to ask the people … citizens' assemblies … the people can decide. (Marcus, 2021)

The trees have now gone and the greenery around the estates is slowly disappearing under the diggers' persistent hunger to destroy. New high-rise blocks are appearing where trees used to stand defiantly. A defeat, perhaps, as with many community campaigns fighting back against forms of 'social cleansing' by taking direct action, however this campaign continues to be fluid in the memory of those residents and their supporters who took part.

Alternative community vision

One strategy for community campaigns opposing developers' plans, which is a growing area of community resistance, are coalitions with university academics in producing co-designed alternative community-led plans to those proposed by developers. A useful example of this is the work of Pablo Sendra, University College London, and his participatory approach in working with community groups (for example, see the Trellick Tower Campaign, 2024) in producing co-designed residents' visions for their urban estates and communities (Sendra, 2023). Alongside this, community groupings, such as Just Space that brings together over 80 community groups across London on planning issues, offers support and a guide to community-led planning (2024a).

Wards Corner campaign

Two examples of producing community-led alternative plans demonstrate this. First, the successful Wards Corner campaign in Tottenham, North London, known as the 'Latin Village', based at an indoor market in one of the London Borough of Haringey's 'poorer' neighbourhoods. This was a 15-year battle by the predominately Colombian community traders and their small businesses operating from the site, supported by residents and activists against a property developer determined to demolish the existing site (Rosa, 2021, 2022). Transport for London, which partly owns the site along with the London Borough of Haringey, has accepted the campaign's 'community plan' after the developer, Grainger PLC, pulled out (London Borough of Haringey, 2022; 2023a).

The 'community plan' that evolved over a number of years during this struggle to secure the site now presents a 'community led development' with the Wards Corner Community Benefit Society, a new body created by the campaign with the aims of restoring the historic site on behalf of the market traders and the community (Wards Corner Community Plan, 2022; Wards Corner Community Benefit Society, 2024). Recognized by the Sheila McKechnie Foundation

(2022) as a 'best community campaign', its success can be viewed as due to a number of factors, including a determined grassroots community campaign that staged mass community events and protests. It ran legal campaigns, fundraised and succeeded in getting the site accepted as an 'asset of community value'. Recognized by the United Nations as a 'unique cultural centre' for London's Latin South American communities, it won a successful judicial review, and gained planning permission for the community plan and demonstrated its financial viability. Overall summed up by the following:

> People said there was no way we could beat the developers … communities around London are being destroyed by regeneration … but an alternative model of regeneration is possible … one that put communities in control … the Wards Corner community plan will bring the market and historic building into community ownership. (Wards Corner Community Voices, 2022)

Their now almost 20-year campaign struggle continues despite the site being largely closed due to the COVID-19 pandemic and the refurbishing of the market space with the impact that has had on the market traders and visitors. The Wards Corner Benefit Society is working to implement the community plan (Di Fazio, 2023) and the appointment of a number of staff to support its realization.[1]

Supporting this is the positive report from the Common Wealth 'think tank' on the Public-Commons Partnership model that referenced Wards Corner and its measurable social value economically to the local community:

> Communities that wish to pursue this third way of development are united in the belief that wealth that is generated locally should be used to enrich those who live within the community. Wards Corner offers an exemplary case study for those who wish to replicate the model across Britain and beyond. (Almeida, 2023: 6)

Hope, therefore, for the future, with the London Borough of Haringey publicly announcing that '[t]he council has been acquiring land previously in private ownership putting it in a unique position to implement a new public sector-led approach to improve and invest in Wards Corner and reconfirms the council's commitment to the Community Plan' (London Borough of Haringey, 2023b).

Alton Action

The second example is the campaign on the Alton Estate across London in the Southwest London Borough of Wandsworth. Situated near to Richmond

Park, famous for its population of red and fallow deer, and surrounding properties which sell for millions of pounds. The 1950s brutalist concrete designed estate, one of the biggest in London, of mixed tenure, had since 2014 has been under the threat of regeneration. In 2017 the developer Redrow, in partnership with the then Conservative-led council, proposed some 300 existing council homes for demolition on this prime real estate, non-affordable investment properties for incomers and retail opportunities. With many existing residents being largely displaced (Radical Housing Network, 2022).

However the developer 'pulled the plug' in 2020, citing a mixture of scaling back its operations in London, increasing costs and the 'two-tier' planning system (Marshall, 2020), as well as the residents' campaign against the proposed regeneration. Working in partnership with academics from the Bartlett School of Planning, University College London and the London communities network Just Space, an 'Alton Estate Peoples Plan' was co-designed in 2021.

This community-led imaginative vision included 'refurbishing' properties rather than demolishing them, aiming for higher environmental standards, recreating lost community facilities and providing 'infill' properties that did not produce higher density nor higher blocks (Sendra and Fitzpatrick, 2020; Estate Watch, 2022b; Sendra, 2023). Mellen describes the process in an interview with one of the key Alton Action campaign group members about how the campaign offered an alternative vision for the regeneration of the estate (2022; Alton Action, 2022).

With the developer pulling out, the then Conservative-led council pushed ahead with the scheme. In doing so it clashed with the mayor of London concerning the consultation process with residents, and how the limited social housing would be segregated, however the mayor agreed the scheme. However, in May 2022, before the then Conservative council could restart the procurement process seeking a new development partner, the Labour Party gained control of the council in Wandsworth for the first time since 1978. This ended some 40-plus years of the former UK Prime Minister Margaret Thatcher's 'favourite Conservative council'. Meetings followed with the newly elected Labour Party councillors and officers. Presenting the plan, for the campaign, was at the forefront to get the new council to adopt the 'People's Plan' (Alton Action Petition, 2022). The Conservative Party Masterplan was officially scrapped, with the new administration favouring more council homes at social rent and deciding to seek new options for regenerating the estate.

As one resident commented:

> [We] don't need anything really to be knocked down, we just need things to be refurbished … if they knock it down it isn't for us, and actually it isn't for the investment of the community. It doesn't create a local economy, it doesn't build a community, it just creates more isolation. (Lillywhite, 2023)

A council community consultation process followed in late 2023, led by a private consultancy outfit, contracted by the local authority, one of many now plying their trade in the field of regeneration. It was, however, heavily criticized by the campaign for being 'community input, then radio silence' (Alton Action Campaign member, 2024).

The campaign is still awaiting a response from the local authority following the consultant's report, on a new proposed regeneration plan. As a campaign member recently stated:

> [T]he new Council administration are still 'looking at options' for the type of regeneration that they want to propose ... but they are doing everything in secret and 'behind closed doors' with Councillors and officers and no community input ... they may just propose their favoured single option and give people a yes/no choice ... not really democratic or participatory! (Alton Action Campaign member, 2024)

The campaign remains active and continues to support other similar London communities' attempts at co-designing and imagining their communities. For example, members speak at other London campaigns, such as the Morning Lane People's Space in Hackney, a campaign in East London fighting for the community's voices to be heard in the form of a 'people's plan' for proposals for the development of a Tesco store site in central Hackney.

As with the Alton campaign, with community-led regeneration the key message is that community co-design is not a 'public consultation' exercise as employed by developers and local authorities. Rather it is, as Sendra reminds us, a process that involves 'collective thinking' and 'collective intelligence' and not the request for individual inputs once a regeneration proposal has already been agreed (2023).

Challenging regeneration

Across London at any one time a number of campaigns are fighting to stop the 'top-down' regeneration and the redevelopment of their communities using a range of tactics and strategies. From Brixton and Peckham in South London, across the River Thames in Brick Lane, East London, and over to Ealing in West London, there are many, as the following examples illustrate.

Save Nour. Save Brixton

In Brixton, in the London Borough of Lambeth, a successful campaign has halted a Texan millionaire's plans to build a controversial 20-storey high-rise office block in the middle of Brixton. Grouped around the developer's actions following serving an eviction notice on the popular Nour Cash and Carry shop, the Save Nour social media campaign, alongside a struggle against the general gentrification of the Brixton area, came into being (Firth, 2023; Save Nour: Fight the Tower, 2024).

With over 35,000 households on the London Borough of Lambeth's housing waiting list as of 31 March 2023, the highest of all 32 London boroughs (Local Government Association, 2024), Hondo, the development company, with an extensive ownership of Brixton market already and seemingly offering no benefit to the local Brixton community's real needs, eventually withdrew its plans. It did so before the London mayor 'called in' the plans to make a decision on the development (Burford, 2023).

The Brixton community's campaign raised over 10,000 objections to the proposal, canvassed extensively locally and had a clear mission, highlighting a good example of a community's view of how they wished to see their community grow and develop:

> Our mission is clear – we stand up for our home and fight to give Brixtonians a say over what happens to their neighbourhood. We organise horizontally and work together with other community initiatives to centre the voices of those our council and their co-conspirators hope to push out of our area – the poor, the racialised, the marginalised. (Save Nour: Fight the Tower, 2024)

Aylesham Community Action

Up the road from Deptford in Peckham, the location of the popular 2023 rom-com, *Rye Lane* (British Comedy Guide, 2023), the community is mobilizing to 'save the soul' of the high street and its environs from going the same way as the gentrification of Brixton and Hackney with their organic coffee shops and associated retail outlets.

One of London's foremost developers, responsible for regenerating huge chunks of London, Berkeley Homes, is seeking planning permission to develop the prime site of the nondescript 1980s Aylesham Shopping Centre. Hundreds of new homes are envisaged, along with a new shopping facility. However, a now familiar story of limited consultation with the community and local businesses persists.

Aylesham Community Action campaigned against the development, with a 7,000-signature petition resulting in the developer returning to the drawing board and engaging another architect to redraw the plans.[2] With its regular community meetings and use of Twitter/X to highlight its campaign, the campaign is presenting an alternative narrative to the developer that supports 'real' affordable homes and commercial space for growing local businesses (Aylesham Community Action, 2024). As one resident commented: 'How about investing in the original communities that were there instead of invading it with the same bland culture' (Bloomfield, 2024). Likewise, a member of the campaign stated: 'We want this development to make Peckham better for the people who live here and for newcomers. The community needs to be involved in deciding what's done with the site. What people don't want is this sort of gentrified citadel being plonked into it' (Tapper, 2023).

'Stop the Towers'

Across the other side of the River Thames, in the leafy green West London Borough of Ealing, a collaboration of residents and their supporters began challenging what they saw as the 'overdevelopment' of their borough with high-rise buildings, or 'towers', in 2019. The campaign group 'Stop the Towers' was formed in 2019.[3]

With a well-organized, informative website, links to social media platforms, Facebook, Twitter/X and Instagram, organized community events to publicize the campaign and repeated objections to developers' planning applications, they have produced visually impressive computer-generated imagery of proposed high-rise (towers) developments across the borough and their impact on local communities (see Stop the Towers, 2024). These also included the proposed redevelopment of the council's offices in the town centre, which would see a 26-storey tower and several new blocks of almost 500 mostly private housing units. Having previously approved the developer's scheme the council subsequently rejected it on the grounds of cost, for example, building materials, with the site being retained as council offices, and local businesses and community space (Salisbury, 2023).

A key aspect of their ongoing campaign is fighting for 'truly affordable housing that would relieve the Council's housing waiting list', demonstrated by their wide-ranging tactics including the aforementioned in addition to an information pack for Ealing councillors entitled 'The true cost of ultra-high housing density' (Stop the Towers, 2021).

Save the Brick Lane Coalition

In London's East End the 'Save the Brick Lane Coalition' campaign is fighting the plan to turn the historic Truman Brewery site into a shopping mall with some offices. Against the wishes of local residents, businesses and local historic groups such as the Spitalfields Trust, the developer's planning application received over 7,000 letters of objection, with only 82 in support, and with 100 businesses and some 500 residents against the redevelopment.

Based in an area of East London with some 'previous' of standing up for itself, for example, Begum's story of the Bengali squatters (2021, 2023), the coalition launched a media-savvy campaign that gained support from a wide range of news outlets (Russell-Jones, 2021; Sherwood, 2021; Curry, 2022). The campaign organized a benefit concert and launched a Crowd Justice appeal, 'Save Brick Lane', that successfully raised over £21,000 for a fighting fund to seek a legal judicial review in 2022. This challenged the London Borough of Tower Hamlets' decision to grant planning permission for the redevelopment (The Gentle Author, 2022; Palin, 2022). Unfortunately, later in September 2022, a High Court Judge ruled against the campaign's legal challenge (Gregory, 2022a; Kehoe, 2023). This was followed by an appeal in the summer of 2023 with the Court of Appeal upholding the right of local authorities on planning committees to restrict elected councillors from voting on planning applications (Francis Taylor Building Chambers, 2023).

At the time of writing, April 2024, the Supreme Court in London, the final court of appeal in the UK for civil cases, and for criminal cases from England, Wales and Northern Ireland, has granted permission to the Spitalfields Historic Building Trust to appeal against the previous decision by the Court of Appeal. A key stakeholder in the campaign, the Trust has for over 50 years been leading the fight against what they call the 'exploitative development' of the area (Battle for Brick Lane, 2024). The Court of Appeal's decision to reject their challenge to the London Borough of Tower Hamlets was in regard to the council's standing-orders and committee voting by councillors being present for the entirety of the Planning Committee (Carey, 2024).

While awaiting this hearing, which effectively has put on hold the shopping mall application, the owners of the Truman Brewery are, as they put it, asking local residents to 'help shape our plan' with the launch of a 'consultation website' in preparation to submitting a planning application (Whitehouse, 2023; Truman Brewery Consultation, 2024). What one un-named local commentator viewed as an attempt to 'build office blocks across their whole site and create an enormous corporate plaza'. In response to this, the Save Brick Lane Campaign are intending to regroup and relaunch the campaign to continue the fight.

Buying communities with 'dirty money'

Another form of community resistance are campaigns highlighting who is buying property in communities and where does the financing for it come from. As Wessie du Toit notes, '[s]ince the Nineties, London has found a new role as a safe deposit box for global wealth, especially through its property market' (2022). It is an issue in London that has been known about for some years, and which the UK Parliament Foreign Affairs Committee recently reported on:

Illicit finance, as dirty money is politely known, spreads corruption across the United Kingdom and costs every home and every community. It undermines our national security by supporting corrupt and autocratic regimes around the world, subverts our rule-of-law systems to hide and protect ill-gotten assets, deprives the world's poorest communities of resources, prices citizens out of our housing market. (UK Parliament Foreign Affairs Committee, 2022)

In the Royal Borough of Kensington and Chelsea, for example, the Kensington Against Dirty Money campaign is successfully highlighting the money coming into the borough allegedly from Russian oligarchs and other millionaires from around the world who purchase property in the Kensington and Chelsea area (2022). Allies of Vladimir Putin are no exception, with their ownership of high-priced luxury homes in Kensington despite the UK government's sanctions following the Russian war on Ukraine (Burford, 2024).

It is one of the wealthiest local authority areas in the UK, with expensive properties. As Tarver notes: 'If you are thinking of purchasing a home in Kensington, the average property price of a home in this neighbourhood is £ 2,568,533 million pounds or roughly $3.21 million' (2022: 1).

A campaigning group supported by a range of politicians, local activists, community organizations, charities, national campaigns and publicly known individuals, Kensington Against Dirty Money is asking for 'comprehensive national legislation to provide transparency over anonymous foreign owned property in Britain and for proper financing to the National Crime Agency to crack down on financial crime' (Kensington Against Dirty Money, 2022; see also Powell, 2024).

Why is this needed? As Knowles highlights in her 'walking tour' of the 'posh' parts of London, including Kensington and Chelsea, she describes the daily lifestyles of the 'super rich', their 'gated communities, expensive house and flats, and secretive and isolated daily lives away from mixing socially with any other. A form of existence whereby their wealth is reimagining their parts of London, through their eyes, and where any form of "social reproduction" with outsiders is strictly taboo' (Knowles, 2022).

These overseas buyers, including offshore companies (Transparency International, 2015), have for some years been purchasing property within the Kensington and Chelsea borough. Many not to reside in, but as investments which then inflate property prices and do absolutely nothing to provide affordable housing for those on the housing waiting list, nor people born in the borough who wish to remain living and working there (Kensington Against Dirty Money, 2022).

Across London there are a number of estimates of some £20 billion worth of residential property lying empty with some £2 billion in Kensington and

Chelsea (Pitcher, 2023) and in the combined neighbourhoods of Westminster and Kensington and Chelsea, over 50 per cent of expensive homes are unoccupied, with no lights on in the evenings (Boyle and Stone, 2023).

The argument is now that increasing numbers of housing stock in the wealthy areas of London have increasingly become a commodity for the 'super-rich', in all their varying disguises. Rather than housing being seen as both shelter, and a necessary 'human right', it is becoming a highly contested area for campaigns to progressively engage with as housing is seen as a speculative investment by the few to the detriment of the many in London in housing need.

Conclusion

This chapter has highlighted how corporate interests, developers and the wealthy seeking profits by their 'land-grabs' in the displacement of working-class communities, often in 'high-value' inner-city London areas, are being challenged. The resistance to this from communities, as we have shown, comes in many forms, all of which aim to fight over 'contested urban spaces' that affect and change for ever their lives and those of their families, friends and their sense of place, their community.

From challenging 'social cleansing' with its urban social engineering and privatization, to the production of community plans as alternative narratives to the anti-council housing lobby, and how organizing varying forms of resistance to developers' 'master plans' is fought using tactics grounded in community organizing and participation. All are, as Watt has noted, 'a form of trench warfare' (2021: 365) with gains and losses over periods of time.

When highlighting who are buying expensive properties and land in these communities, we are reminded of Terry Eagleton, writing in 2011, arguing how capitalism is essential 'antisocial' when it is profitable to do so, which is usually the case! (Eagleton, 2011: 8).

The richness and diversity of all these different campaigns in raising awareness and support, while different to the earlier forms of community resistance to developers, demonstrate the innovative ways in which communities continually fight back and challenge the hegemony of the powerful intent on ordering their lives (Gourevitch, 2017). As Foster has noted in his review of the Max Wilkinson play, *Union*:

> The real purpose of gentrification. ... It's meant to sweep away any community spaces or cultural elements that do not fit neatly into the categories created by the rich and corporations. The conclusion of this vision is segregation between the impoverished and the affluent, creating spaces where only the wealthy are welcome. The displacement

of the working class from their homes is a product of capitalist rationality. (Foster, 2023)

In doing so, he reminds us to ask why should London or indeed any UK city or any other city around the world be left to the market forces of profit and greed rather than community and social need? Why also the challenge for us is how we organize together to bring about participatory action that ensures real grassroots community democratic representation and change that not only, as Massey puts it, opens up 'cracks in the neoliberal front' (2022: 239), but also advances the combined forces of the left, and progressive, labour and social movements for a better world. This is the task for us to outline to you, the reader, in the concluding chapter.

7

Whose City? Communities versus Capital

Roger Green and Keith Popple

Introduction

We have titled the final chapter 'Whose City? Communities versus Capital' as that is at the heart of this book. We have shown how neoliberalism's corrosive impact on democratic society, its institutions, the lives of people, their communities, and politics in general, is a global phenomenon. It has encroached on many, if not all, aspects of our daily lives. It has produced a stupefied version of 'goggles' through which we view what is happening to us, and around us, with its destruction of the 'social' as normal, as 'common sense'. We are still experiencing the effects of the COVID-19 pandemic, of the 2007/2008 global financial crisis with excuses to burden the people of the Earth with more austerity and further inequality. These events, and many more within national boundaries, have produced catastrophes exacerbated by neoliberal greed and government negligence, with global income inequality substantially increasing (Deaton, 2021), so the rich get richer and more powerful. Meanwhile, the rest of us get poorer, with the growing numbers of those at the bottom of the socioeconomic ladder now out of sight.

The neoliberal 'takeover' of London by corporate developers, global investors and the 'super-rich', with profits for shareholders paramount, irrespective of the impact on working-class communities who are deemed as mere collateral damage, is but one example of where this is happening and which forms the central argument of this book. Cities such as London, together with those across the UK and indeed the world, are evolving in the image of those with the power and the money to determine citizens' futures.

The 'fight back'

Capital, though, is not having it all its own way, as we have shown. The example we have presented here is one of a working-class London community that continues to challenge the global developers. The unique key example of the Voice4Deptford campaign, along with other examples from across London, shows what is possible when communities come together to 'fight back' and demand their voices are heard. Communities, such as in Deptford, are seeking their democratic rights, demanding that their voices should be heard, and working to radically reset the power imbalances in their communities brought about by corporate developers and their supporters.

We contend that there are important lessons to be learnt from this Voice4Deptford campaign and the other community campaigns by highlighting the practice of generating the voices of communities and acting when confronted by powerful external and internal forces, such as developers with a global reach, and local power holders who pay lip service to democracy.

We argue for an act of mobilizing embryonic social capital, albeit in circumstances not of our choosing, that produces an 'insurrection of subjugated knowledge' (Pilger, 2006: 3). An organic community co-production engagement approach in urban community spaces such as Deptford that challenges both existing capitalist power arrangements and existing ideas of working with communities.

One of the key lessons from these community campaigns is seeing the importance of sharing information and experience, the lessons learned, for example, promoting each other's campaigns on their websites or Facebook pages. The *We Are Grenfell United* website that campaigns for justice for survivors and bereaved families from the fire in June 2017 that broke out in the 24-storey Grenfell Tower in London is but one example of this (Grenfell United, 2024). Carter (2017) views this process as being crucial and argues that community campaigns against redevelopments and regeneration are recorded and curated to enable them to be shared by other existing or future community activism. Similarly, the HOPE not hate Charitable Trust's Hopeful Towns project, in discussing rapid social change, see it as being '[i]nterventions which foster connections between new and existing communities and allow residents to shape the direction the community takes' (2020: 104).

Related to this is understanding how taking back the power is to have a shared voice. Alemanno (2017), among others, argues that civic empowerment and engagement in the light of community power differentials, whether it be regeneration or another aspect that brings community disengagement, calls for lobbying strategies that re-empower community voices. Many campaigns across London and indeed other cities in the UK, for example, Manchester, have produced information DIY guides for fighting back against developers and landlords (Greater Manchester Tenants Union, 2024). In Grimsby, East Marsh United, an organically grown community group, are taking action themselves in transforming their community by finding practical solutions to how their neighbourhood grows and develops, such as buying up old houses and renovating them for local people (East Marsh United, 2024). Both examples are aimed at ensuring people's voices are heard and support their struggles to act themselves and 'fight back'.

Further, the now widely circulated London Tenants Federation's response to the London mayor's *Good Practice Guide on Estate Regeneration* provides important information and tactics for residents and community action. It argues that any demolition and redevelopment of a council housing estate should not proceed without the full and fair involvement and consultation with tenants, and their role in challenging this (Turnbull and Hollis, 2017).

Likewise, Sendra and Fitzpatrick's (2020) collaborative work with residents from several London housing estates shows how communities can build solidarity, knowledge and take action to protect themselves, their estates and have a voice in their futures. Similarly, the 'anti-gentrification handbook' and information built on the experiences of residents living on council estates gives communities ideas for organizing against regeneration plans (London Tenants Federation et al, 2014; Estate Watch, 2022a).

Yet despite the immense challenges faced by communities across London, most if not all community campaigns and action against proposed regeneration and redevelopments have a finite 'shelf-life'. They emerge to challenge a top-down remaking of a community and end in victory or a defeat. Irrespective of the future outcome, communities continue to 'fight back', they are demanding a voice, putting forward alternatives to developers' plans. Arguing for a realignment of local power, engagement and decision making and seeking a re-democratization of power at the local level. Brown refers to this as the 'lived experience at the frontline' (2019: 3).

Taking sides in working with communities

Our work with Voice4Deptford is exactly that: working WITH the community. We took this view early on, Green from his first meeting with Cadman and the establishment of the Convoys Wharf Community Group, and Popple as a supporter of the campaign from his first contact when attending the campaign 'pop-up shop'.

When writing and compiling this book, along with the contributions and involvement of campaign members and supporters, there was a clear belief in key values: democracy, equality and anti-discrimination, social justice, collective action, and community empowerment. By holding true to these values, it is impossible not to take sides when the power differential is so great. To witness and analyse the wreckage and damage neoliberalism has done to our communities, to families, to individuals and to the global community is both anger-producing and yet liberating.

The anger comes from observing the result of economic and social injustices that are for all to see, and both witnessing and experiencing how the political structures largely fail to respond to these injustices but instead support and collude with the powerful, the hegemony. Working with groups like Voice4Deptford in our view must be a political activity, not a professional undertaking. Engaging in this way is liberating. It is what Gramsci calls the *war of position*. We are not meaning here in the grand way Gramsci wrote about the *war of position* but rather it is recognizing that there is place for developing broad alliances that confront the hegemonic power. Gramsci considered civil society as key in class struggles and of popular-democratic struggles. To quote Simon (1991: 27): 'Civil society is the sphere of class struggles and of popular-democratic struggles. Thus it is the sphere in which a dominant social group organises consent and hegemony. It is also the sphere where the subordinate social groups may organise their opposition and construct an alternative hegemony – a counter-hegemony.'

The *war of position* was also an aspect of the activity of the environmental social movements and campaigns that were discussed in Chapter 2. These social movements and campaign groups, while usually working separately and independently, are often part of wider networks of alliances. In London these group include the London Tenants Federation, Just Space, London Renters Union, Defend Council Housing, and Action on Empty Homes. These and other groupings act both individually and collectively as voices for Londoners, providing at one level useful information and advice, networking, policy input, such as the London Plan, and the informal sharing of campaign activities. Additionally, and crucially, they offer alternative and critical collective responses from the grassroots to the hegemony of neoliberalism and its objectives regarding the destruction and redevelopment of working-class communities (Carroll and Ratner, 2010). What is important in the counter-hegemonic approach is the respect these groups have for the autonomy of others. In this manner, counter-hegemonic groups and movements can build common conceptions of the world which are at odds with the ideology of the powerful.

Important too is to challenge what is known as 'common sense' which emanates from the dominant ideology. We noted this regarding neoliberalism, which is considered to be the 'natural order of things'. It is 'common sense'. Yet as we have observed throughout this book, neoliberalism works for the benefit of the few at the expense of the many. 'Common sense' is a term used to indicate and legitimate cultural domination. It occurs when people believe and accept the prevailing cultural norms of society. They accept the dominant ideology that works to favour the elite. Working with communities provides a platform for the 'common sense' understanding to be deconstructed and, in its place, develop a consciousness that transcends former ways of thinking. A new, sharper and more liberating, equal, democratic and questioning position.

Taking Gramsci further, we are also cognizant of the term 'organic intellectuals'. This is at the centre of working with communities as 'organic intellectuals' where we were not imposing our ideas on those we met and worked with, rather we engaged in a dialogical process with them. It is about helping everyone, including academic researchers and community activists like us, to draw a distinction between intellectuals of the bourgeoisie and those of the majority. These ideas are expanded upon by Valeriano Ramos, Jr (1982) in his seminal article on the concepts of ideology, hegemony and organic intellectuals. Another seminal test in this area is by Louis Althusser (1970), who explains how the ideological state apparatuses are the sites of ideological conflict among social classes in society.

A way forward

The Voice4Deptford campaign has always attempted to undermine the hegemony of the developer and their supporters, elements of the London Borough of Lewisham, the mayor, cabinet members, local councillors and the planners. It has done this while offering an alternative vision of the Deptford brownfield dockyard site. The outcome is an alternative working-class counter-hegemony.

It is on this basis that we offer a 'way forward', a proposed 'radical rethink', where we argue for organizing and 'taking sides' when working with communities. An argument for real democracy, and community action, that involves resistance and change for urban communities that are facing forced change and destruction. This is based on the lessons learnt from the Voice4Deptford struggle and other campaigns across London against developers and their powerful corporate investors and supporters. This 'way forward' is grounded in Gramscian theory that demands an alternative narrative to the existing hegemonic power we currently confront. This demands a reconstruction of thinking, power, democracy and action, whereby urban communities engaging with these powerful neoliberal capitalist forces unify against discrimination based on social class, race, gender, sexuality, disability, discrimination, and social and economic injustice

Our argument throughout this book has been to explain and offer some hope, some ideas, some examples of different forms of action against the neoliberal attempts to destroy London and recreate the environs in its own image, in doing so highlighting the unique Voice4Deptford campaign. Communities facing such threats can be overwhelmed and become indifferent and passive when faced with seemingly powerful forces who are often in collusion with democratically elected politicians and local authority planning department staff.

A way forward, we argue, is to create alternative counter-hegemonic patterns of community democracy, 'ways forward', that 'face up' to developers and their supporters. That challenges what is seen as hegemonic 'common sense', that promote new forms of 'citizens' gatherings' or 'assemblies' as mandatory elements of the planning process. Alongside 'community activism' as shown in the Voice4Deptford example and the other campaigns discussed, all of which create political agency. The aim to create 'new ground', which promotes in communities in fights with developers that there is something to fight for, worth saving, could be grown for the communities' benefit and children's futures, and not just simply provide oppositional voices against.

We do not offer a 'manifesto'. Helpful such as they are, for example, at a strategic level Just Space's Manifesto for London and its communities arguing for innovatory change across a wide range of areas (Just Space, 2024a). But as the late Doreen Massey has argued, we do not always require intellectual knowledge in understanding and answering the world around us (Featherstone and Kelliher, 2022). Rather, arising from the Voice4Deptford campaign, the stimulus comes from engaging in political and social action, movements highlighting and challenging aspects of the local state which now encompasses the heavy boots of the corporate developer.

Moving forward: ways of fighting back

Our message is to be aware how neoliberalism operates. It is not your friend. It has sharp fangs and coldness of spirit. It has a high degree of cunningness together with ersatz (not real or genuine) emotions while spewing the kind of temperate language that is designed to convince you that it cares. It does not. Don't be intimidated by developers and their consultants in suits, politicians who say they know what's best for you, and planning officers making decisions behind closed doors.

'Speak truth to power'

Our starting point is Jacobs' seminal work on urban planning and cities: 'Cities have the capability of providing something for everybody, only because, and only when, they are created by everybody' (Jacobs, 1961: 238). So shout. Make a noise. Get out there. Organize. Door knock. Put up community notices. 'Be realistic, demand the impossible' (Davies, 2012: 21). Use social media. Call meetings. Create alternatives. Seek total community involvement. Go for real community consultation. Organize, and find out the needs of a community. Protest is a right and is vital to democracy. Go for peaceful acts of civil resistance. Take back your streets (Taylor, 2024). Let's have more of it. Housing must be a human right not a commodity. Demand that all new housing is for social need not exclusively profit. Argue for more 'social housing', council, local authority and public housing. Think big and demand big. Go for 'community land trusts' (Astbury, 2023) and 'community benefit societies' (East Marsh United, 2024). Settle for nothing that you do not want. It's your infrastructure, you know what your community needs, not the developers. You are 'stakeholders' not passive providers of information for those with power. Urban design around 'legitimate shared goals' to address both your community and wider city problems. 'Rebel against the "blandification" of our streets and make buildings that nourish our senses' (Heatherwick, 2023:1). Demand inclusive regeneration and architecture from the ground up. Support 'urban empathy' (Reid, 2021). Ensure new developments include children and young people's ideas and demands. Involve older citizens, ensure everyone's voices are heard. Seek 'public luxury', with more community facilities, not 'private luxury' (Monbiot and Hutchison, 2024). Argue for democratic decision making. Climate change is real, make sure you have a voice in designing new green-friendly housing. Make contact and share learning and ideas with other community campaigns, relevant supportive 'social movements', and others such as Extinction Rebellion (XR). Share experiences. Work together. 'Above all, refuse the category consumer. Select the category citizen' (Farrelly, 2021: 358). Lastly, remember it's your future, your community, not theirs, they move on. As Percy Bysshe Shelley wrote: 'Rise like Lions after slumber, In unvanquishable number, Shake your chains to earth like dew, Which in sleep had fallen on you – Ye are many – they are few' (Shelley, 1995: 77).

Notes

Chapter 1
1. Two leading sources of research focusing on UK homelessness are the national charities Crisis and Shelter, and greater detail on this key area of social policy and practice can be found at www.crisis.org.uk and www.shelter.org.uk.
2. To pursue research on US inequality further, please refer to www.inequality.org, which provides up-to-date and extensive information and statistics.
3. Further information on the work Trussell Trust can be found at www.trussell.org.uk.

Chapter 2
1. Further information on the Seaford Environmental Alliance can be found at www.seafuture.org.

Chapter 4
1. See http:/www.convoys-wharf.com/.
2. See https://www.mosaf.org.uk/ and https://deptfordpeoplesheritagemuseum.cargo.site/.

Chapter 6
1. See https://wardscorner.org/cbs.
2. See https://twitter.com/ACA.
3. See http://www.stopthetowers.org/.

References

Abell, S. (2019) *How Britain Really Works: Understanding the Ideas and Institutions of a Nation*, London: John Murray.
Ackroyd, P. (2000) *London: The Biography*, London: Chatto & Windus.
Addley, E. (2024) 'The Tory years: how it all went down – and down, and down', *The Guardian*, 4 July.
Advani, A., Bangham, G. and Leslie, J. (2020) *The UK's Wealth Distribution and Characteristics of High-wealth Households*, London: Resolution Foundation.
Against Social Cleansing Catford (2021) [Printed flyer], Lewisham, London.
Alemanno, A. (2017) *Lobbying for Change: Find Your Voice to Create a Better Society*, London: Icon Books.
Allain, J., Bales, K., Donington, K., Jeffery, H., Nelson, R., Oldfield, J., et al (2019) *Antislavery Usable Past*, AHRC-funded project, 2014–2019, University of Nottingham. Available from: http://antislavery.ac.uk/project [Accessed 11 May 2022].
Allegretti, A. (2021) 'London mayor to rally capital for action on threat from climate crisis', *The Guardian*, 23 September.
Almeida, A. (2021) *Pushed to the Margins: A Quantitative Analysis of Gentrification in the 2010s*, Runnymede and CLASS Report, London: Runnymede.
Almeida, A. (2023) *Social Value Index: Building the Case for the Democratic Commons in Tottenham*, Report, Common Wealth. Available from: https://www.common-wealth.org/publications/social-value-index-building-the-case-for-the-democratic-commons-in-tottenham [Accessed 1 April 2024].
Alonson, L.J.M.A. (2016) *Crony Capitalism and Neoliberal Paradigm (Part II)*, London: London School of Economics.
Althusser, L. (1970) *Ideology and Ideological State Apparatus: Notes towards an Investigation*. Available from: www.marxists.org/reference/archive/althusser/1970/ideology.htm [Accessed 28 November 2023].
Alton Action (2022) Available from: https://www.altonaction.org/ [Accessed 18 August 2022].
Alton Action Campaign member (2024) Email correspondence, April.
Alton Action Petition (2022) Available from: https://www.altonaction.org/petition [Accessed 14 August 2022].

Amnesty International (2024) *Amnesty International Report April 2024: The State of the World's Human Rights*, London: Amnesty International.

Anderson, P. (2017) *The H-Word: The Peripeteia of Hegemony*, London: Verso.

Anim-Addo, J. (1995) *Longest Journey: A History of Black Lewisham*, London: Deptford Forum Publishing Ltd.

Archer, T. and Cole, I. (2023) *The Invisible Hand that Keeps on Taking*, Sheffield Hallam University. Available from: https://www.shu.ac.uk/centre-regional-economic-social-research/publications/the-invisible-hand-that-keeps-on-taking [Accessed 25 July 2024].

ARUP (2020) *Meanwhile Use London: A Research Report for the Greater London Authority*. Available from: https://www.london.gov.uk/sites/default/files/meanwhile_use_for_london_final.pdf [Accessed 21 July 2020].

Astbury, J. (2023) 'Archio creates white brick housing block for London Community Land Trust'. Available from: https://www.dezeen.com/2023/04/14/archio-citizens-house-white-brick-housing-block-london-community-land-trust/?utm_medium=email&utm_campaign=Dezeen%20Debate%20811&utm_content=Dezeen%20Debate%20811+CID_59f395e75aa29b0fc1c7e88e7b5caf9f&utm_source=Dezeen%20Mail&utm_term=Read%20more [Accessed 3 March 2024].

Atkinson, R. (2020) *Alpha City: How London was Captured by the Super-rich*, London: Verso.

Atkinson, R. and Mingay, M. (2024) 'Arrive and retreat: London's ultra-prime apartment blocks as dark urban renaissance', *Analysis of Urban Change, Theory, Action* 28(3–4): 495–511.

Atkinson, R., Tallon, A. and Williams, D. (2019) 'Who is responsible for incorporating the notion of "Public Interest" into Sustainable Urban Developments? A case study of three sites in the south-west of England'. Available from: https://www.researchgate.net/profile/David-Williams-49/publication/313061062_Who_is_responsible_for_incorporating_the_notion_of_%27Public_Interest%27_into_Sustainable_Urban_Developments_A_case_study_of_three_sites_in_the_south-west_of_England/links/588f286945851567c9405b96/Who-is-responsible-for-incorporating-the-notion-of-Public-Interest-into-Sustainable-Urban-Developments-A-case-study-of-three-sites-in-the-south-west-of-England.pdf [Accessed 20 April 2021].

Ayers, A.J. and Saad-Filho, A. (2014) 'Democracy against neoliberalism: paradoxes, limitations, transcendence', *Critical Sociology* 41(4–5): 597–618.

Aylesham Community Action (2024a) Available from: https://twitter.com/ACA [Accessed 15 March 2024].

Aylesham Community Action (2024b) Available from: https://www.ayleshamcommunityaction.co.uk/ [Accessed 15 March 2024].

REFERENCES

Babb, S. and Kentikelenis, A. (2018) 'International financial institutions as agents of neoliberalism', in M. Cooper, D. Primrose, M. Konings and D. Cahill (eds) *The SAGE Handbook of Neoliberalism*, Los Angeles: SAGE International, pp 16–17.

Babb, S. and Kentikelenis, A. (2021) 'Markets everywhere: the Washington Consensus and the sociology of global institutional change', *Annual Review of Sociology* 47(1): 1–26.

Back, L., Sinha, S., Bryan, C., Baraku, V. and Yembi, M. (2018) *Migrant City*, London: Routledge.

Bagehot (2022) 'The rise and fall of Londongrad', *The Economist*, 5 March.

Baker, N. (2020) *… And What do You Do? What the Royal Family Don't Want You to Know*, London: Biteback Publishing.

Bambery, C. (2006) *The Rebel's Guide to Gramsci*, London: Bookmarks Publications.

Barnes, M., Newman, J., Knops, A. and Sullivan, H. (2003) Constituting 'the public' in public participation, *Public Administration* 81(2): 379–399.

Basketter, S. (2011) '1911: the great unrest', *Socialist Worker*. Available from: https://socialistworker.co.uk/features/1911-the-great-unrest/#:~:text=The%20Times%20reported%20that%20at,half%2Dholiday%20in%20the%20week [Accessed 22 February 2024].

Baston, L. (2019) 'Lewisham: council by-election holds for Labour despite small swings against', *On London*, 8 May. Available from: https://www.onlondon.co.uk/lewisham-council-by-election-holds-for-labour-despite-small-swings-against/ [Accessed 30 April 2021].

Battle for Brick Lane (2024) Available from: https://battleforbricklane.com/ [Accessed 5 April 2024].

Baxter, R. (2013) 'Home and inhabitation: a biography of the Aylesbury Estate'. Available from: https://www.leverhulme.ac.uk/early-career-fellowships/home-and-inhabitation-biography-aylesbury-estate [Accessed 2 March 2024].

BBC Two (2018) *The Secret History of Our Streets, Deptford*. Available from: https://www.youtube.com/watch?v=kEam6jk9LFQ&ab_channel=NS [Accessed 3 December 2021].

Beckett, A. (2016) 'The fall and rise of the council estates', *The Guardian*, 13 July. Available from: https://www.theguardian.com/society/2016/jul/13/aylesbury-estate-south-london-social-housing [Accessed 2 March 2024].

Begum, S. (2021) 'From Sylhet to Spitalfields: exploring Bengali migrant homemaking in the context of a squatters' movement, in 1970s East London', PhD thesis. Available from: https://qmro.qmul.ac.uk/xmlui/bitstream/handle/123456789/77341/Shabna%20Begum%20Final%20Thesis%20April%202022%20%28Library%29.pdf?sequence=4&isAllowed=y https://qmro.qmul.ac.uk/xmlui/handle/123456789/77341 [Accessed 29 July 2024].

Begum, S. (2023) *From Sylhet to Spitalfields: Bengali Squatters in 1970's East London*, London: Lawrence Wishart.

Belfield, A. (2015) *Deptford Demographics*, London: Deptford Neighbourhood Action.

Benham and Reeves (2023) 'Benham and Reeves estate agents, analysis of inside Airbnb data, Airbnb-style short let sites pose huge threat to London's rental market', *Evening Standard*, 14 May. Available from: https://www.standard.co.uk/homesandproperty/renting/renting-in-london-landlords-airbnb-b1120844.html [Accessed 28 July 2024].

Berry, S. (2021) 'Estate redevelopment in London: Have things improved under the current mayor? A briefing', 15 January. Available from: http://www.sianberry.london/news/2018_03_23_mayor-betrays-34-estates-over_ballot/ [Accessed 14 March 2021].

Betjeman, J. (2006 [1937]) 'Swindon, town tours', in S. Games (ed) *John Betjeman, Trains and Buttered Toast*, London: John Murray.

Better Homes Enfield (2023) 'The planning game', 24 July. Available from: https://betterhomes-enfield.org/2023/07/24/the-planning-game/ [Accessed 31 July 2024].

Bibby, A. (2009) 'Small scale utopia: the Coin Street's case', *a + t Architecture Publishers*, 19 January. Available from: https://aplust.net/blog/_small_scale_utopia_the_coin_streets_case/ [Accessed 5 July 2022].

Blakeley, G. (2019) *Stolen: How to Save the World from Financialisation*, London: Repeater Books.

Block, I. (2019) 'Record-breaking 541 skyscrapers proposed for London as planning approvals soar'. Available from: https://www.dezeen.com/2019/03/07/nla-london-tall-buildings-survey-2018-architecture-news/ [Accessed 19 February 2021].

Bloomfield, R. (2024) 'Are we witnessing the slow death of Peckham? How residents are battling big business to save the area's soul', *The Evening Standard*, 14 February.

Blyth, M. (2014) *Austerity: The History of a Dangerous Idea*, Oxford: Oxford University Press.

Boffey, D. (2022) 'UK "weakening threat to Kremlin by failing to close property loophole"', *The Guardian*, 20 February. Available from: https://www.theguardian.com/politics/2022/feb/20/uk-weakening-threat-to-kremlin-by-failing-to-close-property-loophole [Accessed 21 June 2022].

Bogdanor, V. (2022) 'Choosing the Conservative leader: a view from history', *The Political Quarterly* 93(4): 564–575.

Booth, R. (2020) 'Revealed: London councils take funds from developers to pay for planning guidelines', *The Guardian*, 23 August. Available from: https://www.theguardian.com/politics/2020/aug/23/revealed-councils-accept-payments-from-developers-to-fund-planning-guidelines [Accessed 23 April 2021].

Booth, R. (2021) 'Thousands of affordable UK homes "won't be built because of safety crisis"', *The Guardian*, 17 October. Available from: https://www.theguardian.com/business/2021/oct/17/thousands-of-affordable-uk-homes-wont-be-built-because-of-safety-crisis [Accessed 24 October 2021].

Booth, R. (2023) 'London council spending thousands on art and security patrols in opulent wards. Kensington and Chelsea, one of most unequal boroughs in UK, allocating social infrastructure funds in wards where homes go for millions', *The Guardian*, 9 May. Available from: https://www.theguardian.com/uk-news/2023/may/09/london-council-spending-thousands-on-art-and-security-patrols-in-opulent-wards [Accessed 29 July 2024].

Boughton, J. (2018) *Municipal Dreams: The Rise and Fall of Council Housing*, London: Verso Books.

Boyle, D. and Stone, I. (2023) 'London's empty mansions: how up to 53% of homes in multi-million pound neighbourhoods of Westminster, Kensington and Chelsea are deserted', *MailOnline*, 18 April. Available from: https://www.dailymail.co.uk/property/article-11973211/Londons-homes-65-properties-plush-city-centre-unoccupied.html [Accessed 18 April 2023].

Brady, H.E. and Kent, T.B. (2022) 'Fifty years of declining confidence and increasing polarization in trust in American institutions', *Daedulus* 151(4): 43–66.

Branson, A. (2019) 'What Boris Johnson becoming prime minister could mean for planning'. Available from: https://www.planningresource.co.uk/article/1589882/boris-johnson-becoming-prime-minister-mean-planning [Accessed 23 October 2023].

Briggs, M. (2020) Interview, Deptford, London.

British Comedy Guide (2023) 'Rye Lane'. Available from: https://www.comedy.co.uk/film/rye-lane [Accessed 13 April 2024].

Brooke, M. (2020) 'Even Thames Armada and sheep couldn't stop Docklands invasion of Isle of Dogs', *East London Advertiser*, 2 October 2017, updated 14 October 2020. Available from: https://www.eastlondonadvertiser.co.uk/news/even-thames-armada-and-sheep-couldn-t-stop-docklands-invasion-3571848 [Accessed 20 June 2022].

Brown, R. (2019) 'Developing trust – conference report. Strengthening public participation in London's planning system', 1 August, Centre for London. Available from: https://www.centreforlondon.org/reader/developing-trust/public-participation-planning/#context [Accessed 2 August 2021].

Budden, G. and Caless, K. (eds) (2012) *Acquired for Development: A Hackney Anthology*, London: Influx Press: Hackney.

Buildner (2022) 'Urban redevelopment of the London Docklands'. Available from: https://architecturecompetitions.com/urban-redevelopment-of-the-london-docklands [Accessed 24 June 2022].

Bullock, A. and Trombley, S. (eds) (1999) *The New Fontana Dictionary of Modern Thought*, London: HarperCollins.

Bullough, O. (2022) *Butler to the World: How Britain Became the Servant to Tycoons, Tax Dodgers, Kleptocrats and Criminals*, London: Profile Books.

Burford, R. (2023) 'Texan billionaire DJ's controversial 20-storey Brixton tower plan scrapped', *The Evening Standard*, 18 July. Available from: https://www.standard.co.uk/news/london/texan-brixton-taylor-tower-plan-scrapped-campaign-b1095113.html?utm_source=Sailthru&utm_medium=email&utm_campaign=News%20email%2018/7/2023&utm_term=ES_News_Daily_CDP [Accessed 27 February 2024].

Burford, R. (2024) 'Calls to urgently close legal loopholes that allow Vladimir Putin's allies to evade sanctions in London', *The Evening Standard*, 6 March.

Byrne, L. (2024) *The Inequality of Wealth: Why it Matters and How to Fix It*, London: Head of Zeus.

Cadman, M. (2021) Interview with Malcolm Cadman, Deptford, London.

Cadman, M. (2024) Interview with Malcolm Cadman, Deptford, London.

Cahill, D. (2012) 'The embedded neoliberal economy', in D. Cahill, L. Edwards and F. Stilwell (eds) *Neoliberalism: Beyond the Free Market*, Cheltenham: Edward Elgar, pp 132–152.

Calafate-Faria, F. (2014) *Urban Regeneration in Deptford*, London: Goldsmiths. Available from: https://www.gold.ac.uk/news/comment-urban-regeneration-in-deptford/ [Accessed 16 May 2022].

Cameron, D. (2021) 'Air pollution cuts billions of lives short around world', *The Guardian*, 1 September.

Campbell, D. (2023) 'Record rise in people using private healthcare amid NHS frustration', *The Guardian*, 24 May.

Campbell, D. (2024) 'Addiction to junk food costs UK £268bn a year', *The Guardian*, 16 November.

Campkin, B. (2013) *Remaking London: Decline and Regeneration in Urban Culture*, London: Tauris.

Carey, A. (2024) 'Supreme Court to hear appeal in challenge concerning standing orders and committee voting', *Local Government Lawyer*, 2 February. Available from: https://www.localgovernmentlawyer.co.uk/governance/396-governance-news/56317-supreme-court-to-hear-appeal-in-challenge-concerning-standing-orders-and-committee-voting [Accessed 6 April 2024].

Carpenter, J. (2014) 'Regeneration and the legacy of Thatcherism', *Metropolitics*, 15 October. Available from: https://metropolitiques.eu/Regeneration-and-the-Legacy-of.html [Accessed 25 October 2020].

Carroll, W. and Ratner, R. (2010) 'Social movements and counter-hegemony: lessons from the field, new proposals', *Journal of Marxism and Interdisciplinary Inquiry* 4(1): 7–22.

Carter, E. (2017) '"Setting the record straight": the creation and curation of archives by activist communities. A study of activist responses to the regeneration of Elephant and Castle, South London', *The Journal of the Archives and Records Association* 38: 27–44. Available from: https://www.tandfonline.com/doi/abs/10.1080/23257962.2016.1260532 [Accessed 3 March 2022].

Catford Struggle (2022) 'Catford against social cleansing', *Twitter/X*. Available from: Tweet @CatfordStruggle [Accessed 10 July 2024].

Cavaye, J. (2004) *Understanding Community Development*. Available from: https://increate.med-ina.org/static/assets/uploads/share/Step6-tools/Understanding-Community-Development-2004.pdf [Accessed 26 August 2024].

Centre for Ageing Better (2021) *Good Homes for All. A Proposal to Fix England's Housing*. Available from: https://ageing-better.org.uk/sites/default/files/2021-09/good-homes-for-all-a-proposal.pdf [Accessed 22 December 2021].

Centre for Cities (2019) *A Decade of Austerity*. Available from: https://www.centreforcities.org/publication/cities-outlook-2019/ [Accessed 30 June 2023].

Chamberlain, D. (2020) 'Greenwich Council's £30,000 planning deal over gasholder branded "astonishing"', *853*, 25 August. Available from: https://853.london/2020/08/25/greenwich-councils-30000-planning-deal-over-gasholder-branded-astonishing/ [Accessed 9 March 2021].

Chandler, M. (2013) 'Boris Johnson takes control of £1bn Deptford Convoys Wharf plans', *News Shopper*, 31 October. Available from: https://www.newsshopper.co.uk/news/10776943.boris-johnson-takes-control-of-1bn-deptford-convoys-wharf-plans/ [Accessed 15 October 2022].

Change.org (2022) 'Lewisham Council stop the social cleansing of Catford'. Available from: https://www.change.org/p/lewisham-council-stop-the-social-cleansing-of-catford#:~:text=%E2%80%9CCatford%20Against%20Social%20Cleansing%E2%80%9D%20is,The%20London%20Borough%20of%20Lewisham [Accessed 18 July 2022].

Chatterton, P. (2019) *Unlocking Sustainable Cities: A Manifesto for Real Change*, London: Pluto Press.

Chen, W. (2017) 'Examining the Beijing Consensus in context', in W. Chen (ed) *The Beijing Consensus? How China has Changed Western Ideas of Law and Economic Development*, Cambridge: Cambridge University Press, pp 95–96.

The Childhood Trust (2021) *London Child Poverty Report 2021*, London: The Childhood Trust.

China Daily (2022) 'World's top 10 real estate industry billionaires', 6 May. Available from: http://global.chinadaily.com.cn/a/202205/06/WS62745249a310fd2b29e5add9_1.html [Accessed 11 May 2022].

CIA Landlords (2022) 'The UK cities worst affected by the housing crisis', *Landlord News*, 24 May. Available from: https://www.cia-landlords.co.uk/news/vacant-homes-and-their-impact-on-the-housing-market-crisis/ [Accessed 6 June 2022].

CITY A.M. (2013) 'Boris Johnson calls in plans for £1bn Convoys Wharf scheme'. Available from: https://www.cityam.com/boris-johnson-calls-plans-1bn-convoys-wharf-scheme/ [Accessed 3 September 2021].

Clark, T. (2021) 'Housing association housebuilding completions drop by fifth', *Inside Housing*, 30 September. Available from: https://www.insidehousing.co.uk/news/news/housing-association-housebuilding-completions-drop-by-fifth-72715 [Accessed 19 May 2022].

Clemance, M. and King, L. (2023) 'Trust in politicians reaches its lowest score in 40 years', *IPSOS*. Available from: www.ipsos.com/en-uk/ipsos-trust-in-professions-veracity-index-2023 [Accessed 11 October 2024].

Coad, E.D. (2020) *The Most Unequal Borough in Britain – Revisited: Inequality and Inequity in Kensington and Chelsea*, London: Kensington Labour Party. Available from: https://www.dropbox.com/s/87fjaogenl945ws/The%20Most%20Unequal%20Borough%20in%20Britain%2021.10.20.pdf?dl=0 [Accessed 22 July 2021].

Coats, A. (2018) 'Five hundred years of Deptford and Woolwich Royal Dockyards and counting', in P. MacDougall (ed) *Five Hundred Years of Deptford and Woolwich Royal Dockyards*. Transactions of the Naval Dockyards Society, conference held at the National Maritime Museum Greenwich, 20 April 2013. West Sussex: The Naval Dockyards Society, pp 1–17.

Cochrane, A. and Jonas, A. (1999) 'Reimagining Berlin: world city, national capital or ordinary place?', *European Urban and Regional Studies* 6(2): 145–164.

Cohn, T.H. and Hira, A. (2020) *Global Political Economy: Theory and Practice*, New York: Routledge.

Coin Street (2021) 'About us. Our story'. Available from: https://coinstreet.org/about-us/our-story [Accessed 16 April 2021].

Coin Street (2024) *Passionate About Our Neighbourhood*, Coin Street Community Builders.

Coles, T.J. (2016) *The Great Brexit Swindle: Why the Mega-rich and Free Market Fanatics Conspired to Force Britain from the European Union*, West Hoathly: Clearview Books.

Convoys Wharf Community Forum (2022) Available from: https://convoys-wharf.com/community-forum/ [Accessed 2 September 2022].

Cooper, A.E., Hubbard, P. and Lees, L. (2020) 'Sold out? The right-to-buy gentrification and working-class displacements in London', *The Sociological Review* 68(6): 1354–1369. Available from: https://journals.sagepub.com/doi/pdf/10.1177/0038026120906790 [Accessed 1 August 2021].

Cooper, L. (2021) *Authoritarian Contagion: The Global Threat to Democracy*, Bristol: Bristol University Press.

Corporate Watch (2017) 'Lendlease. Development creeps'. Available from: https://corporatewatch.org/lendlease-development-creeps/ [Accessed 25 May 2023].

Corporate Watch (2018a) 'Tidemill: Peabody Housing Association – from social landlord to big business', 12 November. Available from: https://corporatewatch.org/tidemill-peabody-housing-association-from-social-landlord-to-big-business/ [Accessed 30 July 2024].

Corporate Watch (2018b) 'Tidemill: the Lewisham councillors pushing demolition and gentrification', 12 November.

Corporate Watch (2019) 'Who's gentrifying Deptford? 15 development schemes and the investors behind them'. Available from: https://corporatewatch.org/whos-gentrifying-deptford-15-development-schemes-and-the-investors-behind-them/ [Accessed 13 February 2022].

Corry, O. and Reiner, D. (2021) 'Protests and policies: how radical social movement activists engage with climate policy dilemmas', *Sociology* 55(1): 197–217.

Cotton, J. (2021) 'Looking forward', Labour Housing Group Newsletter, December. Available from: https://labourhousing.org/wp-content/uploads/2021/12/LHG-newsletter-December-2021.pdf [Accessed 27 January 2022].

cSPACE (2021) 'Docklands poster project'. Available from: https://cspace.org.uk/category/archive/docklands-community-poster-project/ [Accessed 17 May 2021].

Cuffe, G. (2020a) 'Lewisham provides details on approved affordable housing', *News Shopper*, 23 October. Available from: https://www.newsshopper.co.uk/news/18817250.lewisham-provides-details-approved-affordable-housing/ [Accessed 7 August 2021].

Cuffe, G. (2020b) 'Many people on Lewisham's housing waiting list will never be moved into social homes, according to new report', *London News Online*, 14 November. Available from: https://londonnewsonline.co.uk/many-people-on-lewishams-housing-waiting-list-will-never-be-moved-into-social-homes-according-to-new-report/ [Accessed 9 March 2022].

Curry, A. (2022) 'Controversial Brick Lane plans could change as mayor looks at "alternative"', *MyLondon*, 1 June. Available from: https://www.mylondon.news/news/east-london-news/controversial-brick-lane-plans-could-24121390 [Accessed 7 August 2022].

Dalrymple, W. (2019) *The Anarchy: The Relentless Rise of the East India Company*, London: Bloomsbury.

Darling, A. (2012) *Back from the Brink: 100 Days at Number 11*, London: Atlantic Books.

Davies, A. (2025) 'Biden warns "dangerous" oligarchy taking shape in farewell address', *BBC News*, 16 January. Available from: www.bbc.co.uk/news/articles/c1weqzl3ydro [Accessed 16 January 2025].

Davies, M. (2012) *Be Realistic, Demand the Impossible*, Chicago: Haymarket Books.

Davis, K. (2015) 'Can pop-up shops improve my community? Exploring the linkages between tactical urbanism and community development', Applied Research Paper, Georgia Institute of Technology, USA. Available from: https://repository.gatech.edu/server/api/core/bitstreams/1772dfbe-e365-4f18-968c-4f3f87c55f74/content [Accessed 7 March 2019].

Deaton, A. (2021) *COVID-19 and Global Income Inequality*, London: LSE Public Policy Review. Available from: https://ppr.lse.ac.uk/articles/10.31389/lseppr.26 [Accessed 10 August 2024].

Deloitte (2021) 'The London mayor's planning powers', 17 May. Available from: https://www.deloitte.com/uk/en/Industries/real-estate/research/the-london-mayors-planning-powers.html [Accessed 3 October 2023].

Dench, G., Gavron, N. and Young, M. (2006) *The New East End: Kinship, Race and Conflict*, London: Profile Books.

Deptford Dame (2014) 'Lewisham Strategic Planning Committee "rejects" application', 17 January. Available from: https://deptforddame.blogspot.com/ [Accessed 16 January 2024].

Deptford Dame Blogger (2020) 'Barclays' branch closure set to make Deptford a banking desert', 11 October. Available from: https://deptforddame.blogspot.com/2020/ [Accessed 7 January 2022].

Deptford Resident (2022) 'The Battle for Deptford', YouTube. Available from: https://www.youtube.com/watch?v=kzSjSrRuQGo&t=6s&ab_channel=HarrietVickers [Accessed 21 February 2024].

Di Fazio, F. (2023) 'The local community has until mid-February to have their say on the project', *Haringey Community Press*, 16. Available from: https://haringeycommunitypress.co.uk/wp-content/uploads/2023/02/HCPFeb23_ForWeb.pdf [Accessed 3 April 2024].

Dixon, T. and Adams, D. (2008) 'Housing supply and brownfield regeneration in a post-Barker world: is there enough brownfield land in England and Scotland?', *Urban Studies* 45(1): 115–139.

Dorling, D. (2012) *The No-nonsense Guide to Equality*, Oxford: New Internationalist.

Dorling, D. (2015) *Injustice: Why Social Inequality Persists*, Bristol: Policy Press.

Dorling, D. (2018) *Peak Inequality: Britain's Ticking Time Bomb*, Bristol: Policy Press.

Dorling, D. (2019) *Inequality and the 1%*, London: Verso.

Dorling, D. (2023) *Inequality and the Geography of a Failing State*, London: Verso.

Dorling, D. (2024) *Peak Injustice: Solving Britain's Inequality Crisis*, Bristol: Policy Press.

Duncombe, S. and Lambert, S. (2021) *The Art of Activism*, New York and London: OR Books.

Dunn, P. and Leeson, L. (2022) *For Walls with Tongues*. Available from: https://www.forwallswithtongues.org.uk/artists/dr-loraine-leeson-docklands-poster-project/ [Accessed 5 March 2022].

Eagleton, T. (2011) *Why Marx Was Right*, New Haven: Yale University Press.

East London Lines (2016) 'Goldsmiths lecturers join in strike action'. Available from; https://www.eastlondonlines.co.uk/2016/05/goldsmiths-lecturers-join-in-strike-action/ [Accessed 18 February 2024].

East Marsh United (2024) Available from: https://eastmarshunited.org/ [Accessed 23 November 2024].

The Economist (2023) 'No really. Rishi Sunak is a right-winger', 27 July.

Ejiogu, A. and Denedo, M. (2022) 'How stigma shapes social housing policy in England'. Available from: https://redbrickblog.co.uk/2022/11/how-stigma-shapes-social-housing-policy-in-england/ [Accessed 31 July 2024].

Elliott, L. (2014) 'The shape we're in: strong GDP growth issues is masking UK'S deep structural issues', *The Guardian*, 19 August.

Elliott, L. (2021) 'To really reduce emissions we need to create a fairer world', *The Guardian*, 12 August.

Elliott, L. (2022) 'Wealth of the world's 10 richest people doubles since start of pandemic', *The Guardian*, 12 January.

Elms, R. (2019) *London Made Us*, Edinburgh: Canongate Books.

Elvery, M. (2019) 'The wealthiest and most deprived areas of London have been revealed', *MyLondon*, 30 October. Available from: https://www.mylondon.news/news/zone-1-news/wealthiest-most-deprived-areas-london-17171816 [Accessed 23 February 2022].

Engels, F. (1887) *The Housing Question*, Paris: Foreign Languages Press, 2021 [a reprint of the edition published by Progress Publishers, Moscow, Third Printing, 1970]. Available from: https://foreignlanguages.press/wp-content/uploads/2021/03/C13-Engels-The-Housing-Question-1st-Printing.pdf [Accessed 24 June 2022].

Erasmus, A. (2002) 'London's dubious past in slavery', *This is Local London*, 30 July. Available from: https://www.thisislocallondon.co.uk/news/307822.londons-dubious-past-in-slavery/ [Accessed 2 April 2022].

Estate Watch (2021) 'Tenant-led regeneration: alternatives to demolition'. Available from: https://www.estatewatch.london/images/Handout_3.pdf [Accessed 5 August 2021].

Estate Watch (2022a) Available from: https://www.estatewatch.london/ [Accessed 19 August 2022].

Estate Watch (2022b) 'Alton Estate'. Available from: https://www.estatewatch.london/estates/wandsworth/altonarea/ [Accessed 17 August 2022].

Evans, E.J. (2013) *Thatcher and Thatcherism* (3rd edn), London: Routledge

Evening Standard (2022) 'Homes and property', 16 February.

Evening Standard (2024) 'First stay: London's largest penthouse', 30 July.

Farrell, T. (2012) 'Sir Terry Farrell, British architect, Convoys Wharf Master Plan'. Available from: https://www.youtube.com/watch?v=AVknPpsQxwk [Accessed 3 March 2024].

Farrelly, E. (2021) *Killing Sydney: The Fight for a City's Soul*, Sydney: Picador.

Featherstone, D. and Kelliher, D. (2022) 'Massey', in *Doreen Massey: Selected Political Writings*, London: Lawrence & Wishart.

Ferguson, J. (2022) '"Housing has become a commodity": how investors reshaped London's skyline and communities', *Investigate Europe*, 21 December. Available from: https://www.investigate-europe.eu/posts/housing-has-become-a-commodity-how-investors-reshaped-londons-skyline-and-communities [Accessed 1 August 2024].

Ferm, J. and Jones, E. (2016) 'Mixed use "regeneration" of employment land in the post-industrial city: challenges and realities in London', *European Planning Studies* 16. Available from: https://www.london.gov.uk/sites/default/files/ad_62_ferm_jones_eps_article_2016_mixed_use_regeneration_of_employment_sites_-_accepted_version.pdf [Accessed 13 November 2021].

Firth, R. (2023) 'Brixton campaigners celebrate as 20-storey Hondo tower plan scrapped after Texan millionaire DJ pulls project', *Mylondon*, 18 July. Available from: https://www.mylondon.news/news/south-london-news/brixton-campaigners-celebrate-20-[storey-27343708 [Accessed 14 January 2024].

Fisher, M. (2013) 'Map: how 35 countries compare on child poverty (the U.S. is ranked 34th)', *The Washington Post*, 15 April.

Forgacs, D. (ed) (1988) *A Gramsci Reader*, London: Lawrence & Wishart.

Forrest, A. (2022) '"Worse than feared": Brexit to blame for £33 bn loss to UK economy, study shows', *Independent*, 20 December.

Forrest, R., Koh, S. and Wissink, B. (eds) (2017) *Cities and the Super-rich*, London: Palgrave Macmillan.

Foster, T. (2023) 'New play takes a stab against gentrification', *Socialist Worker*, 8 August. Available from: https://socialistworker.co.uk/reviews-and-culture/new-play-takes-a-stab-against-gentrification/ [Accessed 5 January 2024].

Francis, A. (2017) *The Deptford Royal Dockyard and the Manor of Sayers Court, London*, London: Museum of London Archaeology.

Francis Taylor Building Chambers (2023) 'The Court of Appeal upholds the power of local authorities to restrict voting on planning applications by elected members', *Francis Taylor Building Chambers*, 31 July. Available from: https://www.ftbchambers.co.uk/news/news-view/the-court-of-appeal-upholds-the-power-of-local-authorities-to-restrict-voting-on-planning-applications-by-elected-members [Accessed 12 April 2024].

Fredericks, J., Tomitsch, M., Hespanhol, L. and Mc Arthur, I. (2015) *Digital Pop-Up: Investigating Bespoke Community Engagement in Public Spaces*, OzCHI '15: Proceedings of the Annual Meeting of the Australian Special Interest Group for Computer Human Interaction. Available from: https://dl.acm.org/doi/abs/10.1145/2838739.2838759 [Accessed 23 January 2019].

Freedman, D. (2020) 'Goldsmiths strike: why we're fighting the marketisation of higher education', *openDemocracy*. Available from: https://www.opendemocracy.net/en/opendemocracyuk/goldsmiths-strike-universities-fighting-marketisation-higher-education/ [Accessed 18 February 2024].

Freeland, C. (2000) *Sale of the Century: Russia's Wild Ride from Communism to Capitalism*, New York: Crown Business.

Freidman, S. and Laurison, D. (2020) *The Class Ceiling: Why it Pays to be Privileged*, Bristol: Policy Press.

Freire, A.M. and Macedo, D. (eds) (1995) *The Paulo Freire Reader*, New York: Continuum Publishing Company.

Freire, P. (2014) *Pedagogy of the Oppressed: Thirtieth Anniversary Edition*, London: Penguin.

Friedman, M. (1962) *Capitalism and Freedom*, Chicago: University of Chicago.

Friedman, M. (1993) *Why Government is the Problem*, Stanford: Hoover Institute Press.

Friedman, M. and Freidman, R. (1980) *Freedom to Choose: A Personal Statement*, San Diego: Harcourt.

Gamble, A. (2015) 'Austerity as statecraft', *Parliamentary Affairs* 68(1): 42–57.

Gans, H.J. (1962) *The Urban Villagers: Group and Class in the Life of Italian-Americans*, New York: The Free Press.

Garcia, F. (2021) 'Goodbye, Catford? When planners label your childhood haunt an "opportunity area"', *The New Statesman*, 16 February.

Garner, J. (2022) 'Deptford: the London high street voted one of the world's coolest', *BBC*, 4 September. Available from: https://www.bbc.co.uk/news/uk-england-london-62693537 [Accessed 16 January 2024].

Gayle, D. and Horton, H. (2024) '"A travesty of justice": supporters cry foul', *The Guardian*, 20 July.

Gelder, S. (2021) 'Robert Jenrick's "unlawful" approval of Tory donor's £1bn development is reversed', *Big Issue*, 19 November. Available from: https://www.bigissue.com/news/housing/tory-sleaze-jenricks-unlawful-approval-of-1bn-development-reversed/ [Accessed 5 March 2023].

Generation Rent (2023) 'Housing in a hostile environment'. Available from: https://www.generationrent.org/wp-content/uploads/2023/07/GR_Migrant-Private-Renters-Report_Digital2.pdf [Accessed 4 June 2024].

The Gentle Author (2022) 'Six days left to save Brick Lane! Tonight is the benefit concert at Rich Mix to raise money for next week's Judicial Review at the High Court', *Spitalfields Life*, 22 June. Available from: https://spitalfieldslife.com/2022/06/22/six-days-left-to-save-brick-lane/ [Accessed 12 April 2024].

Geoghegan, P. (2021) *Democracy for Sale: Dark Money, and Dirty Politics*, London: Head of Zeus.

GEOGRAFREEDRISCOLL (2018) 'Once a player always a player? Reflections on gentrification'. Available from: https://geogra-free.com/2018/05/30/once-a-player-always-a-player-reflections-on-gentrification/ [Accessed 4 August 2021].

Gilbert, J. (2020) *Twenty-first Century Socialism*, Cambridge: Polity Press.

The Golden Hinde Ltd. (2020) 'A ships fate'. Available from: https://www.goldenhinde.co.uk/blog/268-golden-hinde-fate [Accessed 11 May 2022].

Goldsmiths University and College Union (2024) Available from: https://goldsmithsucu.org/news/ [Accessed 20 February 2024].

Good Law Project (2022) 'Help stop the great British public space sell-off'. Available from: https://goodlawproject.org/news/public-spaces/#:~:text=Locality%2C%20a%20campaign%20group%20fighting,every%20year%20in%20England%20alone [Accessed 23 June 2022].

Goodier, M. and Anguilar Garcia, C. (2024) 'Companies linked to key Tory donors given £8.4bn in public contracts since 2016', *The Guardian*, 28 June.

Gould, K. (2014) 'Boris backs £1bn wharf revamp', *Mercury*, 9 April.

Gourevitch, A. (2017) 'Beyond resistance', *Jacobin*, 13 February.

GOV.UK (2024) 'Community infrastructure levy'. Available from: https://www.gov.uk/guidance/community-infrastructure-levy#:~:text=The%20Community%20Infrastructure%20Levy%20(the,support%20development%20in%20their%20area [Accessed 23 April 2024].

Gramsci, A. (1971) *Selections from the Prison Notebooks* (ed and trans Q. Hoare and G. Nowell Smith), London: Lawrence & Wishart.

Gramsci, A. (1975) *Letters from Prison* (selected and trans J. Lawner), London: Jonathan Cape.

Gramsci, A. (1977) *Selections from Political Writings 1910–1920* (ed Q. Hoare), London: Lawrence & Wishart.

Gramsci, A. (1978) *Selections from Political Writings 1921–1926* (ed Q. Hoare), London: Lawrence & Wishart.

Grant, H. (2022) 'Communities fight back developers with "greener" plans for UK housing', *The Guardian*, 18 April. Available from: https://www.theguardian.com/society/2022/apr/18/communities-fight-back-developers-with-greener-plans-for-uk-housing [Accessed 9 October 2023].

Gray, M. and Barford, A. (2018) 'The depths of the cuts: the uneven geography of local government austerity', *Cambridge Journal of Regions, Economy and Society* 11(3): 541–563.

Greater London Authority (2014) 'Convoys Wharf, Deptford in the London Borough of Lewisham', Representation Hearing Report, 31 March.

Greater London Authority (2018) 'London brownfield sites review', 30 November. Available from: https://data.london.gov.uk/dataset/london-brownfield-sites-review [Accessed 19 June 2021].

Greater London Authority (2021) 'London plan'. Available from: https://data.london.gov.uk/dataset/households-local-authority-waiting-list-%09borough [Accessed 20 July 2024].

Greater Manchester Tenants Union (2024) *Researching Developers and Landlords: A Tenants How-to Guide*.

Green, R. (2014) *Convoys Wharf Street Survey*, Centre for Community Engagement Research, Goldsmiths, University of London.

Green, R. (2021) *Listening to the Voices of the Community. Engaging with Residents and the Community of the Royal Borough of Kensington and Chelsea*, Research Report, Royal Borough of Kensington and Chelsea.

Green, R. and Ferguson, J. (2014) *Audit of Community and Voluntary Organisations and Groups in Deptford*, Centre for Community Engagement Research, Goldsmiths, University of London.

Green, R. and Baker, C. (2020) 'Re-empowering into voice: experiments in organic community coproduction', *Community Development Journal* 57(2): 277–294.

Gregory, A. (2021) 'Test and trace: £37bn system "failed in its bold ambitions"', *The Guardian*, 27 October.

Gregory, R. (2022a) 'Old Truman Brewery plans: campaigners lose legal challenge, 16th September', *East London Advertiser*. Available from: https://www.eastlondonadvertiser.co.uk/news/21822418.old-truman-brewery-plans-campaigners-lose-legal-challenge/ [Accessed 10 April 2024].

Gregory, R. (2022b) 'Lamborghinis, empty flats and plenty of anger – life in the London neighbourhood that's been dubbed Dubai-on-Thames', *MyLondon*. Available from: https://www.mylondon.news/news/south-london-news/lamborghinis-empty-flats-plenty-anger-24125348 [Accessed 20 June 2022].

Grenfell United (2024) Available from: https://grenfellunited.org.uk/ [Accessed 15 December 2024].

The Guardian (2024) 'Economics is a discipline in disarray that holds too much sway over politics', Leader comment, 29 April.

Gurran, N. and Whitehead, C. (2011) 'Planning and affordable housing in Australia and the UK: a comparative perspective', *Housing Studies* 6(7–8): 1193–1214.

Hajdukiewicz, S.M. (2021) *High Hopes: Voices from the Streets of Lewisham*, Documentary film. Available from: https://vimeo.com/655432342 [Accessed 6 February 2022].

Hall, S. (1982) 'Introduction essay: reading Gramsci', in R. Simon, *Gramsci's Political Thought: An Introduction*, London: Lawrence & Wishart, pp 7–10.

Hall, S. and Jacques, M. (1983) *The Politics of Thatcherism*, London: Lawrence & Wishart.

Harding, C., Cottell, J., Tabbush, J. and Mahmud, Z. (2023) 'Homes for Londoners: London's homes today', Centre for London. Available from: centreforlondon.org/reader/londons-homes-today/chapter-2/ [Accessed 25 July 2024].

Harris, J. (2016) 'The end of council housing', *The Guardian*, 4 January. Available from: https://www.theguardian.com/society/2016/jan/04/end-of-council-housing-bill-secure-tenancies-pay-to-stay [Accessed 3 December 2021].

Harvey, D. (2005) *A Brief History of Neoliberalism*, Oxford: Oxford University Press.

Harvey, D. (2013) *Rebel Cities: From the Right to the City to the Urban Revolution*, London: Verso.

Hatherley, O. (2011) 'Regeneration? What's happening in Sheffield's Park Hill is class cleansing', *The Guardian*. Available from: https://www.theguardian.com/commentisfree/2011/sep/28/sheffield-park-hill-class-cleansing [Accessed 28 September 2023].

Hayek, F.A. (1944) *The Road to Serfdom*, Chicago: University of Chicago Press.

Hayek, F.A. (1948) *Individualism and Economic Order*, London: Routledge.

Hayek, F.A. (1978) *The Constitution of Liberty*, Chicago: University of Chicago Press.

Heatherwick, T. (2023) 'Boring buildings are making us ill – let's make London beautiful again', *The Standard*, 23 October.

Hefler, E. (2018) '"We want able Blacks": The British East India Company's African slave trade'. Available from: https://www.vanderbilthistoricalreview.com/post/we-want-able-blacks-the-british-east-india-company-s-african-slave-trade [Accessed 11 May 2022].

Held, D. (2006) *Models of Democracy* (3rd edn), Cambridge: Polity.

Helm, T. and Inman, P. (2022) 'Revealed: the £30bn cost of Liz Truss's disastrous mini-budget', *The Observer*, 12 November.

Henderson, C. and Mendick, R. (2024) 'The million pound London properties owned by Putin's regime', *The Telegraph*, 25 May.

Hennessy, P. (1986) *The Great and the Good: An Inquiry into the British Establishment*, London: Policy Studies Institute.

Hersh, B., Pęchorzewski, D. and (Xiohang) Yu, S. (2012) *Redeveloping Waterfront Brownfields: Ideas, Plans and Experiences for Regeneration of Shipyards on Three Continents*. Available from: https://www.academia.edu/29587259/Redeveloping_Waterfront_Brownfields_Ideas_Plans_and_Experiences_for_Regeneration_of_Shipyards_on_Three_Continents?email_work_card=view-paper [Accessed 30 October 2020].

Hilber, C. and Schoni, O. (2021) 'In the United Kingdom, home ownership has fallen whilst renting is on the rise'. Available from: https://www.brookings.edu/essay/uk-rental-housing-markets/ [Accessed 7 August 2021].

Hildyard, L. (2024) *Enough: Why it's Time to Abolish the Super-rich*, London: Pluto Press.

Hill, D. (2023) 'Major London developers publish proposals for unlocking urban regeneration', *On London*, 25 August. Available from: https://www.onlondon.co.uk/major-london-developers-publish-proposals-for-unlocking-urban-regeneration/ [Accessed 28 July 2024].

HOPE not hate Charitable Trust (2020) *Understanding Community Resilience in Our Towns*, London: Hopeful Towns Project.

House of Commons Committee of Public Accounts (2021) *Test and Trace 2*, 21 October. https://committees.parliament.uk/work/1299/test-and-trace-2/publications/

Howard Boyd, E., Leigh, G. and Sutton, J. (2024) *London Climate Resilience Review*, London: Greater London Authority.

Hunt, T. (2006) 'Charge of the heavy brigade', *The Guardian*, 4 September.

Hyde, M. (2024) 'Dear royals, the Prince Andrew problem is one for you: own it', *The Guardian*, 18 December.

The Independent (2024) 'Westminster scandals: all the MPs who are suspended or have lost the whip', 18 April.

Ingram, H. and Schneider, A. (1991) 'The choice of target populations', *Administration and Society* 23(3): 333–356. Available from: https://journals.sagepub.com/doi/10.1177/009539979102300304 [Accessed 27 March 2021].

Inman, P. (2021) 'Boris Johnson's legacy could be the concreting over of England', *The Guardian*, 22 May. Available from: https://www.theguardian.com/business/2021/may/22/boris-johnsons-legacy-could-be-the-concreting-over-of-england [Accessed 14 August 2021].

Institute of Health Equity (2024) *Health Inequalities, Lives Cut Short*, London: University College London, Institute of Health Equity.

Intelligence and Security Committee of Parliament (2020) *Russia*. Presented to Parliament pursuant to section 3 of the Justice and Security Act 2013. Ordered by the House of Commons to be printed on 21 July. https://isc.independent.gov.uk/wp-content/uploads/2021/03/CCS207_CCS0221966010-001_Russia-Report-v02-Web_Accessible.pdf

Inwood, S. (2005) *City of Cities: The Birth of Modern London*, London: Macmillan.

IPCC (Intergovernmental Panel on Climate Change) (2023) *Intergovernmental Panel on Climate Change Sixth Assessment Report*, Geneva: IPCC.

Jacobs, J. (1961) *The Death and Life of Great American Cities*, New York: Random House.

Jarvis, D., Berkeley, N. and Broughton, K. (2012) 'Evidencing the impact of community engagement in neighbourhood regeneration: the case of Canley, Coventry', *Community Development Journal* 47(2): 232–247. Available from: https://doi.org/10.1093/cdj/bsq063 [Accessed 24 August 2024].

Jayanetti, C. (2021) 'Revealed: overcrowding in private rentals doubled in pandemic', *The Observer*, 25 April.

Jenkins, S. (2017) 'If we keep on building towers, empty London will be a grim reality', *Evening Standard*, 11 April. Available from: http://www.standard.co.uk/comment/comment/simon-jenkins-if-we-keep-on-building-towers-empty-london-will-be-a-grim-reality-a3512541.html [Accessed 19 April 2021].

Jenkins, S. (2020) 'Jenrick, and a system rotten at its heart', *The Guardian*, 26 June.

Jessop, B. (2018) 'Neoliberalization, uneven development, and Brexit: further reflections on the organic crisis of the British state and society', *European Planning Studies* 26(9): 1728–1746.

Johnson, C. (2020) 'Let's talk about South Carolina', *Jacobin* 38: 12–18.

Joint Docklands Action Group (2021) Available from: https://cspace.org.uk/category/archive/docklands-community-poster-project/ [Accessed 16 April 2021].

Jones, A. (2017) 'Every flat in a new South London development has been sold to foreign investors', *Vice*. Available from: https://www.vice.com/en_uk/article/qkq4bx/every-flat-in-a-new-south-london-development-has-been-sold-to-foreign-investors [Accessed 14 May 2019].

Jones, H. (2017) 'City of London says tax take backs case for Brexit banks deal', *Reuters Business News*, 27 November.

Jones, O. (2015) *The Establishment: And How They Got Away with It*, London: Penguin Books.

Jones, O. (2025) 'Young people are abandoning democracy for dictators. I can understand their despair', *The Guardian*, 14 January.

Joseph, J. (2002) *Hegemony: A Realist Analysis*, London: Routledge.

JRF (Joseph Rowntree Foundation) (2024) *UK Poverty 2024: The Essential Guide to Understanding Poverty in the UK*, York: Joseph Rowntree Federation.

Just Space (2024a) *2024 Manifesto. A Different Kind of London – for People and Communities*, London: Just Space.

Just Space (2024b) Available from: https://justspace.org.uk/about/ [Accessed 7 March 2024].

Kaplinsky, R. (2022) *Sustainable Futures: An Agenda for Action*, Cambridge: Polity Press.

Katona, R. (2020) Notes on the Convoys Wharf heritage and its context (Late Deptford resident and Voice4Deptford supporter).

Kehoe, C. (2023) 'The Truman Brewery development: the community reaches boiling point', *Whitechapel LDN*, 26 June. Available from: https://whitechapellondon.co.uk/truman-brewery-development-community-reaches-boiling-point/ [Accessed 2 April 2024].

Kensington Against Dirty Money (2022) Available from: https://www.kensingtonagainstdirtymoney.com/supporters [Accessed 7 July 2022].

Keynes, J.M. (1936) *The General Theory of Employment, Interest and Money*, London: Palgrave Macmillan

Keyte, S. (2020) 'Over 300,000 of us have told the government: don't push through bad planning changes', *CPRE*, 8 December. Available from: https://www.cpre.org.uk/news/over-300000-of-us-sign-petition-against-planning-changes/ [Accessed 9 June 2022].

Kings Fund (2022) *The NHS Budget and How it Has Changed*, London: Kings Fund.

Klein, N. (2007) *The Shock Doctrine: The Rise of Disaster Capitalism*, London: Allen Lane.

Knowles, C. (2022) *Serious Money: Walking Plutocratic London*, London: Allen Lane.

Krugman, P. (2012) *End this Depression Now!* New York: W.W. Norton.

Krugman, P. (2024) 'The "unforced error" of austerity: Conservatives deserve to lose owing to the legacy of the Cameron years', *The Guardian*, 28 June.

Labiak, M. (2021) 'London authorities sitting on £1.29bn of CIL and S106 cash', *Property Week*, 12 March. Available from: https://www.propertyweek.com/news/london-authorities-sitting-on-129bn-of-cil-and-s106-cash/5113111 [Accessed 1 January 2022].

Ladywood Unite (2024) Ladywood Regeneration Residents Group, Birmingham. Available from: https://ladywoodunite.com/ [Accessed 28 July 2024].

Landler, M. and Castle, S. (2022) 'UK moves to tighten laws on oligarchs: critics say it's too late', *The New York Times*, 1 March.

Lanktree, G. (2019) 'The great Section 106 and CIL scandal', *Property Week*, 27 September. Available from: https://www.propertyweek.com/insight/the-great-section-106-and-cil-scandal/5104449.article [Accessed 9 March 2021].

Lawrence, I. (2022) 'These 122 council estates in London might be demolished: thousands of homes could be knocked down amid widespread "regeneration"', *Time Out*, 24 August.

Lean (2019) 'A picture of Lewisham 2019'. Available from: https://www.leanarts.org.uk/advice/picture-lewisham-2019 [Accessed 30 April 2021].

Lee, R. and Edwards, M. (2020) 'Preface', in P. Sendra and D. Fitzpatrick (eds) *Community-Led Regeneration: A Toolkit for Residents and Planners*, London: UCL Press, pp 13–15.

Lees, L. and Ferreri, M. (2016) 'Resisting gentrification on its final frontiers: the case of the Heygate Estate in London (1974–2013)', *Cities* 57: 14–24.

Lees, L. and White, H. (2019) 'The social cleansing of London council estates: everyday experiences of "accumulative dispossession"', *Housing Studies On-line* 35(10): 1701–1722. Available from: https://www.tandfonline.com/doi/full/10.1080/02673037.2019.1680814 [Accessed 15 March 2021].

Lees, L., Just Space, The London Tenants' Federation and Snag (2013) *The Social Cleansing of Council Estates in Regeneration Realities. Urban Pamphleteer#2*, London: UCL Press.

Lees, L., Hubbard, P. and Tate, N. (2017) *Gentrification, Displacement, and the Impacts of Council Estate Renewal in C21st London*, ESRC. Available from: http://gtr.rcuk.ac.uk/projects?ref=ES%2FN015053%2F1 [Accessed 24 August 2020].

Leeson, L. (2019) *Our Land: Creative Approaches to the Redevelopment of London's Docklands*, Middlesex University Research Repository. Available from: https://eprints.mdx.ac.uk/21524/1/Our%20Land%20-%20Creative%20approaches%20to%20the%20redevelopment%20of%20London%E2%80%99s%20Docklands.pdf [Accessed 7 July 2022].

Lendlease (2021) Available from: https://www.elephantpark.co.uk/ [Accessed 19 April 2021].

Lewis, S. (2021) 'The fossil fuel industry is the enemy of progress', *The Guardian*, 11 August.

Lillywhite, C. (2023) 'Massive South London estate plagued by damp and mould "needs to be revamped instead of knocked down" say residents. Wandsworth Council scrapped old proposals for the Alton Estate last year', *MyLondon*, 20 March. Available from: https://www.mylondon.news/news/south-london-news/massive-south-london-estate-plagued-26514761?utm_source=mynewsassistant.com&utm_medium=referral&utm_campaign=embedded_search_item_desktop [Accessed 5 April 2024].

Lim, L. (2017) *Democratic Disorder: Why Modern Democracy is Failing and its Alternatives*, London: Grin Verlag.

Local Government Association (2018) *Moving the Conversation On*, London: Local Government Association.

Local Government Association (2024) 'Total households on the housing waiting list at 31st March in Lambeth'. Available from: https://lginform.local.gov.uk/reports/lgastandard?mod-metric=105&mod-period=1&mod-area=E09000022&mod-group=AllBoroughInRegion_London&mod-type=namedComparisonGroup [Accessed 3 March 2024].

London Assembly (2014) 'Mayor approves plans for major new development at Convoys Wharf'. Available from: https://www.london.gov.uk/press-releases/mayoral/development-at-convoys-wharf [Accessed 3 March 2021].

London Borough of Haringey (2022) 'Scrutiny review: the future of the Seven Sisters market site (Wards Corner)'. Available from: https://www.minutes.haringey.gov.uk/documents/s131317/Scrutiny%20Review%20into%20Seven%20Sisters%20Market%20Final.pdf [Accessed 19 February 2024].

London Borough of Haringey (2023a) 'Placemaking plans for Seven Sisters and the Wards Corner site'. Available from: https://www.haringey.gov.uk/regeneration/tottenham/tottenham-high-road/placemaking-plans-seven-sisters-and-wards-corner-site [Accessed 5 March 2024].

London Borough of Haringey (2023b) 'Work begins to allow market traders to return to Wards Corner'. Available from: https://www.haringey.gov.uk/news/work-begins-allow-market-traders-return-wards-corner [Accessed 5 March 2024].

London Borough of Lewisham (2017) 'Working together to tackle poverty in Lewisham', the final report of the Lewisham Poverty Commission.

London Borough of Lewisham (2019) *Joint Strategic Needs Assessment, Picture of Lewisham 2019 Part A*. Available from: https://www.leanarts.org.uk/sites/default/files/info/a_picture_of_lewisham_-_full_document_2019-20_part_a.pdf [Accessed 29 April 2021].

London Borough of Lewisham (2024) *Catford Town Centre Framework*. Available from: https://lewisham.gov.uk/inmyarea/regeneration/catford-regeneration/catford-town-centre-framework [Accessed 12 February 2024].

London Councils (2019) *Indices of Deprivation 2019*. Available from: https://www.londoncouncils.gov.uk/members-area/member-briefings/local-government-finance/indices-deprivation-2019 [Accessed 22 February 2022].

London Group of the Anarchist Federation (2016) *Making London the Rebel City*, *London's Anarchist Paper*, 1.

London Radical Histories (2018) 'Today in London strike history, 1739: chips on their shoulders, Deptford shipwrights strike'. Available from: https://pasttense.co.uk/2018/10/20/today-in-london-strike-history-1739-chips-on-their-shoulders-deptford-shipwrights-strike/ [Accessed 21 February 2024].

London Tenants Federation (2020) *The London Tenants Guide to 'Genuinely Affordable Housing' 2020*. Available from: https://londontenants.org/publication/the-london-tenants-guide-to-genuinely-affordable-housing-2020/ [Accessed 26 June 2022].

London Tenants Federation (2024) 'Over 35,000 homes on 100 plus London estates are at risk of demolition'. Available from: https://londontenants.org/ [Accessed 1 March 2024].

Loussouarn, S. (2022) *Brexit and its Aftermath*, London: Bloomsbury

MacFarlane, L. (2021) 'Developers' contributions are going unspent by local authorities', *Showhouse*. Available from: https://www.showhouse.co.uk/news/developers-contributions-are-going-unspent-by-local-authorities/ [Accessed 1 January 2022].

Madden, D. and Marcuse, P. (2016) *In Defense of Housing: The Politics of Crisis*, London and New York: Verso.

Malik, N. (2024) 'Emerging from the landslide is a sad truth of Britian's politics', *The Guardian*, 15 July.

Mansfield, M. (2009) 'Blood, sweat and tears: the Miners Strike 1984–85', *Socialist Lawyer* 52: 16–18.

Marcus (2021) Interview with Roger Green, 19 February.

Marlowe Society (2022) *Marlowe's Life*. Available from: http://www.marlowe-society.org/christopher-marlowe/life/ [Accessed 5 April 2022].

Marshall, J. (2020) 'Redrow walks away from London estate revamp', *Housing Today*, 6 August. Available from: https://www.housingtoday.co.uk/news/redrow-walks-away-from-london-estate-revamp/5107403.article#:~:text=Redrow%20has%20pulled%20out%20of,in%20Roehampton%20in%20March%202017 [Accessed 2 April 2024].

Martin, D. (2017) 'Gentrification comes to Walford, with craft beer, Nimbys – and riots', *The Guardian*. Available from: https://www.theguardian.com/tv-and-radio/shortcuts/2017/sep/05/gentrification-walford-albert-square-eastenders-craft-beer-and-riots [Accessed 12 January 2020].

Martini (2017) *Doors Wide Open: Corruption and Real Estate in Four Key Markets*, Berlin: Transparency International. Available from: https://images.transparencycdn.org/images/2017_DoorsWideOpen_EN.pdf [Accessed 29 December 2021].

Marx, K. and Engels, F. (1848) *The Communist Manifesto*, London: Penguin.

Massey, D. (2007) *World City*, Cambridge: Polity Press.

Massey, D. (2022) 'Exhilarating times', in D. Featherstone and D. Kelliher (eds) *Doreen Massey: Selected Political Writings*, London: Lawrence & Wishart, pp 46–61.

McCarthy, J. (2018) 'Students back Goldsmiths' lecturers at start of strike action over pension changes', *East London Lines*. Available from: https://www.eastlondonlines.co.uk/2018/02/students-back-goldsmiths-lecturers-start-strike-action-pension-changes/ [Accessed 20 February 2024].

McChesney, R.W. (2011) 'Introduction', in N. Chomsky (ed) *Profit Over People; Neoliberalism and Global Order*, New York: Seven Stories Press, pp 7–18.

McFadyen, J. (2022) 'I have a love and hate relationship with London', *The Guardian*, 5 February.

McKenzie, L. (2021) '"Class cleansing" is killing London, as poor people are removed from communities like vermin', *Labour Heartlands*, 7 June. Available from: https://labourheartlands.com/class-cleansing-is-killing-london-as-poor-people-are-removed-from-communities-like-vermin/ [Accessed 2 February 2024].

Meade, R., Shaw, M. and Banks, S. (eds) (2016) *Politics, Power and Community Development*, Bristol: Policy Press.

Mee, A. (1937) *London*, London: Hodder & Stoughton.

Mellen, H. (2022) 'Alton Action planning for a community-led regeneration of the estate', *Planning Aid for London*. Available from: https://planningaidforlondon.org.uk/stories/altonaction-3-2/ [Accessed 14 August 2022].

Milne, S. (2014) *The Enemy Within* (4th edn), London: Verso Books.

Minton, A. (2017a) *Big Capital. Who is London For?*, London: Penguin.

Minton, A. (2017b) 'The great London property squeeze', *The Guardian*, 25 May. Available from: https://www.theguardian.com/society/2017/may/25/london-property-squeeze-affordable-housing [Accessed 25 May 2023].

Monbiot, G. (2014) *Rewilding the Land, Sea and Human Life*, London: Penguin.

Monbiot, G. (2017a) *How Did We Get into this Mess?* London: Verso Books.

Monbiot, G. (2017b) *Out of the Wreckage: A New Politics in the Age of Crisis*, London: Verso.

Monbiot, G. (2022) *Regenesis: Feeding the World without Destroying the Planet*, London: Penguin.

Monbiot, G. (2024) 'Protest is vital for democracy: that's why our leaders ban it', *The Guardian*, 19 July.

Monbiot, G. and Hutchison, P. (2024) *The Invisible Doctrine: The Secret History of Neoliberalism (& How it Came to Control Your Life)*, London: Allen Lane.

Morning Lane People's Space (2024) Website. Available from: https://morninglanepeoplesspace.org/get-involved/ [Accessed 4 April 2024].

MoSaF (Museum of Slavery and Freedom) (2020) Available from: https://www.mosaf.org.uk/legacy/ [Accessed 22 March 2022].

Mudlark121 (2020) 'Uncrowned kings: slavery, wealth and statues in London – part 2, past tense – London radical histories and possibilities', 14 June. Available from: https://pasttenseblog.wordpress.com/2020/06/14/uncrowned-kings-slavery-wealth-and-statues-in-london-part-2/ [Accessed 2 April 2022].

Murdoch, J. (2007) *The Place Based Strategic Philanthropy Model*, Houston: Center for Urban Economics.

Murky Depths (2021) 'Shared ownership units fail to sell at Woolwich estate redevelopment', [blog] 26 March. Available from: https://www.fromthemurkydepths.co.uk/2021/03/26/shared-ownership-units-fail-to-sell-at-woolwich-estate-redevelopment/ [Accessed 20 April 2021].

Murphy, M. and Baker, G. (2024) 'UK election: what's happened and what comes next', *BBC*. Available from: www.bbc.co.uk/news/articles 4 July [Accessed 4 July 2024].

Murray, J. (2024) '"It's economic violence": Birmingham resident fight to save homes', *The Guardian*, 23 July.

Museum of London Archaeology (2017) *The Deptford Royal Dockyard and Manor of Sayes Court, London. Excavations 2000–2012*, Monograph 71, London: MOLA.

Naval Dockyards Society (2018) *Five Hundred Years of Deptford and Woolwich Royal Dockyards*, Transactions of the Naval Dockyards Society, Volume 11, Conference held at the National Maritime Museum, Greenwich, 20 April 2013, West Sussex, UK.

Neate, R. (2018) 'Ghost towers: half of new-build luxury London flats fail to sell', *The Guardian*, 26 January. Available from: https://www.theguardian.com/business/2018/jan/26/ghost-towers-half-of-new-build-luxury-london-flats-fail-to-sell [Accessed 20 April 2021].

Neate, R. (2022a) '"Tax us now": super-rich say system rigged in their favour', *The Guardian*, 19 January.

Neate, R. (2022b) 'UK's richest people avoid social housing rules in £1.2bn London flats project. Westminster gave exemption for Hinduja brothers' Old War Office development in return for £10m payment', *The Guardian*, 2 October. Available from: https://www.theguardian.com/news/2022/oct/02/luxury-flats-richest-people-social-housing-hinduja-old-war-office [Accessed 24 July 2024].

Newman, J., Barnes, M., Sullivan, H. and Knops, A. (2004) 'Public participation and collaborative governance', *Journal of Social Policy* 33(2): 203–223.

NewsLine (2023) 'Ambulance workers call for a general strike!', 24 January. Available from: https://wrp.org.uk/news/ambulance-workers-call-for-a-general-strike/ [Accessed 13 January 2023].

OBR (2024) *Brexit Analysis*, London: Office for Budget Responsibility.

The Observer (2024) 'Only a Labour government can make Britain a fairer and greener place', Leader comment, 30 June.

Old Royal Naval College, Greenwich (2022) *Black People in Greenwich and Deptford*. Available from: https://ornc.org/our-story/today/discover/bgp-online/greenwich-and-deptford/ [Accessed 1 April 2022].

ONS (2023) *Average Household Income, UK: Financial Year Ending 2022*, London: Office for National Statistics.

Our Tottenham (2021) Available from: https://ourtottenham.wordpress.com/about/ [Accessed 9 May 2022].

Oxfam (2023) *Survival of the Richest*, Oxford: Oxfam.

Palin, H. (2022) 'Save Brick Lane'. Available from: https://www.crowdjustice.com/case/save-brick-lane/?s=09 [Accessed 10 August 2022].

Parker, L. (2019) 'How London became the centre of the world', *National Geographic*, August.

Passino, C. (2024) 'The history behind London's latest power station conversion', *Country Life*, 9 April. Available from: https://www.countrylife.co.uk/property/the-history-behind-londons-latest-power-station-conversion-267648 [Accessed 7 August 2024].

Pearson-Jones, B. (2021) 'Why would you ever leave? Millennials are snapping up "all-in-one" apartments that come with gyms, shops and roof gardens – after pandemic leaves them "craving community living"', *Daily Mail*, 21 March. Available from: https://www.dailymail.co.uk/femail/article-9122297/Millennials-moving-apartment-buildings-one-gyms-shops-gardens.html [Accessed 5 August 2021].

People's History Museum (2022) 'The sirens last time: an ambulance worker looks back', 20 December. Available from: https://phm.org.uk/blogposts/the-sirens-last-time-an-ambulance-worker-looks-back/ [Accessed 20 January 2024].

Pettifor, A. (2020) *The Case for the Green New Deal*, London: Verso.

Phipps, M. (2024) 'The 2024 general election: things just got a lot more interesting', *Labour Hub*, 5 July.

Piketty, T. (2014) *Capital in the Twenty-first Century*, London: The Belknap Press of Harvard University Press.

Piketty, T. (2020) *Capital and Ideology*, London: The Belknap Press of Harvard University Press.

Pilger, J. (2006) 'The return of people power: John Pilger on what we can learn from global resistance', *The New Statesman*, 4 September. Available from: https://www.newstatesman.com/long-reads/2006/09/the-return-of-people-power-john-pilger-on-what-we-can-learn-from-global-resistance [Accessed 4 January 2025].

Piloti (2013) 'Nooks and corners', *Private Eye*, 3 November.

Pitcher, G. (2023) 'London's empty homes could be worth £20bn: which borough has the most?', *The Standard*, 2 June.

Popple, K. (2015) *Analysing Community Work: Theory and Practice* (2nd edn), Maidenhead: Open University Press.

Popple, K. (2021a) 'Populist politics and democracy in the UK: the implications for community development', in S. Kenny, J. Ife and P. Westoby (eds) *Populism, Democracy and Community Development*, Bristol: Policy Press, pp 165–185.

Popple, K. (2021b) 'Trust and political life: the need to transform our democracy', *Concept: The Journal of Contemporary Community Education and Practice Theory* 12(1): 1–9.

Potts, G. (2008) *Overview of Deptford*, London: BURA.

Powell, J. (2024) https://twitter.com/josephpowell [Accessed 14 April 2024].

Powell, K. (2017) 'Brexit positions: neoliberalism, austerity and immigration – the (im) possibilities of political revolution', *Dialectical Anthropology* 41: 225–240.

Public Law Interest Centre (2024) 'Victory in the High Court: Aylesbury estate residents win; developers told that their submissions "lacked coherence"', 17 January. Available from: https://www.pilc.org.uk/news/victory-in-the-high-court-aylesbury-estate/ [Accessed 6 March 2024].

Qpzm (2022) *Evelyn Demographics* (Lewisham, England). Available from: http://evelyn.localstats.co.uk/census-demographics/england/london/lewisham/evelyn [Accessed 22 February 2022].

Raban, J. (1991) *Hunting Mr Heartbreak*, London: Pan Books.

Radical Housing Network (2022) 'Refurbish don't demolish on Alton Estate', 27 June. Available from: https://www.radicalhousingnetwork.uk/home/altonestate [Accessed 15 August 2022].

Radical Housing Network (2021) Available from: https://www.facebook.com/radicalhousingnetwork/ [Accessed 5 March 2021].

Ramos Jr, V. (1982) 'The concepts of ideology, hegemony, and organic intellectuals in Gramsci's Marxism', *Theoretical Review* 27 March–April. Available from: www.marxists.org/history/erol/periodicals/theoretical-review/1982301.htm [Accessed 4 September 2023].

Redrow (2017) *Creating Britain's New Communities*. Available from: https://www.redrowplc.co.uk/media/2015/creating-britains-new-communities-report-feb-2017.pdf [Accessed 21 April 2021].

Reid, N. (2021) 'Urban empathy: the next big shift', *Quality of Life Foundation*. Available from: https://qolf.medium.com/urban-empathy-the-next-big-shift-9bfee18c9488 [Accessed 20 October 2023].

Researchgate (2021) *Heygate Estate Tenants Displacement Map*. Available from: https://www.researchgate.net/figure/Council-tenant-displacement-from-the-Heygate-Estate-London-Source-Lees-et-al-2013_fig1_337266396 [Accessed 2 August 2021].

The Resident (2016) 'London's new urban villages; where to invest?', *The Resident*, 29 February. Available from: http://www.theresident.co.uk/property-market-london/reinventing-london-regeneration-development/ [Accessed 11 August 2020].

Rhodes, C. (2022) *Woke Capitalism: How Corporate Morality is Sabotaging Democracy*, Bristol: Bristol University Press.

Ringrose, I. (2021) 'Profit hungry developers broke the housing system', *Socialist Worker*, 9 June.

Robbins, G. (2022) 'We don't just need council housing – we need good council housing', *Tribune*, 23 January. Available from: https://tribunemag.co.uk/2022/01/council-housing-estate-south-london-property-developers [Accessed 5 June 2022].

Robeyns, I. (2024) *Limitarianism: The Case Against Extreme Wealth*, London: Allen Lane.

Robson, M. (2023) 'South London exhibition showcases residents' fight against "social cleansing"', *Open Democracy*, 19 April. Available from: https://www.opendemocracy.net/en/aylesbury-estate-exhibition-demolition-southwark-council-regeneration/ [Accessed 23 February 2024].

Romain, L. (2024) 'Austerity, Brexit and Covid: why the Conservatives lost the general election after 14 years in office', *Independent*, 5 July.

Romei, V. (2024) 'UK public trust in political parties collapses to 12%', *The Financial Times*, 1 March.

Romyn, M. (2020) *London's Aylesbury Estate: An Oral History of the 'Concrete Jungle'*, London: Palgrave Macmillan.

Rosa, S.K. (2021) 'How we won: the community that saved Latin village from demolition. Campaigners fought a 15-year battle against property developers', *Novara Media*, 12 August. Available from: https://novarame dia.com/2021/08/12/how-we-won-the-community-that-saved-latin-vill age-from-demolition/ [Accessed 16 August 2022].

Rosa, S.K. (2022) Wards Corner Community Plan, 9 August, @sophiekrosa [Accessed 10 April, 2024].

Rostboll, C.F. (2024) 'Polarization and the democratic systems: kinds, reasons and sites', *Perspectives on Politics*, 16 April.

Rowley, P. (2017) *Class Work*, Grimsby: independently published.

Royal Museums Greenwich (2022) 'East India Company ships at Deptford'. Available from: https://www.rmg.co.uk/collections/objects/rmgc-obj ect-13352 [Accessed 11 May 2022].

Russell, H. (2023a) 'Aylesbury Estate resident reluctantly relocates after years spent defying regeneration', *Southwark News*, 15 November. Available at: https://southwarknews.co.uk/area/walworth/aylesbury-estate-resident-reluctantly-relocates-after-years-spent-defying-regeneration/ [Accessed 6 March 2024].

Russell, H. (2023b) '"Cash over homes": developer pays just under £6 million instead of providing affordable homes in Elephant and Castle', *Southwark News*, 26 April. Available from: https://southwarknews.co.uk/area/elephant-and-castle/cash-over-homes-developer-pays-just-under-6-million-instead-of-providing-affordable-homes-in-elephant-and-castle/ [Accessed 4 September 2023].

Russell-Jones, L. (2021) 'Locals fight plan to turn the Truman Brewery into a shopping mall', *CITYA.M.*, 9 November. Available from: https://www.cityam.com/locals-challenge-plan-to-turn-truman-brewery-into-a-shopp ing-mall/#:~:text=In%20September%20the%20council%20voted,a%20 period%20of%2015%20years [Accessed 7 August 2022].

Safran Foer, J. (2018) *Eating Animals: Should We Stop?* London: Penguin.

Safran Foer, J. (2019) *We are the Weather: Saving the Planet Starts at Breakfast*, London: Penguin.

Salisbury, J. (2020) 'Tough cookie. Biscuits plans pushed through, 2020', *Southwark News*, 21 February. Available from: https://www.southwarkn ews.co.uk/the-paper/27th-february-2020/ [Accessed 15 April 2021].

Salisbury, J. (2023) 'Ealing Council scraps plans 26-storey tower at council HQ which would have created 477 homes', *The Evening Standard*, 10 May.

Sampson, A. (2022) 'Is Battersea the new Belgravia?', *Tatler*, 3 March. Available from: https://www.tatler.com/article/battersea-power-station-most-glamorous-place-to-live-in-london [Accessed 19 June 2022].

Sassen, S. (2014) *Expulsions: Brutality and Complexity in the Global Economy*, Cambridge, MA: Belknap: Harvard University Press.

Save Nour: Fight the Tower (2024) Available from: https://www.savenour.com/ [Accessed 28 February 2024].

Scanlon, K., Whitehead, C., Blanc, F. and Moreno-Tabarez, U. (2017) *The Role of Overseas Investors in the London New-build Residential Market*, final report for Homes for London, London: LSE.

Schneider, A. and Ingram, H. (1993) 'Social construction of target populations: implications for politics and policy', *American Political Science Review* 87(2): 334–347. Available from: https://www.jstor.org/stable/2939044?seq=1 [Accessed 17 April 2021].

Sendra, P. (2023) 'The ethics of co-design', *Journal of Urban Design* 29(1). Available from: https://www.tandfonline.com/doi/full/10.1080/13574809.2023.2171856 [Accessed 17 March 2024].

Sendra, P. and Fitzpatrick, D. (2020) *Community-Led Regeneration: A Toolkit for Residents and Planners*, London: UCL Press.

Service, R. (2011) *Lenin: A Biography*, London: Picador.

Shabrina, Z., Arcaute, E. and Batty, M. (2021) 'Airbnb and its potential impact on the London housing market', *Urban Studies*, 16 January. Available from: https://journals.sagepub.com/doi/full/10.1177/0042098020970865 [Accessed 17 April 2021].

Shah, K. (2022) *Wealth on the Eve of a Crisis*, London: Resolution Foundation.

Sheila McKechnie Foundation (2022) 'Urban regeneration for the people, by the people'. Available from: https://smk.org.uk/awards_nominations/wards-corner-community-plan/ [Accessed 17 August 2022].

Shelley, P.B. (1995) *Shelley*, London: David Campbells Publishers.

Shelter (2021c) 'Health of one in five renters harmed by their home'. Available from: https://england.shelter.org.uk/media/press_release/health_of_one_in_five_renters_harmed_by_their_home [Accessed 19 November 2021].

Shelter (2022) 'What is social housing'. Available from: https://england.shelter.org.uk/support_us/campaigns/what_is_social_housing [Accessed 22 June 2022].

Sherwood, H. (2021) 'Huguenots, Jews, Bengalis … now developers size up London's Brick Lane', *Observer*, 19 September. Available from: https://www.theguardian.com/focus/2021/sep/19/huguenots-jews-bengalis-now-developers-size-up-londons-brick-lane [Accessed 8 August 2022].

Simon, R. (1982) *Gramsci's Political Thought*, London: Lawrence & Wishart.

Simon, R. (1991) *Gramsci's Political Thought: An Introduction*, London: Lawrence & Wishart.

REFERENCES

Sinclair, I. (2017) *The Last London*, London: Oneworld.

Smith, G. (2024) *Abolish the Monarchy: Why We Should and How We Will*, London: Penguin.

Smith, M. (2024) 'Why do Tory members think the party lost the 2024 general election'. 10 September. www.YouGov.co.uk [Accessed 10 September 2024].

Social Metrics Commission (2024) *Measuring Poverty 2024*, London: Social Metrics Commission.

Springer, S., Birch, K. and Macleavy, J. (2016) *The Handbook of Neoliberalism*, London: Routledge.

Stafford, J. (2023) 'Exhibition corrects myth that demolished Brutalist housing estate was unpopular with its residents', *University of Manchester*. Available from: https://www.manchester.ac.uk/about/news/exhibition-corrects-myth-that-demolished-brutalist/ [Accessed 28 July 2024].

Steele, J. (1993) *Turning the Tide: The History of Everyday Deptford*, London: Deptford Forum Publishing Ltd.

Steerpike (2023) 'Green co-leader denies party is "institutionally racist"', *The Spectator*, 7 October.

Stein, S. (2019) *Capital City: Gentrification and the Real Estate State*, London: Verso.

Stop the Towers (2021) *Councillor Information Pack*. Available from: https://stopthetowers.info/wp-content/uploads/2020/09/Stop-the-Towers_Councillor-Pack-V3-DC-amended.pdf [Accessed 13 March 2024].

Stop the Towers (2024) Available from: https://stopthetowers.info/act-now-before-its-too-late [Accessed 1 March 2024].

Strasser, A. (2020) *Deptford is Changing*, London: CHASE/Goldsmiths.

Summers, C. (2021) Available from: www.sas.org.uk/rep/claire-summers [Accessed 4 June 2022].

Sunday Times (2024) 'Rich list 2024', *The Sunday Times*, 19 May.

Tapper, J. (2023) '"It doesn't need regeneration": Peckham's charm under threat from gentrification plans. The quirky appeal of Rye Lane is threatened by developer's 14 high-rise flats, say residents', *The Observer*, 13 May. Available from: https://www.theguardian.com/society/2023/may/13/it-doesnt-need-regeneration-peckhams-charm-under-threat-from-gentrification-plans [Accessed 12 March 2024].

Tarver, N. (2014) '£1.5bn "community cash" unspent by English Councils', 7 January. Available from: https://www.bbc.co.uk/news/uk-england-25094100 [Accessed 10 March 2021].

Tarver, E. (2022) 'The most expensive neighbourhoods in London', *Investopedia*, 24 May. Available from: https://www.investopedia.com/articles/personal-finance/100115/most-expensive-neighborhoods-london.asp [Accessed 8 August 2022].

Taylor, L. (2024) '"It fees you": Bogota, the city that shuts out cars every Sunday', *The Guardian*, 1 June.

Thoburn, N. (2022) *Brutalism as Found: Housing, Form, and Crisis at Robin Hood Gardens*, London: Goldsmiths Press.

Thompson, E.P. (1974) *The Making of the English Working Class*, Harmondsworth: Penguin Books.

Thorold, P. (1999) *The London Rich: The Creation of a Great City, from 1666 to the Present*, London: Viking.

Toynbee, P. (2021) 'Cronyism is rampant and, worse, it goes unpunished', *The Guardian*, 23 February.

Toynbee, P. and Walker, D. (2020) *The Lost Decade 2010–2020 and What Lies Ahead for Britain*, London: Guardian Books.

Toynbee, P. and Walker, D. (2024) *The Only Way is Up: How to Take Britain from Austerity to Prosperity*, London: Atlantic Books.

Transparency International (2015) 'Unmask the corrupt. How UK property launders the wealth of the global corrupt report', *Transparency International*. Available from: http://www.ukunmaskthecorrupt.org/ [Accessed 15 August 2022].

Transpontine (2010) *Deptford 1911: School and Dock Strikes*. Available from: https://transpont.blogspot.com/2010/12/deptford-1911-school-and-dock-strikes.html [Accessed 20 February 2024].

Transpontine (2011) *Who Owns Convoys Wharf?* Available from: https://transpont.blogspot.com/search?q=rupert+murdoch [Accessed 24 November 2021].

Trellick Tower Campaign (2024) Available from: https://trellicktower.com/develop-trellick [Accessed 2 April 2024].

Truman Brewery Consultation (2024) Available from: https://trumanbreweryconsultation.co.uk/ [Accessed 11 April 2024].

Trust for London (2022) 'Lewisham'. Available from: https://www.trustforlondon.org.uk/data/boroughs/lewisham-poverty-and-inequality-indicators/ [Accessed 5 March 2022].

TUC (1986) 'The Wapping dispute, in numbers'. Available from: https://tuc150.tuc.org.uk/stories/the-wapping-dispute/ [Accessed 22 February 2024].

Tuckett, I. (2021) 'Coin Street: how a community in South London transformed its own neighbourhood', *Landscape Institute*, 15 April. Available from: https://www.landscapeinstitute.org/blog/coin-street-community-builders/ [Accessed 4 July 2022].

Turnbull, P. and Hollis, R. (2017) *London Tenants Federation, 14.03.17, Audio, Response to the London Mayor's Good Practice Guide on Estate Regeneration*. Available from: http://www.londontenants.org/publications/responses/LTF%20response%20to%20LMGPG-ER140317.pdfAA [Accessed 4 March 2022].

Tweneboa, K. (2024) *Our Country in Crisis: Britain's Housing Emergency and How We Rebuild*, London: Trappeze.

UK Government (1990) *Town and Country Planning Act, 1990*. Available from: https://www.legislation.gov.uk/ukpga/1990/8/contents [Accessed 23 June 2021].

UK Parliament Foreign Affairs Committee (2022) 'The cost of complacency: illicit finance and the war in Ukraine', Second Report of Session 2022–23, 30 June. Available from: https://publications.parliament.uk/pa/cm5803/cmselect/cmfaff/168/report.html [Accessed 12 August 2022].

UNEP (United Nations Environmental Programme) (2024) *Emissions Group Report 2024*, New York: United Nations Environmental Programme.

UPI (1986) 'Warehouse for Murdoch's papers burns; company blames ousted printers', *Los Angeles Times*, 3 June. Available from: https://www.latimes.com/archives/la-xpm-1986-06-03-mn-9421-story.html [Accessed 19 February 2024].

Venugopal, R. (2015) 'Neoliberalism as concept', *Economy and Society* 44(2): 165–187.

Vickers, H. (2022) 'The Battle for Deptford', YouTube video. Available from: https://www.youtube.com/watch?v=kzSjSrRuQGo&t=6s&ab_channel=HarrietVickers [Accessed 14 February 2024].

Viet Nam News (2024) 'London Square's spectacular showcase at Rosewood Hong Kong provides a dazzling view of its UK new homes', *Viet Nam News*, 11 June. Available from: https://vietnamnews.vn/media-outreach/1657276/london-square-s-spectacular-showcase-at-rosewood-hong-kong-provides-a-dazzling-view-of-its-uk-new-homes.html [Accessed 7 July 2024].

Waights, S. (2014) *Gentrification and Displacement in English Cities*, London School of Economics. Available from: http://people.lse.ac.uk/waights/default_files/Gentrification_SW_15_09_2014.pdf [Accessed 19 February 2021].

Wards Corner Benefit Society (2024) Available from: https://wardscorner.org/cbs [Accessed 29 March 2024].

Wards Corner Community Plan (2022) Available from: https://wardscorner.org/cbs [Accessed 16 August 2022].

Wards Corner Community Voices (2022) 'Help fund the Wards Corner Community Plan', YouTube video. Available from: https://www.crowdfunder.co.uk/p/wardscornerplan [Accessed 17 August 2022].

Watt, P. (2017) 'Gendering the right to housing in the city: homeless female lone parents in post-Olympics austerity East London', *Cities* 76: 43–51.

Watt, P. (2021) *Estate Regeneration and Its Discontents: Public Housing, Place and Inequality in London*, Bristol: Policy Press.

Watt, P. and Minton, A. (2016) 'London's housing crisis and its activisms', *City* 20(2): 204–221. Available from: https://www.tandfonline.com/doi/abs/10.1080/13604813.2016.1151707 [Accessed 20 July 2020].

Waywell, C. (2018) 'How people power got the Deptford anchor back', *Time Out*, 21 February.

Wehner, P. (2020) 'Councils accused of collusion after developers pay for planning rules', *UK Cities, Investor Guide*, 24 August. Available from: https://www.egi.co.uk/news/councils-accused-of-collusion-after-developers-pay-for-planning-rules/?eg_tr_frm_cmpt=true# [Accessed 29 April 2021].

Weinreb, B. and Hibbert, C. (eds) (1992) *The London Encyclopaedia*, London: Macmillan.

Wessie du Toit (2022) 'The elitism of the river Thames Londoners aren't welcome on the riverside', *UnHerd*, 19 December. Available from: https://unherd.com/2022/12/the-elitism-of-the-river-thames/ [Accessed 30 July 2024].

Whitehead, R., Brown, R., Harding, C., Brown, J., Gariban, S. and Moonen, T. (2020) *London at a Crossroads*, Centre For London. Available from: https://www.centreforlondon.org/project/london-futures/ [Accessed 20 October 2020].

Whitehouse, E. (2023) 'All eyes on the Truman show: public consultation launched for Truman Brewery regeneration', *New Start. The Future of Regeneration*, 12 December. Available from: https://newstartmag.co.uk/articles/all-eyes-on-the-truman-show-public-consultation-launched-for-truman-brewery-regeneration/ [Accessed 12 April 2024].

Widgery, D. (1993) *Some Lives! A GP's East End*, London: Simon & Schuster.

Wilkinson, R. (2005) *The Impact of Inequality: How to Make Sick Societies Healthier*, New York: The New Press.

Wilkinson, R. and Pickett, K. (2010) *Why Equality is Better for Everyone*, London: Penguin.

Wilkinson, R. and Pickett, K. (2018) *The Inner Level: How More Equal Societies Reduce Stress, Restore Sanity and Improve Everybody's Wellbeing*, London: Penguin.

Williams, M. (2022) 'Exclusive: 2,300 people died while waiting for a council house last year', *Open Democracy*, 2 November. Available from: https://www.opendemocracy.net/en/council-house-waiting-list-2300-died-housing-crisis/?utm_source=SEGMENT%20-%20Newsletter%3A%20oD%20weekly&utm_medium=email&utm_campaign=%F0%9F%97%B3%20Christian%20Right%20groups%20behind%20voter%20suppression&_kx=s9W1uLX_7xgW05hk98qJd8ZhxVFJAFfehSDtEU-1qH0%3D.YjCYwm [Accessed 28 July 2024].

Wilmore, J. (2021a) 'Replace Decent Homes Standard with beefed-up version to tackle crisis of poor conditions, urges new report', *Inside Housing*, 17 September. Available from: https://www.insidehousing.co.uk/news/news/replace-decent-homes-standard-with-beefed-up-version-to-tackle-crisis-of-poor-conditions-urges-new-report-72555 [Accessed 24 September 2021].

Wilmore, J. (2021b) 'Court of Appeal upholds council decision over controversial Elephant & Castle regeneration', *Inside Housing*, 7 June. Available from: https://www.insidehousing.co.uk/news/news/court-of-appeal-upholds-council-decision-over-controversial-elephant--castle-regeneration-70974 [Accessed 10 June 2022].

Wilson, S. (2022) ' "It can't be sustainable": the hidden costs of demolishing council housing Estates', *Big Issue*, 14 May. Available from: https://www.bigissue.com/news/environment/it-cant-be-sustainable-the-hidden-costs-of-demolishing-council-housing-estates/ [Accessed 26 July 2024].

Wintour, P. (2025) 'Post-cold war era is over says Lammy as he vows to revamp Foreign Office', *The Guardian*, 9 January.

Wood, J. (2020) 'Children's views should be taken into account when designing urban space', *The Conversation*, 5 November. Available from: https://theconversation.com/childrens-views-should-be-taken-into-account-when-designing-urban-space-148888 [Accessed 16 March 2021].

World Bank Group (2024) *Poverty, Prosperity, and Planet Report: Pathways out of the Polycrisis*, Wahington, DC: World Bank Group

Worthington, A. (2020) 'Two years since the violent eviction of the Old Tidemill Wildlife Garden, Lewisham Council's housing policy still puts profits before people'. Available from: https://www.andyworthington.co.uk/2020/10/30/two-years-since-the-violent-eviction-of-the-old-tidemill-wildlife-garden-lewisham-councils-housing-policy-still-puts-profits-before-people/ [Accessed 15 February 2024].

Yellow book ltd (2017) 'Barriers to community engagement in planning: a research study', *Scottish Government*. Available from: https://www.gov.scot/binaries/content/documents/govscot/publications/factsheet/2017/05/barriers-to-community-engagement-in-planning-research/documents/barriers-community-engagement-planning-research-study-pdf/barriers-community-engagement-planning-research-study-pdf/govscot%3Adocument/Barriers%2Bto%2Bcommunity%2Bengagement%2Bin%2Bplanning%2B-%2Ba%2Bresearch%2Bstudy.pdf [Accessed 3 August 2021].

Yorke, H., Pogrund, G. and Urwin, R. (2022) 'How Boris Johnson's friendship with Evgeny Lebedev deepened despite MI6 concerns', *The Sunday Times*, 12 March.

Young, H. (2013) *One of Us*, London: Pan.

Yu, E. and Kantor, A. (2022) 'Chinese parents seek flats for their kids in London's new towers', *Bloomberg UK*, 18 May. Available from: https://www.bloomberg.com/news/articles/2022-05-18/chinese-parents-seek-flats-for-their-kids-in-london-s-new-towers [Accessed 10 June 2022].

Index

References to figures and photographs appear in *italic* type.

A

action 106
  direct 126–127
  see also strike action
Advani, A. 22
affordable housing 59–61, 63, 66, 71, 80, 125, 132
  see also non-affordable housing
air pollution 48
Airbnb 63
Alemanno, A. 138
Alliance for Childhood 71
alternative community visions 110–113, 127–130
  see also counter-hegemonic practices and visions
Althusser, L. 141
Alton Action 128–130
ambulance strikes 88
armchair revolution 106
art 122
ARUP report 70
Atkinson, R. 24–25, 64
Atkinson, R. and Mingay, M. 62
austerity measures 15–16, 56
Ayanda Capital 33
Aylesbury Estate 125–126
Aylesham Community Action 131–132

B

Battle of Orgreave 14
Belt Road Initiative 19
Berkeley Homes 131
Bermondsey 59
Betjeman, J. 55
Biden, J. 51
Big Lottery programme 96
Birmingham 75
Blakeley, G. 14
Blyth, M. 16
Brexit 10, 35–37

Brick Lane, Save the Brick Lane Coalition 132–133
Briggs, M. 71, 72–73, 100
British Land 67
Brixton 130–131
Brown, R. 139
brownfield sites 63–64
Bullough, O. 41
Byrne, L. 22

C

Cadman, M. 67, 75, 91, 92–93, 94, 96, 98, 100, 101
Calarion Housing 61
Campkin, B. 55
capitalism 45, 50, 135
Carpenter, J. 68
Carter, E. 138
Catford Against Social Cleansing 124–125
Celosse, V. 96, 99, 100
Centre for European Reform 10
Chatterton, P. 57
Cheung Kong Holdings 80
child poverty 8, 20, 25, 78, 84
children 70–73
China 19
Church of England 38
City of London 24
civil society 27, 140
class cleansing 124
climate emergency / climate crisis 2–3, 43–45, 48, 49
coastal erosion 48
Cochrane, A. and Jonas, A. 55
Coin Street Action Group 121, 122–123
Coles, T.J. 36
common sense 11, 27, 140–141
communities
  global challenges 2–3
  working with 139–141
community alliances 102–103

178

INDEX

community campaigns 120–136
　alternative community visions 127–130
　challenging dirty money 133–135
　challenging regeneration 130–133
　creative resistance 123–127
　historical lineage 121–123
　key lessons 138–139
　see also Voice4Deptford (V4D)
community consultation 67–71, 130
　children and young people 71–73
　Convoys Wharf development 94, 97, 106–109
community forums 108, 118
community groups *see* community campaigns; Convoys Wharf Community Group (CWCG); Voice4Deptford (V4D)
Community Infrastructure Levy (CIL) 65–67
community involvement 67
　see also community consultation
community meetings
　Convoys Wharf Community Group (CWCG) 94–96
　Convoys Wharf development 107–108
　Voice4Deptford campaign 98–100, 103, 112
community plans 127–128, 129
community visions 110–113, 127–130
community voices 138–139
Conservative government
　austerity programme 56
　Brexit 35–37
　cronyism 33–35
　sleaze, scandal and corruption 32–33
　see also Thatcher government
Conservative Party 39, 42, 65, 129
Convoys Wharf Community Forum 108, 118
Convoys Wharf Community Group (CWCG) 94–98
Convoys Wharf development 72, 80, 86–87, 92
　alternative vision for 110–113
　community consultation 94, 97, 106–109
　judicial review 109–110
　resistance to 87–88 (*see also* Voice4Deptford (V4D))
Convoys Wharf Property Ltd 107, 108
Convoys Wharf site 2, 4, 79–80, *114–115*
Corporate Watch 85
corruption 32–33, 64–67
　see also dirty money
Corry, O. and Reiner, D. 99
cost of living crisis 9
council estates 55–58, 123
　Aylesbury Estate 125–126
　community consultation 68–69
　Heygate Estate 58
　Ladywood Estate, Birmingham 75
　Morris Walk Estate 60
　Pepys Estate 82
　Right to Buy 59
　Robin Hood Estate 57–58
　Winstanley council estate 126
　York Road council estate 126
counter-hegemonic groups 140
　see also community campaigns; environmental social movements
counter-hegemonic practices and visions 43–51
　way forward 141–143
　see also alternative community visions
COVID-19 pandemic 3, 16, 32, 33–35
cronyism 33–35
Cuckmere Haven 47–48
cultural hegemony 2, 26–27, 50, 140–141
　see also counter-hegemonic practices and visions; establishment, hegemonic power of
Cultural Steering Group 108
Cummings, D. 34

D

Darling, A. 15
Davis, K. 104
Death and Life of Great American Cities, The (Jacobs) 73
Decent Homes Standard 56
democracy 30–32
　lack of trust in 31, 32–39
Dennis, A. 125–126
deprivation 78
Deptford 1–2, 69, 77–89
　Convoys Wharf 2, 4, 79–80, *114–115*
　forgotten history 81–82
　housing waiting list 84
　maritime history 78–79
　regeneration 83–87
　resistance to injustice 87–88
　slave trade 80–81
　see also Convoys Wharf development; Voice4Deptford (V4D)
Deptford Lives 111
Desmond, R. 65
direct action 126–127
dirty money 133–135
Dixon, T. and Adams, D. 63
Docklands *see* Convoys Wharf site; Joint Docklands Action Group
Dorling, D. 21
Drake, F. 79, 81
Duncombe, S. and Lambert, S. 122
Dunn, P. and Leeson, L. 122
Dyson, J. 10

E

Eagleton, T. 135
Ealing *see* Stop the Towers campaign

Earth First 51
East India Company 81
East Marsh United 139
EastEnders 57
economic growth 45–46
Elephant Park 58
Enclosure Acts 124
Engels, F. 74
environmental campaigns 47–48
environmental groups, cooperation with political parties 46–47
environmental social movements 44–47, 48–49, 50–51, 140
Equiano, O. 81
Erasmus, A. 80–81
establishment, hegemonic power of 37–39
Estate Watch 56, 123
ethnic diversity 24, 48–49, 78
European Union (EU) 10
  see also Brexit
Evelyn, J. 79
Evening Standard 42, 60, 62, 83
Extinction Rebellion (XR) 44–45, 46, 50

F

Farage, N. 35, 36
Farah, W. 85–86, 100
financial crisis 14–15, 27–28
food banks 22
fossil fuel industry 45, 47, 48, 50
Foster, T. 135–136
Fredericks, J. 104
Freire, P. 106, 122
Friedman, M. 12
funding 96, 133

G

Gamble, A. 16
Gans, H.J. 73
Gatter, H. 111
gentrification 84, 85, 88, 123, 131, 132, 135–136
Geoghegan, P. 33
Gilbert, J. 16–17
'Give Deptford a voice' *117*
global challenges 2–3
global climate crisis see climate emergency / climate crisis
global corporations 3
  see also international corporations; transnational corporations
global financial crisis 14–15, 27–28
globalization 18–19
Goldsmiths University 88, 94, 104, 111
Gooch, N. 67
Good Law Project 34
Gove, M. 34, 36
Gramsci, A. 2, 11, 25–27, 140

Great Unrest 1911 87
Green Party 45, 46, 48–49
Green, R. 91, 92, 96, 100, *116*
Greenstone, M. 48
Grenfell high-rise fire 61, 138
Grimsby 139
Guardian 105, 124

H

Hancock, M. 34
Hanshaw, P. 121–122
Harding, D. 34
Hatherley, O. 124
healthcare 9, 13
  see also National Health Service (NHS)
Hefler, E. 81
hegemonic power 37–39
  see also counter-hegemonic practices and visions; cultural hegemony
Hersh, B. 63
Heygate Estate 58
Hillier, M. 34
Hinduja brothers 61
Hinduja, G. 10
HOPE not hate Charitable Trust 138
housing see affordable housing; non-affordable housing
housing associations 61, 123
housing developments
  brownfield sites 63–64
  community consultation 67–71
  children and young people 71–73
  Deptford 80, 83–87 (see also Convoys Wharf development)
  resistance to 87–88 (see also Voice4Deptford (V4D))
  new communities 61–63
  non-affordable housing 58–61
  planning process 64–67
  resistance to see community campaigns
  threat to council estates 55–58, 123
housing market 10, 53, 134–135
housing waiting lists 58–59, 60, 84, 131
Hunt, J. 32
Hunt, T. 14
Hutchinson Property Group 80, 91
Hyde, M. 25

I

income deprived children 78
inequality 9, 11, 19–22, 23–25
  see also super-rich
Inequality.org 20
infrastructure 65–67
Institute for Policy Studies 20
Intergovernmental Panel on Climate Change (IPCC) 44

INDEX

international corporations 19
  see also global corporations;
  transnational corporations
International Monetary Fund 15

J

Jacca, J. 86–87, 98, 100, 109
Jacobs, J. 73, 142
Jenkins, S. 62
Jenrick, R. 65
Johnson, B. 32, 34, 36, 42, 65, 80, 93
Johnson, C. 53
Joint Docklands Action Group 121–122
Jones, O. 38–39, 43
judicial reviews 109–110, 125–126, 128
Just Stop Oil (JSO) 44–45, 46, 50

K

Katona, R. 79, 100
Kensington Against Dirty Money 134
Keynesian economic policies 12
Khan, S. 49, 59
King Charles III 38
knowledge networks 99
Knowles, C. 134
Krugman, P. 16
Kwarteng, K. 32

L

Labiak 67
Labour government 9, 33, 37
Labour Party 129
Ladywood Estate, Birmingham 75
Landler, M. and Castle, S. 42
Landsec 67
Lawrence, I. 56
Lebedev, E. 42
Lee, R. and Edwards, M. 53
Lees, L. 68, 124
Leeson, L. 68
Lendlease 64
Lewis, S. 48
liberal democracies 30–31
local authority planning departments 64
local environmental campaigns 47–48
local infrastructure 65–67
local power 98–99
London
  brownfield sites 63–64
  climate change 49
  community campaigns 120–136
  (*see also* Voice4Deptford (V4D))
    alternative community visions 127–130
    challenging dirty money 133–135
    challenging regeneration 130–133
    creative resistance 123–127
    historical lineage 121–123
    key lessons 138–139

community consultation 67–71
  children and young people 71–73
council estates 55–58, 123
housing market 53
housing waiting lists 58–59, 60, 84, 131
inequality 23–25, 53
new communities 61–63
non-affordable housing 59–61
planning process 64–67
Russian oligarchs 41, 134
urban structural transformation 54–55
see also Convoys Wharf development;
  Deptford; Peckham
London Docklands *see* Joint Docklands Action Group
London Government Act 1963 78
London Tenants Federation 123, 139
low-income countries 15

M

Madden, D. and Marcuse, P. 73
Malik, N. 37
Marlowe, C. 79
mass consumption 45–46
Massey, D. 136, 142
McChesney, R.W. 17
McFadyen, J. 54
Mee, A. 79
miners' strikes 13–14, 87
Monbiot, G. 17, 46, 50
Monbiot, G. and Hutchinson, P. 13, 15, 17, 53
Morning Lane People's Space 130
Morris Walk Estate 60
Mudlark121 81
Multilingual Capital 24
Murdoch, R. 80, 87
Murky Depths 60

N

National Health Service (NHS) 9, 16
nationalism 18
neoliberalism 11, 27–28, 45–46, 142
  and Brexit 35–37
  as 'common sense' 140–141
  emergence and development 12–19
  see also counter-hegemonic practices and visions
networks 99
new communities 61–63
News International 80, 87
News Shopper 60
Nickson, T. 104
Nine Elms development 62
Nixon, T. 100
non-affordable housing 58–61, 101
nuclear power 45

O

older people 70
organic intellectuals 141
Oxfam 20

P

Packham, C. 50
Parker, L. 63
parliamentary sleaze 32–33
Partygate 32
Patriotic Millionaires 22
Peckham 84
People's Plan for the Royal Docks 122
Pepys Estate 82
Phipps, M. 37
police violence 14
political parties
  cooperation with environmental groups 46–47
  see also specific parties
political representation 3
pop-up shops 104, *116*
Popple, K. 27
populism 31
poverty 8, 9, 20, 22, 84
  see also child poverty
power 37–39, 98–99
power dynamics 103
private education 13
Private Eye 80
private healthcare 9, 13
private rented sector 60
private sector 10
pure activism 106

R

Raban, J. 64
Radical Housing Network 123
Raleigh, W. 79
Ramos, V., Jr 141
Ratcliffe, J. 10
Reading Pepys 82
Redrow 62
Rees-Mogg, J. 36
reflection 106
regeneration
  brownfield sites 63–64
  community consultation 67–71
    children and young people 71–73
  community-led 130
  Deptford 80, 83–87 (*see also* Convoys Wharf development)
    resistance to 87–88 (*see also* Voice4Deptford (V4D))
  new communities 61–63
  non-affordable housing 58–61
  planning process 64–67
  resistance to *see* community campaigns
  threat to council estates 55–58, 123

resistance 87–88
  see also community campaigns; environmental social movements; Voice4Deptford (V4D)
Riddell, P. 34
Right to Buy 59, 71
Robbins, G. 58
Robin Hood Estate 57–58
Rotherham 14
royal family 38
Russia 39–43, 45
Russian oligarchs 41, 134

S

Save Nour. Save Brixton 130–131
Save the Brick Lane Coalition 132–133
scandals 32–33
school strikes 1911 87
Seaford Environmental Alliance 47
Secret History of Our Streets, The 82
section 106 agreements 65–67, 95, 96, 97, 108
segregation 24
Sendra, P. 130
Sendra, P. and Fitzpatrick, D. 139
Shah, K. 20
Shelley, P.B. 143
Simon, R. 140
Sinclair, I. 55
slave trade 80–81
sleaze 32–33
social capital 138
social change 138
social cleansing 123, 124
  Catford Against Social Cleansing 124–125
social housing 101
  see also affordable housing; council estates; housing associations
Social Metrics Commission 8
social mobility 17, 21
social movements *see* environmental social movements
social rent 59, 61
Spitalfields Trust 132, 133
Sriskandarajah, D. 20
state surveillance 13, 14
Steele, J. 69, 81
Stein, S. 74
Stop the Towers campaign 132
Strasser, A. 83
strike action 87–88
  see also miners' strikes
Structural Adjustment Programmes 15
student protests 88
Sumners, C. 47
Sunak, R. 32–33
Sunday Times Rich List 10

super-rich 3, 20
  London 24, 25, 62, 134–135
  UK 10, 21, 22
  see also Russian oligarchs
Surfers Against Sewage 47
surveillance 13, 14

T

Tarver, N. 134
tax 22, 24, 45, 47
technology 18–19
Test and Trace programme 34
Thatcher government 13–14, 68
Thatcherism 23
Thoburn, N. 55–56, 57
Thomas, K.M. 103
Thompson, E.P. 124
Time Out magazine 84
Times 87
trade unions 13, 87, 88
transnational corporations 18
  see also global corporations; international corporations
Transparency International 41, 62
tree protectors 126–127
Trinity House 79
Truman Brewery 132, 133
Trump, D. 31–32
Truss, L. 32, 33
Trussell Trust 22
Turner, A. 94–95, 100, 107

U

UK Parliament Foreign Affairs Committee 133–134
Ukraine 40
un-affordable housing *see* non-affordable housing
UN Convention on the Rights of the Child 72
unemployment 13
Union (Wilkinson) 135–136
United Kingdom (UK)
  Brexit 10, 35–37
  Enclosure Acts 124
  hegemonic power of the establishment 37–39
  inequality 21–22
  Russian influence 39–43

super-rich 10, 21, 22
  see also London
United Nations 128
United Nations Climate Change Conference (CO29) 44
United States 20, 31–32
Urban Heat Island effect 49
urbanization 3

V

Voice4Deptford (V4D) 2, 3–4, 90–119, 138
  alternative vision for Convoys Wharf 110–113
  beginnings 91–94
  campaign 98–103, *116*
  communication and campaigning 105–106
  community consultation 106–109
  Convoys Wharf Community Group (CWCG) 94–98
  'Give Deptford a voice' *117*
  judicial review 109–110
  logo *117*
  ongoing work 118–119
  pop-up shop 104–105
  pop-up shops *116*
  reflections 113–118
Voice4Deptford Wall 105
von Hayek, F. 12

W

Wapping dispute 1986 87
war of position 140
Wards Corner campaign 127–128
Washington Consensus 19
Watt, P. 124, 135
We Are Grenfell website 138
wealth 22
  see also establishment, hegemonic power of; inequality; Russian oligarchs; super-rich
wealth taxes 22
welfare system 13
Wessie du Toit 133
Widgery, D. 89
Winstanley council estate 126
Wood, J. 70–71
World Bank Group 9

Y

York Road council estate 126
young people 39, 70–73

www.ingramcontent.com/pod-product-compliance
Lightning Source LLC
Chambersburg PA
CBHW051548020426
42333CB00016B/2148